Pauline Ugliness

Series Board

James Bernauer

Drucilla Cornell

Thomas R. Flynn

Kevin Hart

Richard Kearney

Jean-Luc Marion

Adriaan Peperzak

Thomas Sheehan

Hent de Vries

Merold Westphal

Michael Zimmerman

John D. Caputo, *series editor*

Perspectives in
Continental
Philosophy

OLE JAKOB LØLAND

Pauline Ugliness
Jacob Taubes and the Turn to Paul

Fordham University Press
New York ▪ 2020

Copyright © 2020 Fordham University Press

All rights reserved. No part of this publication may be reproduced, stored in a retrieval system, or transmitted in any form or by any means—electronic, mechanical, photocopy, recording, or any other—except for brief quotations in printed reviews, without the prior permission of the publisher.

Fordham University Press has no responsibility for the persistence or accuracy of URLs for external or third-party Internet websites referred to in this publication and does not guarantee that any content on such websites is, or will remain, accurate or appropriate.

Fordham University Press also publishes its books in a variety of electronic formats. Some content that appears in print may not be available in electronic books.

Visit us online at www.fordhampress.com.

Library of Congress Cataloging-in-Publication Data

Names: Løland, Ole Jakob, author.
Title: Pauline ugliness : Jacob Taubes and the turn to Paul / Ole Jakob Løland.
Description: First edition. | New York : Fordham University Press, 2020. | Series: Perspectives in continental philosophy | Includes bibliographical references and index. | Summary: "Jacob Taubes radically changed our conceptions of Paul the apostle. Loland shows how we can approach Paul's letters with the distinctive perspective of this Jewish rabbi steeped in continental philosophy. This book emphasizes Paul's Jewishness as well as the political explosiveness of the apostle's revolutionary doctrine of the cross, which the author terms Pauline Ugliness"—Provided by publisher.
Identifiers: LCCN 2019028526 | ISBN 9780823286553 (hardback) | ISBN 9780823286546 (paperback) | ISBN 9780823286546 (epub)
Subjects: LCSH: Bible. Epistles of Paul—Criticism, interpretation, etc. | Paul, the Apostle, Saint. | Taubes, Jacob—Influence. | Philosophical theology.
Classification: LCC BS2650.52 .L65 2020 | DDC 227/.06—dc23
LC record available at https://lccn.loc.gov/2019028526

Printed in the United States of America

22 21 20   5 4 3 2 1

First edition

Contents

	Introduction	1
1	The Historical and the Philosophical: A Contemporary Scene	13
2	Jacob Taubes's Path to Paul: From the Eschatologist to the Paulinist	22
3	Paul and Philosophy: Taubes's Contradictory Paul	52
4	Paul as Predecessor to Psychoanalysis: Taubes's Introspective Paul	100
5	Paul against Empire: Taubes's Political Paul	140
	Conclusion	177
	Acknowledgments	*185*
	Notes	*187*
	Bibliography	*219*
	Index of Biblical References	*229*
	General Index	*231*

Pauline Ugliness

Introduction

> One of the remarkable features of the present time is the dramatic rediscovery and reactivation of Paul not so much, as one might imagine, within the church, but outside of it, or on its very edge, in the whole raft of continental philosophers, of whom Slavoj Žižek and Alain Badiou are perhaps the best known.
>
> —John M. G. Barclay, "Paul and the Philosophers: Alain Badiou and the Event"

The biblical scholar John M. G. Barclay is one of those who have highlighted the drama in the turn to Paul in recent continental philosophy. To sustain the notion of drama in these academic circumstances Barclay pointed to the rediscovery of Paul outside the apostle's traditional religious reading circles. Indeed, a philosopher like Alain Badiou assured his readers that Paul could be reclaimed for wholly secular purposes. Moreover, the allegedly secular concern in Badiou's readings of the Pauline epistles appeared not only to be a sensational reactivation of Paul but also aimed at reinventing the political left. Given that radical leftist philosophers such as Slavoj Žižek and Giorgio Agamben felt the need at the turn of the the millenium to reactivate the apostle's legacy, we were left with the impression that Paul was somehow indispensable or necessary for this kind of philosophical radicalism. Paul appeared to be one of the figures that united them in a common philosophical movement: Here appeared a group of leftist-oriented philosophers who turned to Paul simultaneously and engaged in a common interrogation of the apostle's relevance for contemporary politics. Among the other figures that united their philosophical orientations were Marx, Freud, and Nietzsche. In other words, Paul became woven together with so many modern intellectual figures, including the three pillars of modern critical theory. Paul the apostle is nowadays, at least potentially, also a name for critical theory. This foundational figure of early Christian religion has been made into one of the contemporary symptoms of the blurring of the religious-secular distinction.

How did this come into being? And how is the Pauline legacy refigured in light of this recent philosophical interest?

One of the ways to answer these two questions is to introduce the absent four in this list of philosophers that at some point turned to Paul: Jacob Taubes (1923–87) was a Jewish rabbi who worked as a philosopher in various universities in the United States, Israel, and West Germany until he died in 1987. Barclay may be right that Badiou and Žižek are the best known, but the commentaries and secondary literature about Giorgio Agamben's *The Time That Remains* have also been massive. Nonetheless, Taubes may be regarded as a forerunner to all three. As a leftist activist and thinker within the continental philosophical tradition he was the first of them, with his lectures on Paul from 1987, published as *The Political Theology of Paul*.[1] Badiou's book on Paul was published in 1997, Žižek started to engage with Paul in his 1999 book *The Ticklish Subject*, and Agamben's reading of the Letter to the Romans was published in 2000.[2] Agamben declares that his work on Paul is dedicated to Taubes and is in fact the one of the three that is most concerned with Taubes.[3] Although some of Taubes's readings of Paul (such as the Paul-Benjamin parallel) appear to be crucial for Agamben's work, Agamben leaves out many aspects of Taubes's Paulinism. Žižek limits his engagement with Taubes to an appraisal of his work in a footnote.[4] Furthermore, Taubes appeared to be somehow left in the dark by the secondary literature. Articles were seldom focused on Taubes's Paul, and no English-speaking monograph was dedicated to his readings of Paul. When Taubes was included in the discussions it was sometimes done indirectly, as if he were difficult to integrate within the dominant frames of interpreting the turn to Paul or the philosophical turn to religion. It was fascinating, for instance, that Hent de Vries included a discussion of Taubes's lectures on Paul in his *Philosophy and the Turn to Religion* from 1999, but in the form of a footnote of two full pages.[5] Why was it difficult to include Taubes within the main discussions about philosophy and religion? What made Taubes's Paulinism resistant toward such integrations? In order to explain this, it is necessary to investigate the origins of Taubes's Paulinism, particularly with regard to the disciplinary boundaries that define philosophy as distinctive and different to history. Hence, there is a need to discern the method that is operative in Taubes's approaches to Paul. And we may ask: How can we understand Paul's texts on the background of Taubes's readings of them?

Pauline Ugliness is a notion that surges in Taubes's works through an explicit and deliberate transgression of the boundaries set between history and philosophy. It comes to fore in an essay from 1968 entitled, "The Justification of Ugliness in Early Christian Tradition."[6] Here Taubes declares that the aphorisms and polemics of the philosopher Friedrich Nietzsche contain a "historical insight" that remains "unsurpassed by the New Testament exegetes." In other words, the experts of historical criticism within modern biblical scholarship have yet to see what Nietzsche saw: Paul's doctrine of the cross as foolishness in the First Epistle to the Corinthians 1:20 constituted no less than a transvaluation of the religious, ethical, and aesthetic values of Antiquity. This text is where the conflict between the slave morality and the noble morality first appears, according to Nietzsche, and Taubes agrees with the polemical philosopher. He praises Nietzsche's historical knowledge and devalues the claims made by the historical and exegetical experts. According to Taubes, the historians have not perceived the deadly conflict that goes through the history of the West in what is considered Nietzsche's true version of it, between the ugliness of the cross of the oppressed and the aesthetic beauty of the aristocracy.

"The Justification of Ugliness in Early Christian Tradition" was written by Jacob Taubes for the research group "Poetik und Hermeneutik" in 1966.[7] The paper was presented to this group of German intellectuals, comprising theorists such as Reinhart Koselleck, Hans Robert Jauss, Wolfgang Iser, and Hans Blumenberg. This strikingly overlooked paper anticipates Taubes's widely discussed lectures on Paul from Heidelberg in 1987. While philosophers constituted Taubes's primary audience for the reading of Paul in 1966, exegetes from the school of historical criticism were the explicit addressees for the Heidelberg lectures. Nonetheless, in Heidelberg Taubes repeated his main perspective on Paul from the 1966 paper: He confessed that Nietzsche had been his best teacher on Paul.[8] His readings effected not only a blurring of the dichotomy between the religious and the secular, but also of the powerful historical-philosophical distinction.

If we are to understand how Taubes contributed to the recent philosophical turn to Paul, we also need to pay close attention to how notions of the historical and philosophical function in Taubes's reception of Paul. To analize this particular form of reception it is necessary to clarify the function of the various and complex layers of reception that produce Taubes's Paul. This variety and complexity can be analyzed and viewed through the careful work of the genealogist.

In recent discussions biblical scholars have sometimes ignored, dismissed, or criticized the philosophers' readings of Paul's letters on the basis of what are historically false or true assumptions about the historical context in which these letters were produced. From the viewpoint of reception theory, claims about the historically accurate or inaccurate readings of Paul's letters can themselves be considered examples of reception of Paul. They also, unavoidably, like philosophical or theological readings, contribute to the afterlife of these ancient texts. To contextualize texts is not to reflect meaning embedded in an original context but to produce meaning selectively informed by perceptions of that context, which inevitably produces parts of ever new layers in the reception of these texts.

Moreoever, these strategies of qualifying or disqualifying readings in terms of right and wrong stand in tension with the mode within which this book is written: the mode of commentary that, according to Michel Foucault, may guide the work of the genealogist.

Reception and Deconstruction

Foucault distinguishes the commentary from the textual forms often associated with scientific disciplines, characterized by cateogories of exclusion such as "the prohibition," "reason and madness," and "true and false."[9] While Foucault considers these modes of controlling and delimiting discourse external, the controlling procedures of the commentaries are more internal. These commentaries do not merely construct and add meaning to the authoritative primary texts, but also control them through their principles of classification and ordering.[10] The genre of commentary can be claimed as a room of not only control and classification but also of strategic resistance to and untying of earlier readings in the reception of the supposedly primary texts.[11]

The reader will notice that this work partakes of a certain deconstruction of the reception of Paul. The aim of this study is not so much to catalogue and unify meaning in the philosophers' reception of Paul, although there is always an element of stabilization of meaning in any attempt to order and structure reception. All the same, this study is also an attempt to carefully underscore the multiplicity and ambiguity of meaning in the different layers of reception detectable in these philosophers. Although names of authors are constantly invoked, the premise is not so much that what takes place in these works are dialogues or encounters between philosophers as that there are friction, tension, and play among these different layers. The result of the exposure and investigation of these forces is the manifestation of a plurality of meanings that are connected to the name "Paul" in Taubes's work and in the layers of reception that are linked together in his work. Thereby, assumptions of a unified and stabilized meaning of this name are questioned and indeed targeted. The ultimate goal is not to arrive at a stable truth, as if that would necessarily lead to more secure and definitive truths. An exploration of the ambivalences and multiple meanings of the name "Paul" and the writings ascribed to this name could be just as desirable in order to gain more secure knowledge.

In a similar mode to Derrida's endeavor with the metaphysical tradition, the reception historian may use the resources *within* the interpretative tradition in order to deconstruct it.[12] Said otherwise, the reception historian should acknowledge that there is no place outside this interpretative apparatus or machine often designated as "tradition." There is no urgent need to step out of the mode of commentary. Furthermore, the possible expectation of radically new beginnings or revolutionary readings in the present philosophical turn to Paul should be tempered by this acknowledgment. The ambitions of reading Paul differently in the present academic climate or juridico-politico-philosophical situation will have to be disciplined or qualified through what Michel Foucault characterized as "the gray, meticulous, and patiently documentary" exercise of genealogy. This mode of reading operates on "documents which have been scratched over and recopied many times," a Foucauldian description that is extraordinarily fitted to Paul's letters. Few Western documents have been scratched over to such a degree as some of Paul's letters, which points to the apt name of genealogy for an analysis of the function of the different layers of reception presented in this thesis. In Foucault's words,

> the world of speech and desires has known invasions, struggles, plundering, disguises, ploys. From these elements, however, genealogy retrieves an indispensable restraint: it must record the singularity of events outside of any monotonous finality; it must seek them in the most unpromising places, in what we tend to feel is without history—in sentiments, love, conscience, instincts; it must be sensitive to their recurrence, not in order to trace the gradual curve of their evolution but to isolate the different scenes where they engaged in different roles. Finally, genealogy must define even those instances when they are absent, the moment when they remained unrealized.[13]

This study presupposes that there is no such thing as "a gradual curve of evolution" of ideas, conceptions, or interpretations of texts in history, nor any unifying horizon of meaning that would render credible a Gadamerian *Wirkungsgeschichte*[14]—a term so dear to many reception historians.[15] Hence, it is necessary to "isolate the different scenes where they engaged in different roles" without presupposing an overarching principle that would unify or anchor these diverse settings and scenes. Through a genealogical approach to the material in Taubes, the different layers in the reception of Paul, the various choices made in these readings of the apostle, the unstable meanings of the name "Paul," and even the lost moments with the Pauline legacy might be better understood and recognized.

A Study in the Reception History of the Bible

The tradition upon which a reader situated within biblical scholarship is most dependent upon and by which he is conditioned may not emerge from churches and Christian communities. What are considered historical approaches may be said to constitute another powerful tradition with its specific prohibitions and other procedures of exclusion in Foucault's sense. In his *Displacing Christian Origins* Ward Blanton claims that there is a tendency within New Testament Scholarship to group scholars into "traditional" historians on the one hand and those with "other" kinds of methods on the other.[16] In other words, what is sometimes regarded within this field as traditional is not something considered religious but rather something seen as having an empirical foundation in the reality of the past, in the historical context in which these ancient texts are supposed to have been produced. A parallel division of labor sometimes assumed within New Testament scholarship between scholars reading as traditional historians and scholars applying "theory" (from literary theory to class analysis) divides those traditionally working with the historical origins of the biblical texts on the one hand and those analyzing the reception of these texts on the other. As Brennan W. Breed, one of the winners of the 2016 Manfred Lautenschlaeger Award for Theological Promise, affirms, this division of labor is no less than a constitutive boundary between biblical criticism on the one hand and reception history of the Bible on the other.[17] Breed's *Nomadic Text: A Theory of Biblical Reception History* has reopened and sharpened the debate about where biblical criticism ends and reception history of the Bible begins. When reception historians write about their approach or field as a history of "effects" and "impact" they often implicitly draw on this constitutive boundary of a separation between the original and later meanings of the texts. But where could the limit possibly be set for original meanings of a text? Breed asks in a simple yet provocative manner for biblical criticism, "Yet how can we tell what came after something if we do not know where that something ends?"[18]

Breed argues that when historians read a text in its "original" or "historical" context, the effort of placing the text back into this context is already a result of choosing one out of "multiple irreconcilable points of view from which to read it." Contexts are not "pregiven wholes" for the historian.[19] The historian cannot determine the meaning of a text derived from the historical context in which it was produced, in Breed's mind. There is no such accessible closed context from which to save the historian from being immersed in the reception of the text. Breed concludes, "Reception history, or the study of things other than the original text in its original context, may be all that has ever existed."[20] Biblical criticism cannot escape from always already being partly also reception history.

Other reception theorists have pointed to the need for going beyond the enterprise of reception history of the Bible conceived as a study of the ideas that great theologians have derived from biblical texts. Biblical scholarship, often located within departments of theology, has been preoccupied with the interpreted meanings of words and the literary content of different biblical texts. This has often resulted in presentations of interpretations of particular biblical texts in the theological works of authoritative figures like Augustine and Luther. Such a history of interpretation surely is of great value. All the same, as John Lyons and Jorunn Økland have remarked, one should challenge the tendency within this academic field to treat the use of biblical figures and texts as if this were primarily a question of theological ideas: "What we want to get away from is reception history as an exercise in cataloguing, as reductionist and mono-causal history-writing, or as a descriptive overview of the authoritative readings of particular biblical texts by pillars such as Aquinas, Luther and Calvin."[21] This move away from privileging the interpretative meaning of the biblical texts and its interpreters is one that in my opinion is further carried out by Breed's mandate for biblical critics to change the question "what does this text mean?" to "how might this text function?"[22] If we take Breed as a methodological point of departure and ask what a text can do rather than what it means, we broaden the picture. It becomes necessary to not just ask what kind of ideas Jacob Taubes got from Paul, but also, in a wider sense, what Paul's texts could do within Taubes's broader intellectual engagements. What did his intellectual thought achieve with Paul?

To locate the use of texts in broader historical settings is, however, also to emphasize the material life conditions under which the necessarily embodied forms of reception always take place. Although the intention here is not to write an extensive biography of Jacob Taubes, the biographical and anecdotal aspects Taubes himself brings into his discussion of Paul in the Heidelberg lectures from 1987 make his biography inseparable from his understanding of Paul.[23] The newly published correspondence from the early 1950s between Taubes and his former wife, Susan Taubes (1928–69), has shed some light on this aspect of Jacob Taubes's intellectual life.[24]

To clarify the function of the Pauline texts within Taubes's intellectual life is also to use Taubes's readings as a specific case for demonstrating some particular capacities of these texts, as suggested by Brennan W. Breed's program:

Here is the mandate: demonstrate the diversity of capacities, organize them according to the immanent potentialities actualized by various individuals and communities over time, and rewrite our understanding of the biblical text.[25]

This study is written with the conviction that an investigation into the reception of Paul in the works of Taubes can consist in such a demonstration of the different capacities of texts at various stages in their trajectories through history, which can enrich and broaden our perspectives on Paul's texts. Consequently, by working and proceeding through the various layers and possible aspects of the reception of Paul in some contemporary contexts, this book aims at rewriting and broadening our understanding of the Pauline epistles. This book is not only a product of reading Taubes. It also rests on some specific readings of Paul.

Structure of the Book

The analyses of the various functions of the receptions of Paul in the work of these philosophers can be led by a useful distinction made by Heikki Räisänen for reception history of the Bible. Räisänen outlined a kind of program for biblical scholars who wanted to generate knowledge about the various sort of effects the Bible has had throughout history. As these effects can only be discerned by analyzing complex processes, the biblical scholar proposed to distinguish mainly three effects: effects of specific verses, general effects, like the idea of a holy scripture, and, last, models. For Räisänen a model from the Bible would for example include the idea of a chosen people or Paul's conversion.[26]

In this study attention will primarily be given to effects or uses of sentences or passages that can be traced back to specific verses in Paul's epistles, but also to models that appear without reference to these biblical texts. It is demonstrated how Taubes's Paul can be present as a name—for instance, as a precursor or condition of thought for philosophers. Furthermore, such models function as heuristic devices in my analysis, where some of them appear under the names of "the Introspective Paul" and "the Political Paul."

Chapter 1 extends the discussion of the concepts of the historical and the philosophical from this Introduction by isolating a certain scene from the recent debate on Paul and contemporary philosophy. This sets the stage for the competing paradigms for claims of ownership to the "truth" about Paul between historical and philosophical perspectives through isolating a scene from a recent debate between philosophers (Slavoj Žižek and Alain

Badiou) and biblical scholars. Having already made claims about the supremacy of Nietzsche's understanding of Paul vis-à-vis historically oriented biblical exegetes, Taubes forms part of this disciplinary competition. The chapter deepens the theoretical discussion in the Introduction by lending perspectives from Ward Blanton's *Displacing Christian Origins*, but also through some metaperspectives provided by Taubes himself, particularly as a critic of "historicism."

Chapter 2 is intended to show how Paul emerges as a figure for Jacob Taubes's thought. In the introduction to his Heidelberg lectures from 1987, Taubes himself provides some historical and biographical background for his interest in Paul. In that way, Taubes invites such approaches to his readings of Paul. What is more, as there is a certain self-identification in these lectures with the figure of Paul, aspects of these biographical notes may even be considered part of the reception history of Paul. What is more, Taubes also highlighted events in his life that were crucial for his path to Paul, such as Taubes's highly controversial relation with the former Nazi professor Carl Schmitt.

In Chapter 3, "Paul and Philosophy," aspects of the philosopher's readings of Paul in relation to the historical and the philosophical are a central concern. Some intellectual origins of the presuppositions inherent in the philosopher's readings of Paul are to be found in the Weimar period as well as in the postwar time of European intellectual history. By analyzing how Taubes's interpretations of Paul depend on historical or philosophical perspectives from these periods of European thought, this chapter seeks to discern methods that are explicitly or implicitly at work in the reception of Paul in the philosopher's work, primarily focused on Taubes's readings of 1 Corinthians. The chapter discerns the deconstructive method and Talmudic spirit inherent within Taubes's idiosyncratic readings of Paul. Moreover, this method is applied within specific intellectual debates where Taubes's articulation of Paul as a messianic thinker with a "political theology" constitutes Taubes's efforts to establish a synthesis of the insights of Walter Benjamin and Carl Schmitt. This synthesis also provides Taubes with a powerful device with which to counter a tradition of critical theory, culminating in Adorno, which becomes—in Taubes's view—merely aesthetic and even "indifferent" in relation to the historical struggles of the excluded against the powerful.

Chapter 4, "Paul as Predecessor to Psychoanalysis: Taubes's Introspective Paul" highlights the reception of Romans, and particularly Romans 7, in the work of the philosopher. The title of the chapter draws on the insights of Taubes's former colleague Krister Stendahl and his critique of the Augustinian-Lutheran reading of Paul as the introspective conscience.

Taubes's strategy is to maintain Paul as a figure of introspective consciousness, but a deeply Jewish one, partly by comparing Paul and Sigmund Freud. This unique interpretative strategy with regard to Paul is made by the Jewish rabbi within a post-Holocaust world where biblical scholars have attempted to liberate Paul from Protestant readings of him as the introspective figure *par excellance*. Taubes, however, establishes Paul's Jewishness by other means and comes close to considering Freudian psychoanalysis as a Pauline science. This concept of the introspective apostle also facilitates a discussion of the negotiations of "the Jewish" and "the Christian" that occur in the reception of Paul in Taubes. Since questions about his Jewishness are brought to the forefront in scholarly discussions of Paul, the relevance and legitimacy of Taubes's philosophical readings of Paul may also be illuminated with these categories. The categorization of Taubes's readings of Paul as "Jewish" is tempered by Taubes's reliance on what appear as rather Christian perspectives in the works of Freud and Nietzsche.

Finally, Chapter 5 demonstrates Taubes's peculiar method of reading Paul through key thinkers of twentieth-century European thought, such as Nietzsche, Benjamin, and Barth. The political aspects of the philosopher's readings are analyzed through an extended use of the notions of the historical and the philosophical, in addition to categories of the Jewish and the Christian. It becomes clear that Taubes mainly draws on Romans 1 and 13 when he addresses the political dimensions of Paul's thought. The chapter shows how—even as it amplifies a seething antagonism toward the values of the Greco-Roman world—Taubes's Paul develops a "nihilism" that is actually "quietist" and withdrawn in relation to direct contestation of actually existing authority. Nonetheless, the Pauline impulse is highly explosive for Taubes in a political sense. This is the chapter that connects ideas that result in an unlikely meeting between biblical scholars of our day and Nietzsche, which can occur through Taubes.

The book concludes that the contemporary philosophical turn to Paul, considered by taking Taubes as its prime example, can partly be explained by these philosophers' (Taubes, Badiou, Agamben, Žižek) attraction to Paul as an antinomian figure, a figure of lawlessness and freedom from law that can lead to apocalyptic violence (for Taubes) or pave the way for an existential and political break with the domain of law (for Badiou and Žižek). Jacob Taubes pointed beyond his own readings, however, when he called for wholly new interpretations of Paul. By quoting Freud's *Moses and Monotheism* extensively without any final conclusions about its relevance for the interpretations of Paul to come, Taubes's last words about Paul become more a call to freely reinvent meanings than to be limited by Taubes's opinions of Paul. In the manner of the Talmudic commentators and interlocutors of Taubes's own Jewish intellectual culture, Taubes lets his own philosophy about Paul remain incomplete, as if to await new and unforeseeable interpreters to come. He could not have predicted that thirteen years after his last will in the form of lectures about Paul, an Italian philosopher, Giorgio Agamben, would dedicate his major work on Paul to Jacob Taubes.

When English translations of biblical passages are quoted, the New Revised Standard Version (NRSV) is used in this book. When Koine Greek versions of New Testament texts or expressions are quoted, SBL Greek New Testament (SBLGNT) is used and then latinized.

1

The Historical and the Philosophical
A Contemporary Scene

If reception history is "all that ever existed," in the words of Brennan W. Breed,[1] the difference between readings that rely on history and those that rely on philosophy is not that clear-cut. If we cannot identify definitive boundaries between the original text and its reception, between production and interpretation, the opposition between a historical and a philosophical approach becomes more unstable and problematic. With this in mind the inside and outside of a biblical text is shaken, and the clear dichotomy between exegesis and eisegesis is rendered unsustainable, since the difference between text and reader is not easily drawn.[2]

Nevertheless, assumptions that such disciplinary boundaries can and indeed should be drawn have guided recent discussions on the philosophers' readings of Paul. We may isolate a scene where the view of the philosophical and the historical as irreconcilable entities were reproduced and made an impact on these discussions. This scene is from the 2005 conference at Syracuse University in the United States on April 14–16, documented in *St. Paul among the Philosophers* (2009). Taubes was not a theme during this conference. Badiou and Žižek, however, were among its participants.

Setting the Scene

For this meeting, Linda Martín Alcoff and John D. Caputo gathered philosophers and biblical scholars to discuss Paul. The biblical scholar Paula Fredriksen responded to what she termed the philosopher's "sense of discovery" of Paul as "our contemporary," this latter expression being one of her only two quotations from the philosophers, in this case Alain Badiou.[3]

On the one hand, Fredriksen's two short quotes are representative of the degree of engagement between the two camps of academicians. No wonder then that what struck commentators on this published conference in retrospect was the lack of engagement across these disciplinary formations that are delineated by the nouns "history" and "philosophy."[4] The conversations documented in *St. Paul among the Philosophers* were indications of failed encounters or missed opportunities to go into dialogue, though with some very important exceptions.[5]

On the other hand, Paula Fredriksen's response almost amounted to an argument for the necessity of *not* engaging. Badiou's position of Paul as "our contemporary" was not to be discussed by Fredriksen, but rather declared to be an unacceptable position from a strictly historical point of view. As the title of her paper indicated, Badiou's reading of Paul was the result of an "interpretative freedom," as if this freedom were something in which only philosophers like Badiou could indulge. The contrast to this unrestrained philosophical pleasure was described by another participant at the conference, the Pauline scholar Dale Martin, as "the ascetic point of view of modern historical criticism." This potentially self-critical description of the historians' mode of reading was in Fredrikson's words branded as "historical integrity." This integrity was to be achieved through avoiding the pitfall of an anachronistic reading, which Badiou had run into through his discovery of Paul, his closing of "cultural gaps," according to Fredriksen:

> The frame of reference for historical interpretation is not and cannot be the present. To do history requires acknowledging difference between us and the objects of our inquiry. Historical interpretation proceeds by acceding to the priority of the *ancient* context. Our frame of reference is the *past*. In our particular instance, this morning, for example, my question is not, What *does* Paul mean? that is, to us. Rather, I ask, What *did* Paul mean? that is, to his first-century contemporaries. . . . They, not we, were the audience of his message. He was obliged to be intelligible not to us but to them.[6]

The demarcations between the science that cultivates the virtue of "historical integrity" and the one that reads texts from the past with "interpretive freedom" are presented as clear-cut: past versus present, what an author meant versus what an author means, them versus us.[7] Fredriksen then proceeds in her paper to warn the philosophers, it appears, that the intelligibility with which Paul met his ancient audience was "alarmingly elusive," since "consistency does not rank among Paul's strong suits."[8] Accordingly, one might add another binary constituting the division of labor between historians with "integrity" and philosophers with "freedom": while historians reveal the author's inconsistencies, philosophers read the same author as consistent, systematizing this author's thought. In Fredriksen's words, "Coherence often has to be distilled or imposed."[9]

Processes of Outbidding

These demarcations are not drawn in a vacuum, devoid of powers and struggles. Neither do they represent something radically new. They should rather be characterized as reactions that occur as the result of an interdisciplinary tension, a new mode of what Immanuel Kant in his days described in *The Conflict of the Faculties*, a conflict that needed wise negotiators in order to secure a proper role for reason itself. Though the demarcations between the historical and the philosophical are set along other lines than in Kant's days, there is still an unresolved conflict over the right of ownership to the correct understanding of scripture, of Christianity in relation to modern reason, which is played out in academic debates with such regularity as to be labeled a "small discursive machine."[10]

In *Displacing Christian Origins* Ward Blanton performs an intriguing comparison of Derrida's depiction in this essay to a process of outbidding. While Derrida points to the repeated efforts of modern philosophy to separate itself from religion as pure, secular reason, Blanton gives Derrida's thesis an added force when he applies it to modern biblical scholarship. Not only did this manifestation of modern thought produce its knowledge in interaction and dialogue with the named modern philosophers, but modern biblical scholarship was also in the search for the "origins" of religion, in particular, of Christianity, relying on and further developing distinctions between religion and secular reason. It also had to trust, to believe, or to "gamble." As Blanton states:

> With the insertion of New Testament historiography into the self-transcending economy of modern thought, we immediately double the modes of originariness in view because we double the academic modes in which such gambles to outbid Christianity may be performed.[11]

Paula Fredrikson's stark lines of demarcation between the modes of reading that manifest "historical integrity" and those (like Badiou's) that do not may be regarded as automated productions of Derrida's little machine. Fredrikson's superior version of understanding of this author, this historical person called "Paul," serves the purpose in this discussion of outdoing the other—namely, Badiou's Paul. This "philosophical" Paul is not discerned within what are here regarded as the (or Fredriksen's) limits of historical reason alone. E. P. Sanders's apparent ignorance of or minimal attention toward the philosophers' work on the same occasion might as well be interpreted as a confirmation of this logic of outbidding, rather than just "historical integrity" or "interpretive humility."[12] As Blanton observes, apropos these gestures of apparently not succumbing to normatively laden debates about the meaning of "Paul" in our contemporary situation, the prevailing attitude among New Testament historians to claim cultural relativism for their work does not constitute radicalism in today's academy:

> Far from being radical statements, such confessions (despite their apparent humility) are . . . little more than dogmatisms, and they will not be otherwise as long as scholars are declaring the historicity of their thinking without being able to articulate much about how this thinking participates in the various types of contingency of what genuinely viable alternatives might be available to these forms of analysis.[13]

In this intensified conflict between the faculties of history and philosophy over the ownership of the name "Paul," the philosophers are by no means left unscathed or saved from this process of outbidding. In their declared resistance to "historicism" or their critique of the traditional churches' failure to realize and fulfill Christianity's secular meaning, they are not innocent of exercises of superiority. These are philosophers who have the capacity to "extract a formal, wholly secularized conception of grace from the mythological core,"[14] in the words of Badiou. Or as Žižek puts it, "The subversive kernel of Christianity . . . is accessible *only* to a materialist approach."[15] They have surely announced their own bid in this never-ending spiral of outbidding. The philosophers, like the historians, participate in this "competitive play of images between these disciplines."[16]

It is not only that the two groups of academicians participate in the same sort of logic, described by Derrida and Blanton, when they expose their disagreements over the meaning of the Pauline legacy. It might also be the case that the reason for talking past each other is that both parties lack what Blanton is aiming at in his investigation of the production of modern New Testament scholarship in interaction with modern philosophy. Blanton's declared aim is a deeper historicity that might enable the parties at both sides of this division of academic labor "to articulate much about how this thinking participates in the various types of contingency."[17] In this process scholars will hopefully be able to attain a higher degree of disciplinary memory, of how modern biblical scholarship shaped modern philosophy and vice versa. But we may also get a clearer view of what Blanton has labeled "the excessive nature" of "both the formal, abstract categories of philosophy and the empirical or historical descriptions of New Testament historiography."[18] For as Blanton underlines, each field borrows from the other. At the same time as he evokes a disciplinary memory from the past through the analyses in *Displacing Christian Origins*, Blanton points to the inescapably blurred distinctions and unstable oppositions between history and philosophy in the present. Neither camp has ceased to borrow, as if they were now "pure" disciplines, with a historical method safeguarded against any "speculation" or a philosophical undertaking protected at the outset against any kind of "historicism."

Precisely because there is an intensified interdisciplinary conflict surrounding the name "Paul" and because this competitive play of images is taking place in the activation of the Pauline legacy, one would expect to find traces of this disciplinary contest at work in the philosophers' readings of Paul. In isolating "historical" and "philosophical" aspects of this reading, in order to see the competitive play more clearly, it is crucial to have Blanton's warning in mind concerning "the excessive nature" of the opposition, the difference between these two "origins" or "sources" for reading: history and philosophy. There may also be a danger of privileging the one over the other in terms of epistemology instead of paying close attention to how these "abstract" forces of "history" and "philosophy" are operating in the readings of Paul. This requires the isolation of aspects of these readings as "philosophical" and "historical." For heuristic purposes, then, it will be necessary to work within this opposition without believing too much in its dichotomy or stability without forgetting that ultimately this dichotomy's contrast makes only limited sense.

Taubes: The Disciplinary Disaster

When Jacob Taubes introduces his lectures on Paul's letter to the Romans, he emphasizes the place at which he is speaking. He speaks as if he is not only addressing himself to a specific audience, but is also confronting a scholarly tradition with his reading of the Romans, which amounts to a "monstrous task":

> To broach this Epistle is a monstrous task. Just as, in general, this conference is not lacking in monstrosities. Here I am in Heidelberg, which is the city of Martin Dibelius, of Günther Bornkamm, of Gerd Theissen and other New Testament scholars. What am I doing, carrying coals to Heidelberg?[19]

It is as if Taubes anticipates an imagined reaction from his audience, as if he is just another in a line of people who bring what already exists in great quantity in Heidelberg: interpretations of Romans. Nevertheless, this self-questioning of the necessity or legitimacy of his task to interpret Romans is only a preparation. Taubes does not admire the pillars of New Testament scholarship fully and unreservedly. He is aiming at something more than a regular or even plausible reading of Paul, which would be as unnecessary as "carrying coals." He is launching an attack on some fundamental aspects of the scholarly tradition that great New Testament scholars from Heidelberg represent.

One of these fundamentals is the practice of New Testament scholarship as a historical discipline detached from philosophy. Besides demonstrating the relevance of philosophy in order to read Romans through the lectures, Taubes also attacks the separation of biblical studies and philosophy more openly in the same introduction, because it leads to "ignorance" when the departments of theology and philosophy are separated as "closed units."[20] The imagined disciplinary purity of either biblical studies or philosophy is characterized by the professor of philosophy as a "disaster":

> I think it is a disaster that my students grow up in sheer ignorance of the Bible. I received a dissertation about Benjamin in which twenty percent of the associations were mistaken, for the reason that they were biblical associations. So the student comes to me with the finished product, I read some of it and I say: Listen, you need to go to Sunday school and read the Bible![21]

The criticism of this separation of biblical scholarship and philosophy does not limit itself to the lamentable devaluation of theology and ignorance of the Bible, the remedy for which Taubes now proclaims is in philosophy "more important than a lesson on Hegel."[22] There is also an implicit devaluation of the historical-critical tradition in the theological departments in Taubes's interpretation of Paul in these lectures, an implicit devaluation that takes the form of a polemical attack when the professor of philosophy turns to Nietzsche. For this professor the insights of Heidelberg scholars such as Dibelius, Bornkamm, and Theissen are superseded by Nietzsche. As Taubes declares, "Nietzsche has been my best teacher about Paul," not even primarily in a philosophical sense for Taubes, but in a historical sense. This is a position that Taubes affirms through a reading of Paul's letter to the Corinthians as early as 1968.[23] It is in the essay "The Justification of Ugliness in Early Christian Tradition" that he praises Nietzsche for his ability to grasp Paul in a historical sense:

With their exegetical investigations of the First Letter to the Corinthians along the lines of the history of religion, Walter Schmithals and particularly Ulrich Wilckens—whose work we gratefully invoke—paved the way for an in-depth interpretation of this passage. If today we are to determine the acutely polemical character of the discussion more precisely than Nietzsche could, his historical insight still remains unsurpassed by the New Testament exegetes.[24]

Hence, for (at least) the second time Nietzsche is elevated by Taubes to the status of the "unsurpassed" interpreter of Paul in the Heidelberg lectures, one of several deliberate provocations from Taubes within this interdisciplinary conflict of interpretations. This should not be considered as an attempt to raise a new wall of separation between the two fields, but as a deconstruction of the separation.[25]

Nietszche installs himself as one of the main proponents of a critique of historical reason, especially with his *Vom Nutzen und Nachteil der Historie für das Leben* (1874). On his part, Taubes does not merely position himself outside the historical sciences. He presents himself as a critical voice of "historicism" equipped with knowledge from historical critical scholarship on the Bible, especially New Testament studies, in his first book, *Occidental Eschatology*. If his appraisal of Nietzsche's "historical insight" functions to blur the lines between the historical and the philosophical, then *Occidental Eschatology* could be labeled his first expression of such a distortion of the demarcation between the two perspectives or disciplines. But this distortion is not Taubes's innovation, but rather integrant to the New Testament scholarship on which Taubes based much of his dissertation—for instance, the scholarship performed by Albert Schweitzer and Hans Jonas.

The Rabbi against Historicism

The then young rabbi Taubes could be considered an adherent of a theological anti-historicism, both Jewish and Christian, that again is indebted to a landmark in New Testament scholarship, Albert Schweitzer's *Von Reimarus zu Wrede* (1906).[26] In his search for an authentic Jewish spirituality, confronted by German idealism and the historical sciences, Franz Rosenzweig armed himself with weapons from Schweitzer's conclusions[27] when he launched his attack on "the curse of historicity."[28]

The primacy of hope was to protect authentic spirituality against the historicist ideology that valued the past in its own terms and resulted in a sort of relativism vis-à-vis the various historical persons, events, and epochs. This corresponded to the suspicion of what Rosenzweig referred to as "the gullibility of experience," the lived present experience of the human being, which Rosenzweig regarded as the place for revelation. What Rosenzweig termed "the historical *Weltanschauung*" had rejected tradition and replaced it with the idea of the progress of humanity. Historicism as "the new enlightenment" connected present and future in its confidence in progress.[29]

When Jacob Taubes uses the term *historismus* in *Occidental Eschatology* it is with the same pejorative connotations of Rosenzweig's critique. Like Rosenzweig, Taubes criticizes the historicist ideology from a theological point of view, what Taubes labels "the essence of history." And like Rosenzweig, the young doctoral student rejects the supposed relativism and corresponding teleology and its "ideology of progress":

> Historicism, while indulging in convoluted language and theological embellishment, tends to equate axiology and value: all ages are equally near to God. This statement always collapses into another: all events are of equal value [*gleich gültig*] and therefore indifferent [*gelighgültig*]. This indifferent proximity to God overlooks the essence of history as the pathway to redemption. The ideology of progress, on the other hand, isolates the teleological pole when it devalues each moment of history in favor of an ideal, which it finds in the infinite instead of in the eternal.[30]

The fact that Taubes in this paragraph has a footnote to Paul Tillich (and in another paragraph in this chapter to Barth's *Church Dogmatics*), though the critique is nearly identical to Rosenzweig's, confirms the picture of a common Jewish-Christian theological anti-historicism, with its claims of "the Absolute," "the essence of history" as spelled out in the terms of the early Taubes.

The early Taubes is immersed in this interdisciplinary interaction between history and philosophy. He does not expose the need to separate them or justify the combination of both disciplines for the service of his description of "the nature of eschatology." All the same, the need to polemicize against "historicism" is there, together with theological hope. *Occidental Eschatology* is, after all, an optimistic account of how the messianic spirit of Jewish apocalypticism is reawakened in the revolutionary movements in the modern age, on a dynamic route toward redemption. Interestingly, in the Heidelberg lectures nearly forty years later, this polemic against historicism is absent. The spirit is no longer only pressing "forward," as Taubes wrote as a young student. In Heidelberg at the end of his life, the spirit appears to press backward in the sense that Taubes looks more to the past in order to write a new chapter in his history of the eschatological spirit. Or said differently, it as if the old Taubes slows down, focusing on only one eschatological figure—namely, Paul—to inquire once more what actually happened, especially during Second Temple Judaism. In this period apocalyptic messianism is not yet neutralized and absorbed by the two hegemonic, conservative blocks: Rabbinic Judaism and the Christian church, Jews and Christians.

> With that [i.e., the latter period] the will of the Jewish Christian congregations is broken by both the Jews and the Gentile Christians. What is exciting in Paul is that we are just *before this turning point,* and the balances are different—totally different, in any case, from the way I learned them in my church history lessons in Zurich, from Mr. Blanke.[31]

Taubes is now excited by the past. He can feel *das aufregende bei Paulus* precisely because of this moment of the past, just before the turning point, when everything still seemed open. This excitement toward the historical past is displayed together with a noticeable disillusionment toward the present. The professor is by no means triumphalist on behalf of his commitment to the revolutionary left in the '70s student movement in Berlin,[32] and he appears disillusioned with regard to the prevailing powers of the world.[33]

While the early Taubes polemicized against "historicism" and proclaimed his hope in apocalyptic political revolutions, the later Taubes does not employ his rhetoric against a target called "historicism." Nor does he proclaim any belief in a contemporary political project or ideology. Instead, he is excited by this moment of the past—Paul's moment.

2

Jacob Taubes's Path to Paul
From the Eschatologist to the Paulinist

In the introduction to his lecture on the Epistle to the Romans from 1987, Jacob Taubes tells a story about how he "came to the Letter to the Romans: As a Jew and not as a professor." The story is, briefly retold, about Taubes's first meeting with Carl Schmitt in 1979 when the Jewish rabbi sat down with "the greatest state law theorist of our time" and read Romans 9–11.[1] Being admired by Taubes for his theoretical achievements, Schmitt was all the more infamous for his support of the Nazi regime from 1933 onward. This personal link and meeting between the rabbi and the former Nazi are what Taubes presents as the primary background for his own interest in the Letter to the Romans. It may be regarded as an overstatement and understatement at the same time. It is an overstatement, because there are reasons to doubt whether this meeting with the law theorist actually was as crucial or even necessary for Taubes in order to discover, end up with, or turn to Paul. All the same, it is also an understatement, since Taubes's short narrative about this encounter cannot but leave many things unsaid.[2] Taubes tells the audience about a letter he sent to Schmitt in 1979. He explains to them that it has a broader background but excuses himself for not providing a commentary to it. "But that would have amounted to a conference in itself,"[3] he explains. The picture is, in other words, much larger, according to Taubes himself.

In the following, some hypotheses regarding Taubes's path to the Epistle and the figure of Paul will be presented in an attempt to broaden the picture given in Taubes's own presentation of his background for reading

Paul. First, Taubes wrote his doctoral thesis, which was published in 1947, about the secularized effects of Jewish and Christian eschatology through the history of the West in his *Occidental Eschatology*. This is a theoretical framework that persists as a basis for Taubes's thinking throughout his academic career, which in certain ways leads to Paul. Second, by engaging himself as a Jew with "the second founder of Christianity," Taubes surely crossed some barriers. However, Taubes demonstrated through his whole life a tendency to transgress instituted and imposed limits. This will help explain his attraction to Paul. And third, there was an inescapable reality for Taubes as a Jew in postwar Europe: the horrors of Nazism. This underlies the whole story of Taubes's encounter with Schmitt and is expressed in clear terms in a letter from 1952 to his friend Armin Mohler: "What was so seductive about National Socialism?"[4] This question is raised in the letter against the background of Taubes's intellectual admiration for Carl Schmitt and Martin Heidegger, the two great German thinkers who "welcomed" Nazism.

Theology Is Everywhere

In the same letter to Mohler, Taubes had asked rhetorically, "What is it today that is not 'theology' (apart from theological claptrap)?"[5] Everything was theology for Taubes, in a certain sense.

Taubes's doctoral dissertation was already a demonstration of how underestimated the presence of theological presuppositions was in the modern era, which was considered to have liberated itself from its theological and religious bondage through the process of secularization. Taubes had attempted to show the effects of apocalypticism through the history of the West, including its secularized forms in the modern epoch. The apocalyptic energies that are poured out through messianic expectations of the Kingdom of God on earth are channeled through human history in ever new forms, religious and secular alike, in every movement that wants to break out of history and its immanent forces. Having marked out Paul as an apocalypticist in the revised version of the dissertation that was published as *Occidental Eschatology*,[6] he also belongs to this history of apocalypticism in the West. What Taubes does in the final years of his life and in his published lectures on Paul from 1987 is, in simplified terms, to write another chapter in this history, narrowing or sharpening the focus to the effects and afterlives of Paul's messianism. This theory of the long eschatological history of the West that Taubes develops in his dissertation also leads him to Paul.

Taubes's framework expressed in *Occidental Eschatology* illustrates one of two crucial aspects of Taubes's background. While this type of scholarship was to a high degree a result of the European Enlightenment, Taubes was heavily influenced by Jewish religiosity, politics, and culture, in ways that are apparently less manifested in his writings. One might say that his father, Chaim Zwi Hirsch Taubes (1900–1966), provided the bridge between the devotional and scientific realms, given that his father served as rabbi at the same time as he founded an institute dedicated to the scientific study of the Talmud in Vienna—between the two world wars. It was one of Europe's cultural centers for Jews. Here Taubes's father had also founded a religious counseling center that primarily targeted young men from the still traditional communities of Eastern European Jewry who had come to the metropolis of a former empire. Being born in the Galician town of Czernelica in the periphery of the Austro-Hungarian Empire (today's Chernelytsya of Western Ukraine), Zwi Taubes knew something about the difficulties of adaptation and the possible consequences of the loss of a traditional religious lifeworld in Eastern Europe. In this work, Jacob Taubes's father was assisted by his wife, Fanny (1899–1957), who had studied at the Viennese Hebrew Pädagogium, the institute that educated teachers who were going to work in Jewish schools. In the 1920s, Fanny also knew Martin Buber (1878–1965), as both were activists in the movement Hapoel Hatzair (in English, "The Young Worker"), a non-Marxist, socialist Zionist party that by nonmilitary means gained a foothold for Jewish settlers in Palestine.[7] Thus Jacob, born in Vienna in 1923, grew up in a home marked by intellectualism, religious devotion, and political activism.

In the introduction to his lectures on Paul, Taubes mentions this family background from Eastern Europe briefly when he relates the history of Sabbatianism, though the family ties to this movement remain unclear. "This is before Hasidism. The thousands of Jews in Galicia—I know that area, Lemberg, by the name of Rohatyn, the families are well known—convert to Catholicism."[8] As Taubes was a descendant of Jews in Galicia, the Sabbatean movement might also be part of his more personal history. And still marked by the memories of the mystical and charismatic movement of Hasidism, the Taubes family was, in contrast to many Jews in Western Europe, not assimilated to the more secular culture but continued to adhere to Jewish rituals and mysticism, which were regarded by many "modern" Jews as retrograde superstition.[9] Not only was a figure like Martin Buber, who was aiming at an awakening of and a return to the older Hasidic mysticism, in the Taubes family's surroundings, but with generations of rabbis adhering to Hasidism on both the mother's and the father's side, Jewish mysticism was part of the family's heritage.[10]

Hasidism promoted an oral culture where sermons or stories by the great-souled men, the *Zaddikim*, were preserved as holy words, since these leaders acted as intermediaries between man and God. Marked by this charismatic tradition and confronted with the sober and rational ideals of the Enlightenment, Jacob Taubes was ordained as a rabbi in 1943.[11] This took place in Switzerland, where his family had moved in 1935 after his father was appointed as a chief rabbi in Zurich. Here Taubes finished his studies. Even without a Jewish community where he could serve as a rabbi in the United States in the '50s, Taubes would appear to others as "something of a holy man, a *zaddik*."[12] After publishing his doctoral thesis entitled *Occidental Eschatology* in 1947, he moved from Zurich to New York to work as a research student in the Jewish Theological Seminary (JTS).

The Hasidism that was spread among Jews of the Ukraine, Poland, and White Russia in the eighteenth century rejected the extreme asceticism of former Jewish mystics. Rather, it embraced all features of life as legitimate tools for attaining a holy life. At the core of the movement was God's hidden presence everywhere. This meant that no area was ultimately profane rather than holy. Since God was present in everything, he could be served in every way, a view that brought the movement into conflict or tension with Rabbinic Judaism.[13] This may be reflected in Taubes's discernment of or disposition to see messianic forces or theological concepts from his Jewish background at work in somewhat unexpected places, as in Christian theology and secular political movements. Besides, Taubes manifested no great admiration for Rabbinic Judaism that safeguarded itself against messianic risk, resulting in a "retreat from history."[14] Instead, Taubes adopted ideas that had been historically regarded by the orthodox rabbinic tradition as heretical because of their messianic logic. Together with Scholem, he paid special attention to the Sabbatean movement and treated it as a Jewish phenomenon, not simply a heretical result of influences and forces external to Judaism. The impulse to return to older and recently neglected forms of Judaism, felt by Buber and others, also included a revaluation of what had been previously deemed heresies and deviations from the Jewish faith. But this new openness toward former heresies was, for Taubes's part, based on a loyalty to old Jewish tradition. This loyalty is manifested in Jacob Taubes's correspondence with his first wife, Susan Taubes (1928–69), whom he married in 1949.

Because of their physical separation due to Taubes's stay in Jerusalem in the years 1950–52, the married couple wrote to each other on a nearly daily basis, with philosophical and religious issues at the center of their dialogue beside more personal ones. Susan was the granddaughter of the chief rabbi in Budapest, but her father was a more assimilated and bourgeois psychoanalyst who managed to get the family out of Hungary and migrate to New York in 1939. While Jacob Taubes seemed to consider collective Jewish tradition as a solid foundation in the post–World War II world, Susan was troubled by her Jewishness and felt haunted by what she described as "the ghosts of Judaism."[15] This she wrote during a stay in Paris in 1952, where she prepared her doctoral dissertation in philosophy and met, among others, the Jewish philosopher Emmanuel Levinas.[16] Before her stay she had been with her husband in Jerusalem, where he taught sociology of religion at the Hebrew University and where Gershom Scholem, Martin Buber, and Hugo Bergman figured among the professors.

> I have been told by Bergman, Levinas, and others of my perfect ignorance of what Judaism is. Nevertheless I would hazard to say the following. The positive and imperishable element in Judaism is a sense of fidelity which pierces through the very center of man, sanctifies his earthly bonds and establishes a bond between heaven and himself. You have told me and it is true that by disloyalty to the past we jeopardize our own self-identity. The world of faithfulness becomes tragic when a man loses irrevocably his mate, his friend, his family, his people, his country. How can one remain faithful and continue to live?[17]

For Susan the tension between the faithfulness to the Jewish collective and the need for an authentic individual spirituality constitutes a dilemma that arises as a nerve in many of her letters to Jacob. This came to the fore in a letter she wrote but never sent to Jacob shortly after their wedding in 1949: "Although there is nothing I desire more than to worship in community and not in loneliness I will suffer my loneliness rather than to give myself to hypocrisy and falsehood."[18] The words were written after the two of them had been to the synagogue and Jacob had told Susan that the Torah was his "whole life and truth."[19]

In this intense search for meaning and identity in Jewish circles in the postwar years, religious issues and theological questions were pressing, even in a world that seemed absent of God. Theology was everywhere for Jacob Taubes in the form of the most personal correspondences or in highly sophisticated intellectual debates. In a sense, it was a matter of survival, of how to come to terms with the present, not only for Susan but also for Jacob.

Nevertheless, it was not Judaism that constituted Jacob Taubes's main challenge and problem as a German-speaking Jew in these years. Rather, it was contemporary German thought. As he writes in a letter to Armin Mohler in 1952:

> It remains a problem for me that both C.S. [Carl Schmitt] and M.H. [Martin Heidegger] welcomed the National Socialist "revolution" and

went along with it and it remains a problem for me that I cannot just dismiss by using catchwords such as vile, swinish.[20]

These Nazi commitments in the past remain a problem for Taubes since he cannot but admire and agree with these German thinkers in some of their insights. Taubes poses a rhetorical question in this very same letter, asking, "What is it today that is not "theology?"[21] This question mirrors in a way Schmitt's thesis from his 1922 book on political theology: "All significant concepts of the modern theory of the state are secularized theological concepts."[22]

In the published lecture "Carl Schmitt: Apocalyptic Prophet of the Counterrevolution," Taubes tells about his first encounter with this book. It seems to have made an impact on the nineteen-year-old's mind comparable only to Karl Löwith's *From Hegel to Nietzsche*,[23] which also helps to explain Taubes's lifelong involvement with Schmitt's theories:

> My reading of Löwith's new interpretation of what had been forgotten and neglected in pre-1848 Germany made quite clear to me that here was a signpost from which orientation of the global civil war of our generation could be found.[24]

On the one hand, Taubes had discovered a profound relevance of philosophy for what he perceived as political realities in a world in "global civil war," an expression from Schmitt that often was interpreted as a reference to the deep political and ideological conflicts of modernity. On the other, Löwith's genealogy of the role of Judeo-Christian eschatology in the philosophies of Hegel, Marx, Kierkegaard, and Nietzsche provided Taubes with a historical account of the secularization process that Schmitt affirmed but for which he did not provide data.[25] Schmitt's thesis had consisted of two types of arguments for the political theology at work in modernity.[26] The first part of Schmitt's thesis is genealogical:

> All significant concepts of the modern theory of the state are secularized theological concepts not only because of their historical development—in which they were transferred from theology to the theory of the state, whereby, for example, the omnipotent god became the omnipotent lawgiver.[27]

The second part can be labeled as structural.[28] Schmitt goes on to affirm the necessary or correlated resemblance between political human law and divine law:

> but also because of their systematic structure, the recognition of which is necessary for a sociological consideration of these concepts.

> The exception in jurisprudence is analogous to the miracle in theology. Only by being aware of this analogy can we appreciate the manner in which the philosophical ideas of the state developed in the last centuries.[29]

Here he sets up an analogy between the legal state of exception and the miracle, but he also points to an analogy between the sovereign's infinite authority and God's power in addition to the analogy between "an absolute decision out of nothingness" and the theological *creation ex nihilo*. Theology is still operative in the supposed secular modernity but has erased its traces, allowing it to be "everywhere" without being recognized as theology. Or, in Löwith's words, "We are still Jews and Christians, however little we may think of ourselves in those terms."[30]

To recognize this presence in the modern era, following and extending Löwith's genealogy back to Antiquity,[31] is exactly what Taubes appears to do with his dissertation, *Occidental Eschatology*. In this sense the young Jewish scholar supports Schmitt's position without acknowledging it. In contrast to Löwith, Schmitt does not figure in Taubes's footnotes or in his bibliography. The focus on eschatology and the genealogy of eschatological ideas in modern philosophers in *Occidental Eschatology* is so similar to Löwith's interpretation that this part of the dissertation could appear as a plagiarism.[32] But Taubes's "discovery" of the disguised eschatology in modernity does also resonate with one of his teachers, the Catholic theologian Hans Urs von Balthasar. Taubes had often attended Balthasar's lectures in Basel,[33] and Taubes stands supposedly in debt to the latter's three-volume *Apocalypse of the German Soul* (1937–39), a debt that to a certain extent is also acknowledged through some footnotes.[34]

Israel has a privileged place in Taubes's history of apocalypticism in the West: "The historical place of revolutionary apocalypticism is Israel. Israel aspires and attempts to 'turn back.' . . . The pathos of revolution defines Israel's attitude to life."[35] Nevertheless, this is no exclusive Jewish version of the history. And Taubes does not at all restrict himself to Jewish voices. Though he refers to the Talmud, Baeck, Buber, and Rosenzweig, he also bases his main theological perspectives on Christian theologians like Paul Tillich and Karl Barth. In addition, he draws on different scholars from the so-called *Religionshistorishe Schule*, centered around the University of Marburg, which had been one of the bastions and bulwarks of German Liberal Protestantism.

Taubes even includes Jesus among these apocalypticists who transform history: "Even though salvation is delayed, whoever announces that the end is coming shares the same passionate faith as the others who have done so—from Daniel to Jesus and from Bar Kochba to Sabbatai Zvi."[36] They are all produced by Israel and form part of Jewish history.

These figures are all actors in a transhistorical drama that for Taubes always involves the redemptive possibility of the Kingdom of God and the possibility of evil and catastrophe and destruction. But it is a drama that has temporal history as its stage, where revolutionary forces clash with counterrevolutionary ones. What Taubes had named "a global civil war of our generation" is just another chapter in this long history, which Schmitt also sees and recognizes, with chapter 4 in his *Political Theology* as the clearest sign of this, according to Taubes.[37] That is why he states that "Carl Schmitt thinks apocalyptically, but from above, from the powers that be; I think from the bottom up."[38]

Occidental Eschatology encompasses, like Karl Löwith's *Meaning in History*, more than 2,000 years where the author sees that the very same apocalyptic logic occurs, though not following strictly historical laws but to a large degree depending on human agency and freedom. Nevertheless, apocalyptic themes are taken up by revolutionary thinkers and groups in the Judeo-Christian culture in times of "revolutionary tides" that are

> not trivial and random but rhythmical and inevitable. Ideas and events which transform the nature of man and the features of humanity cannot be compressed into moments but must be seen through; they complete their course within a historical economy which comprises seemingly disparate centuries.[39]

According to Taubes, there is an overarching continuity in history with regard to the afterlife of apocalyptic and also of gnostic themes that makes comparisons between thinkers and philosophies from "seemingly disparate centuries" possible. This means that Taubes can discern the unfolding of a continuing process from Paul to Hegel and Kierkegaard: "The dialectic of Paul's history of salvation is both *quantitative in terms of world history* (Hegel) and *qualitative in existential terms* (Kierkegaard)."[40] Both apocalypticism and Gnosticism inaugurate "a new form of thinking [that] . . . has been preserved into the present and taken up and further developed."[41] Taubes supplements this metahistorical assumption with a historical reconstruction of Paul's role in early Christianity on the basis of Albert Schweitzer's research and his book *The Mysticism of Paul the Apostle*: "Paul marks the exact turning point from Christian apocalypticism to Christian Gnosis; eschatology and mysticism meet in him."[42] Although, at this stage in Taubes's thought, Paul is not a major figure, the ground for an afterlife of Paul in history and especially in modern philosophy is established.

The lamenting tone of how the unacknowledged eschatological meaning appears in and conditions modern philosophy that characterizes Löwith's account is in Taubes replaced with hope on theological grounds. Thereby he reverses the more common assumption, especially after World War II, that political messianism was a corrupted version of religion that would lead to the totalitarian politics of communism and Nazism. Taubes is not criticizing the eschatological view of history in its modern forms as "a perversion of the classic meaning,"[43] as Löwith does. Nor does the young scholar limit himself to a request for the moderation of our utopian expectancies and historical ambitions. Instead, Taubes emphasizes how apocalypticism has always failed, though through its failures it has left behind a legacy of institutional renovation that also has led to greater freedom in human history. Movements fail by their own standards, but unintentionally leave traces of hope for future generations. With references to Augustine and Martin Heidegger, Taubes concludes with a theocentric speech in a rather optimistic mood:

> If, looking into the beauty of the night, man does not mistake it but sees the darkness for what it is; if he recognizes his protective shells as mirages; if he perceives his insistence as dogged resistance and unmasks his self-made measures for the lies and errors they are—then day will dawn in this human world, and the transition from insistence to existence will follow. When day dawns all measures will turn upside down. Man will then be brought home by God and will *ex-ist*, since he will find his center in God.[44]

The subtitle of the book, "Beiträge zur Soziologie und Socialphilosophie," might be read as a response to one of the leading figures in German sociology, Max Weber, and his thesis of modernity as a process of increasing "disenchantment" and "rationalization." Taubes had joined forces with von Balthasar and Löwith, who were united against the notion of a self-constituted modernity that has liberated itself from apocalypticism and other irrational religious impulses or ideas. Within Weber's scheme such mythological phenomena could be explained away as either "modern remnants of an irrational past or contemporary flights from an overly rationalized present."[45] To one of Weber's students, Carl Schmitt, this had appeared as too one-sided, in spite of the fact that he recognized some truth in Weber's narrative of the modern disenchantment of society and its association of Protestantism and modernization. But for Schmitt, religion and theology were not something external to modern rationality. Premodern "irrationality" was not something totally different or alien to enlightenment rationality but, instead, an inherent part of it, however absent this "irrationality" was in the form of political theology. Taubes interpreted Schmitt's *Political Theology* as "a general onslaught on liberal modernity"[46] and immediately connected Schmitt to Weber as "a legitimate, not an illegitimate, son of Max Weber."[47]

Occidental Eschatology showed indirectly that Weber's thesis on a very fundamental level was wrong.[48] Theology, especially in the form of eschatology, was not marginalized, exhausted, or replaced by the modern enlightenment and its "disenchantment." Theology had not disappeared. As Schmitt had pointed out, political theology was latent in every situation that might need legitimation. And as Weber had stated clearly, modernity was characterized by a success in technological progress and a lack of legitimation of these very same successes. Theology had not disappeared. Theology was potentially everywhere, with Paul looming in the background.

The Stranger in Weimar—the Heretical Ideal

Although Taubes wrote *Occidental Eschatology* during the war, the dissertation is to a large extent an intellectual product of the years between the two world wars: the Weimar period. Here are some of the historical roots of Taubes's first work to be found.

The book's "untimely" or "politically incorrect" character is perhaps reflected in the review by Albert Salomon from 1947: "It may seem strange to contemporary Jews that a Jewish scholar should concentrate today on an interpretation of the German contribution to western thought."[49] To affirm any spiritual value in German philosophy in a book published just two years after the war could seem "strange to contemporary Jews," according to Salomon. It could appear as somewhat out of place, illegitimate or irrational in the light of the war and the Shoah. But the bibliography in Taubes's dissertation lists an intellectual production that mainly dates from the interwar period. The fixation on this intellectual period is persistent throughout Taubes's career. Even in the lectures on Paul from 1987 Taubes still struggles with questions that arose from the Weimar period and its intellectuals.

Max Weber's writings could be said to reflect a certain sense of loss or an experience of the loss of an enchanted religious lifeworld. The notion of a loss was on a theological level mirrored in the loss of the former self-confidence of German liberal Protestantism from the nineteenth century, in its union of scientific progress and the optimistic faith in human growth and development. After Schweitzer's groundbreaking and iconoclastic study of historical Jesus images in his 1906 book, Karl Barth's book on Romans attacked the liberal theology at a time when the destructivity and damages of the First World War had already disillusioned his readers about humankind's modern aspirations and abilities.

The crisis years nourished skepticism toward liberal modernity among German Jewish intellectuals who had already found themselves in an ambivalent position with regard to modern ideals. Over a century after Moses Mendelssohn (1729–86), significant parts of German Jewry had experimented with different kinds of assimilationist positions and opted for liberalism in the nineteenth century, as their legal rights were dependent upon the success of liberal politicians and parties. They favored promotion of individual rights, free trade, and more ecumenical versions of religion.[50] This option was made by a Jewry that in modernity was thrown into the tension between a Jewish enthusiasm for emancipation and the Jewish fear of assimilation.

Some Jews had feared that by assimilating themselves to the dominant German culture and leaving behind their own, they risked losing more than they could win. A range of Jewish intellectuals in the years approaching the First World War thereby questioned the Jewish option for liberalism. The optimism of earlier generations of intellectual Jews who chose to adhere more to the German *Bildung* than the Jewish tradition was seriously questioned in these Jews' experiences with political anti-Semitism and the anti-liberal spirit in the German upper classes.[51] The *Deutschum* and the *Judentum* did not appear to approximate each other, coexisting ever closer in harmony, following a progressive evolution as modernity had promised. In fact, they saw tendencies toward the opposite of this cultural progress. In spite of the fact that the Weimar Republic was the first to grant Jews the same legal rights as the other inhabitants, the First World War had already disillusioned so many about the foundation that had legitimated these rights in the first place.[52] The political and cultural assumptions of the post-emancipation epoch were thereby called into question, leading to new intellectual reactions, developments, and innovations among Jews.

One of these reactions is represented by the co-activist of Jacob Taubes's mother, Martin Buber. Buber had called for a reaction against assimilation in the form of a renewal of Judaism by a return to older Jewish sources, especially within Hasidic mysticism. The Jewry had in Buber's eyes to undergo a decisive transformation and personal renovation in order to return to the essential Judaism. Buber's writings just before the outbreak of the war had an "enormous influence among young German-Jewish intellectuals."[53]

Buber's ideas fueled the new skepticism of assimilation and secular liberalism as it also empowered young German Jews in an unseen way. Young

Jewish thinkers such as Walter Benjamin and Gershom Scholem had been empowered and encouraged by Buber's call for self-definition to reflect on their own Jewishness and to draw upon the cultural and religious reservoir of their ancestors' traditions as an alternative to liberalism. The visible result of this in the case of Benjamin, as well as that of Ernst Bloch, is a type of a modern Jewish messianism. This messianic impulse confronted the modern belief in progress with catastrophic and apocalyptic visions that contemplated the *total* renewal of the prevailing order, a restoration of lost meanings. Though more pessimistic, this new messianism committed itself to a utopian future.

In its allergic relation toward the evolutionist aspect of political liberalism, these new Messianic intellectuals might be considered the Jewish counterpart to what in Protestant circles went under the name "crisis theology," epitomized in Karl Barth's commentary on Romans. Although Barth will defend Paul as an orthodox figure, Barth contributes to this new intellectual climate in which the heretic arises as a scientific object on the one hand and a model to follow or experiment with on the other. After all, it was Barth who was accused of being a Marcionite because of his emphasis on the radical otherness of God.[54] In tune with this emphasis on divine otherness, the new Jewish messianism is not only characterized by skepticism toward secular rationalism and its political implications but also by a discontentment with orthodox or normative Judaism. A total renewal of the present state of order implied a search for what the orthodox and restricted versions of messianism had suppressed. The belief in the possibility of restoring and redeeming these lost meanings in the present led to a new interest in heretical ideas that had been excluded in history by the powerful religious orthodoxies.

The new Jewish intellectual attraction to the heretical figure may be delineated in three versions of it: the messianic-apocalyptic, the gnostic, and the pantheist.[55] *Occidental Eschatology* bears most traits of the first two, and in Taubes's view Paul the Apostle stood in the middle of or in the encounter of both positions. He represented the Christian shift from apocalypticism to Gnosticism, categories that were applied in historical disciplines (*Religionshistorishe Schule*) but used in philosophy as well.

These became categories in the interwar intellectual climate among Jewish and Christian thinkers. They were expressions of more fundamental, felt sensibilities in this period: there was a certain truth in Max Weber's disenchantment thesis along with other modernization theses; the Judeo-Christian God from the enchanted and premodern era seemed more absent than ever. For some, this absence led to a declared atheism (as in Ernst Bloch), and for others it led to an even stronger emphasis on God's transcendence and otherness (as in Karl Barth or Rudolf Bultmann) that was pushed in the direction of Marcionism (as in the late Adolf von Harnack). In this intellectual atmosphere Gnosticism was not a surpassed historical phenomenon. In Hans Jonas's work *Gnosis and Spätantiker Geist* from 1934, which also influenced Taubes's dissertation, the concept is rather ahistorical than historical. Gnosticism involves for Jonas a deep structure in the human being-in-the-world. He was speaking of *Dasein*, acclaiming and appropriating Heidegger's philosophical category.[56] Gnosticism became a category that deepened the meaning of the *Dasein*'s Heideggerian homelessness in the world when Jonas linked it primarily to alienation and otherness.[57] It was a category filled with meaning from the new existential philosophy, the Weimar experience of the loss of a religious lifeworld (especially the Protestant experience), and not least, the Jewish intellectual search for what it meant to be a Jew in modern Europe.[58]

That Taubes presents his dissertation as a contribution to the understanding of religious and social history does not have to prevent one from seeing the influence of the personal fate of this European Jew in his philosophical and historical perspectives on 2,000 years of collective experiences. Friedrich Nietzsche once wrote that "however far man may extend himself with his knowledge, however objective he may appear to himself ultimately he reaps nothing but his own biography."[59] Without reducing Taubes's account of the eschatological history of the West to a mere autobiography, it is not difficult to see some of his personal history mirrored in his reflection on how Gnosticism and apocalypticism are interlinked:

> The theme of self-alienation is to be heard for the first time in the context of apocalypticism. Alienness or exile [*die Fremde*] and the topic of self-alienation permeate the whole of apocalyptic, Gnostic literature. . . . To be alien means: to come from elsewhere, not to be at home in this world.[60]

In 1956 Jacob Taubes became naturalized and was given U.S. citizenship. For his whole life, until then, he had been a Polish citizen, without ever living in Poland. This unlikely status was because his parents automatically had become Polish citizens after the breakup of the Habsburg Empire.[61] The condition of being raised by the leader of a religious minority in two foreign countries (Austria and Switzerland) that were nonetheless the countries most familiar to him enforced the sense of alienation and estrangement. When Taubes's father got reports about the fate of European Jewry under Nazi occupation,[62] which included most of the family's relatives, this must have radicalized the sense of living in exile even in the most familiar and dear surroundings. Taubes did not only grow up in a family that had lost its roots, but his roots were to be found in this rootlessness. Paradoxically, this loss of roots did not only have a destructive effect in the life of Jacob Taubes. Jacob Taubes's first geographical or physical uprooting, when his family moved from Vienna to Zurich, was after all what saved his life from the Nazi persecution and killing.

This possibly forms some of the background of the privileged position of the view from the apocalypse, which constitutes the ultimate perspective of estrangement, in *Occidental Eschatology*. Nevertheless, this privileged apocalyptic viewpoint implies the condition of homelessness, and the greatest sense of homecoming is marked by a paradoxical absence:

> The dramatic homecoming that follows, as ordained by the motif of salvation, is the metaphysical history of the light deprived of light, of life in the world deprived of life, of the estranged life in the estrangement of the here and now. History is the path of light into the world, through the world and out of the world.[63]

This experience of estrangement, which is by Taubes and other interwar Jewish intellectuals understood with the categories "Gnosticism" and "apocalypticism," among others, seems to be one of the factors that raises an interest in Taubes for Paul the Apostle—for Paul the Apocalyptic and Gnostic. It is as if the constant oscillation of these categories between the historical discourses and philosophical ones draws Paul closer to the present and makes him ever potentially a contemporary, as in Karl Barth's words:

> The differences between then and now . . . are purely trivial. . . . If we rightly understand ourselves, our problems are the problems of Paul; and if we be enlightened by the brightness of his answers, those answers must be ours.[64]

In *Occidental Eschatology*, Paul is still a figure in between epochs and not the main actor in Taubes's account of the long drama of eschatological discourse. But already the letters of Taubes from the '50s attest to his increasing interest in Paul.[65]

The Wanderer Forever Exiled

This interest arises in a personal context that may be characterized as a new form of exile. The correspondence with his wife, Susan, reflects a situation where, in addition to the geographical distance between the young couple, there was also a personal distance between Taubes and the professors surrounding him in Jerusalem. The editor of this correspondence, Christina Pareigis, writes that from several letters it becomes clear that in Jerusalem Jacob was sometimes in a depressed mood, tied to the bad state of his finances but above all the difficult human relations at the Hebrew University.[66]

Taubes had come to Jerusalem to study under Gershom Scholem, who saw continuity between Taubes's work in his dissertation and his own on the history of Jewish messianism.

Scholem had been impressed by the young Jewish scholar when he stayed in New York in 1949. The older Kabbalist scholar saw a brilliant student in Taubes, whom he had desired to include in his research team in Jerusalem.

All the same, the relation between the two proved to be difficult. Taubes was, after what Scholem thought was a breach of confidence, expelled from the latter's circle and never forgiven.[67] Taubes had developed a friendship with the also young student Joseph Weiss, while Scholem stood at the center of their relation as mentor and patron. By the end of 1950, Weiss had left Israel for England. The unstable political situation in the new state as well as Weiss's eagerness to work abroad resulted in his move. Weiss left Israel with his wife without delay and submitted an unfinished dissertation at the Hebrew University. Scholem rejected the dissertation, but without letting Weiss know immediately. Furthermore, he told Taubes about his rejection and confessed that he "found in it signs of mental illness." While Weiss waited for his master's response in England, Taubes sent him a letter where he revealed what Scholem had told him. When Scholem got to know about this, he no longer allowed Taubes into his circle of students.

The young student was forever to be the *Verräter* in the eyes of Scholem.[68] On his part, Taubes described the incident in a letter more than two decades later as belonging "to the vanity of academic life." Taubes may have confirmed his image as an *enfant terrible* by deeming as unimportant what the old master considered as moral treason.[69] Nor did the young Taubes, like other students of Scholem, remain in Israel in order to contribute to the poor university and build the new state. Taubes instead sought a way out, in spite of the Zionist commitments for which his mother was especially known.

Taubes does not seem to have felt at home in Israel. In fact, he does not appear to have felt at home any place at all. His second wife, Margareta von Brentano, characterized Taubes's life as "restless and torn" and as "homeless in every aspect."[70] Through his life Taubes moved from Austria, to Switzerland, to the United States, to Israel, back to the United States, and finally to Germany. Besides this, Taubes regularly achieved funding in order to travel extensively while serving as professor in a fixed place. While working in the United States, he would go to Europe; while working in Berlin, he would give guest lectures in Paris, New York, or Jerusalem.[71]

Would not the state of Israel give Taubes some firm ground as Jew, in spite of personal problems at the Hebrew University in the new state? It looks as if not. An important factor in this regard is that Taubes did not appear to share Scholem's Zionist enthusiasm. For instance, by highlighting in his published lecture on Carl Schmitt from 1985 how the minister of justice in Israel used Schmitt to write the new state's constitution,[72] he discredited rather than credited the state. When Taubes as a professor in Berlin in the '60s became an advisor for Rudi Dustchke and a public defender of the student protests, the Jewish professor in reality backed a movement like few other professors that identified with the Palestinian cause rather than the Israeli in the conflict. At the end of his life, Taubes went repeatedly to Jerusalem, where he often went to a Hasidic synagogue in the ultra-orthodox quarter Mea Shearim, one of the centers of Jewish resistance against Zionism in Israel.[73] Not to mention his final attack on the Zionist Gershom Scholem, where he warned his former master against the messianism that had "allowed the wild apocalyptic fantasy to take over political reality in the state of Israel," which could lead "straight into the abyss."[74]

It appears that it has rather been detachment than attachment to a land and to a place that has characterized Taubes's self-understanding as a Jew. In spite of his Hasidic appearance, the Hasidic environment in his upbringing, and rehabilitation of "heretical" messianic movements in East European Judaism, he saw a danger in romanticizing it. He criticized in the Jewish and New York—based magazine *Commentary* this tendency:

> The pseudo-Agadic stress in modern Jewish religious thinking on the "romance" of Hasidism, or the romance of a mythologized East European Jewry in general, is in the end no obstacle to the Christianizing of the Jewish people.[75]

In other words, in the attempt to retain a true Jewish identity or tradition one must refrain from idyllic representations of Hasidism. This could be read as an indirect critique or at least a moderation of Martin Buber's call for a return to older traditions, especially Hasidism. A less nostalgic attempt of a return to an authentic Judaism would be found by Taubes in Rosenzweig.

Franz Rosenzweig did not have the background of *Ostjuden*, but originated from a more typically assimilated family of Western European

Judaism. Rosenzweig might be one of the keys to understanding Jacob Taubes's Jewish identity, and some keys are needed since Taubes himself displays this identity in his writings only obliquely. Rosenzweig stands out as the most acclaimed among confessed Jews in Taubes's lecture on Paul. Only Nietzsche and Freud are honored with recitations as long as Rosenzweig's in these lectures, as if his work were scripture or tradition. Then Rosenzweig is also praised as "an ingenious breakthrough"[76] and "among the most astonishing events," because he took on the task "to interpret the religious community through its liturgy."[77]

The homelessness that characterizations of Taubes as well as his own writings attest to finds a theological explanation in Rosenzweig; the uniqueness of the Jewish people is its refusal of identification with territory. While other peoples cling to the land, the Jewish people have manifested an extraordinary capacity for persisting in exile. They have only one land, a nonterritorial one, according to Rosenzweig's view. This is the holy land. Though maintaining themselves in blood, the Jewish people is detached to any physical land: "We were the only ones who trusted in blood and abandoned the land."[78]

This particular Jewish background could help in a portrayal of Taubes's life and intellectual heritage. In a letter quoted by the editors of his lectures on Paul, Taubes describes his "uneasy Ahasueric lifestyle at the borderline between Jewish and Christian, at which things get so hot that one can only (get) burn(ed)."[79] The adjective "ahasueric" refers to the legend of the wandering Jew, proliferated in different European regions and languages. In folklore this figure of the Jew became the symbol of the sins of pride and revolt of the Jewish people.[80] In this tale the wandering is not a blessing, but rather a divine punishment for rejecting the Messiah by not allowing Jesus to rest on his way to the cross. But one could argue that for Taubes his restless wandering was not only a predestined fate, it was also a vocation.

This would account for Taubes's views on exile in *Occidental Eschatology* as not only a historical punishment or something destructive, but as an apocalyptic viewpoint from which to contemplate the essence of human history.[81] It would also partly help to explain how Taubes could make a choice that nearly no other Jew would in the '60s: select Germany as the place of residence.[82] Surely, Taubes could speak in his mother tongue in Germany, though yet again he was in foreign land and, on top of this, among the people that had exterminated millions of his own. Taubes had crossed a border that few others would.

A Vocation for Transgression: Taubes at the Borderline

What Taubes did when he moved to Germany in 1961 was a kind of embodiment of his spiritual and academic trajectories. In his academic and religious life, he always went to the extreme. He was constantly looking for intrigue, rivalry, and conflict, and he found it. Within these controversies, he would deliberately provoke and upset.

Many of Taubes's Jewish colleagues and friends were upset by Taubes's decision to accept the position as a professor in Jewish Studies at the Free University of Berlin. Few of them would visit him in Germany, as this would appear as a kind of treason; some were afraid to travel there.[83] Ethically and politically, Taubes's move was seen both as highly unusual and problematic. Taubes touched a deep rift between Jews and Germans, apparently without any promise of helping it to heal.

What attracted him to Berlin was, among other things, the political environment of an undogmatic new left wing. It was his affiliation in these circles that would also lead to Taubes's public commitment to the radical student movement, including the initial activities of the Baader-Meinhof group.[84] From his network of professors from the other side of the Atlantic was Herbert Marcuse, who became one of the symbols of the '68 movement. This left-oriented commitment did not stop him from maintaining his contacts with intellectuals on the right wing, among them his longtime friend from Switzerland, Armin Mohler. When residing in Jerusalem he would affiliate himself with a terrorist and later right-wing member of the Knesset, Geulah Cohen. She has been referred to as "the mother of the Jewish settlers movement in the West Bank."[85]

During the mid-'70s Taubes became disillusioned with what he perceived as a Leninization of the student uprising, and he suddenly started to attack his friends and allies on the left in a sharp tone.[86] His colleague Peter Szondi at the Free University described him as untrustworthy in a letter to Theodor Adorno,[87] and he was apparently not the only one who regarded Taubes as totally unpredictable. With time his left-wing activism was replaced with his commitment to the legacy of Carl Schmitt. He regarded Schmitt as an apocalyptic like himself, but "from above, from the powers that be."[88] Taubes, in contrast, sought to delegitimize power. But as a Jew on the political left, Taubes's association with Schmitt was regarded as a highly dubious enterprise. There had been a reception of Schmitt on the political left already in the '60s in Germany. It was, however, only after Taubes's death in 1987 that one could witness a major left-oriented academic recognition of Carl Schmitt's thought in the journal *Telos*. To engage with a person who was considered *non grata* was transgressive on various political levels. Taubes's whole oscillation between the political right and left was in itself transgressive of norms reigning in the political sphere.

This transgressive tendency in Taubes's activity was also seen in the academic world. He did not care about disciplinary boundaries like others. This resulted in cooperation, conferences, and workshops with an interdisciplinary dimension that was unlikely at the time, whether as editor at Suhrkamp with Jürgen Habermas or professor at the Free University. Even the basic norms of academia were broken by this reckless professor. Taubes took intellectual freedoms that were unheard of at the time. For one thing, he did not care about writing long monographs or tractates, but still criticized others relentlessly. Blumenberg was one of those who got irritated with what he saw as a kind of double standard. Taubes polemicized without backing his often harsh, though intelligent attacks with either detailed footnotes or his own writing.[89] In fact, he wrote no book after his dissertation from 1947.

Taubes's trajectory was also transgressive in a religious and confessional sense. Taubes would also look for reasons from within Jewish tradition to approach Christianity. Without leaving Jewish tradition, Taubes would seek to live in the intersection of Judaism and Christianity, typically dressed in black garb and the hat of a Christian pastor.

Allergic to what he regarded as superficial ecumenism or formal peace agreements, Taubes would continue to live in his permanent state of enmity. He uncovered conflictive views in apparently harmonic agreements or syntheses, also in the relation between Judaism and Christianity. An essay from 1953, at a time when he is approaching Paul privately (for instance in letters), demonstrates this allergy:

> For all the current popularity of the term "Judeo-Christian" tradition, the differences between the Jewish and Christian religions are not at all solved. They are basic, and their consequences still influence every moment of our lives.[90]

Taubes acknowledges that there are good and indeed pressing social and political reasons for improving relations between Jews and Christians. Nonetheless, it is necessary to acknowledge the differences that have theological origins. He states polemically that "in the last twenty years it has become fashionable to gloss over and distort these differences."[91] There is an almost confessional supplement to this *Commentary* essay to be found in Taubes's correspondence with his wife, Susan. Publicly, Taubes writes in a rather rabbinical tone, apologetically emphasizing the uniqueness of Judaism in relation to Christianity and the centrality of the Jewish law that challenges the Christian "arbitrariness of love."[92] But privately in the years of 1952 and 1953, Taubes somewhat sets out to defend Christianity in the aftermath of Nazism. He declares this motive when referring to preparations for a Hegel seminar at the Hebrew University in Jerusalem:

> I intend to show that between Hegel and us the deluge took place, i.e., the Christian premises for the concepts of truth, science, etc. . . . were taken away.[93]

And in contrast to his *Commentary* essay, where he somewhat pejoratively describes the Christian concept of love as arbitrary, in a letter to Armin Mohler (written eight days after the one sent to Susan) Taubes reveals a search for a love beyond the law. And this search "always leads me, against my will, to St. Paul."[94]

One reason for this search is a step taken in the *Commentary* essay beyond Gerschom Scholem in relation to Sabbatai Zevi. Taubes describes the situation of the early Christians as similar to the situation of the Sabbatians. The catastrophic event, whether Zevi's apostasy or the death of Jesus, could only be overcome by what Taubes calls "a paradox of faith." Both the paradox of a dying Messiah and that of an apostate savior were interpreted through the same prophetic vision, that of the suffering servant. In both cases the collision of the followers' messianic expectations led to the destruction of old values and antinomian positions. This is the first text where Taubes inscribes Paul and early Christianity within Jewish history as "a crisis that is 'typical' in Jewish history."[95] Taubes is on his way to Paul, as a Jew. He has taken a significant step to "the borderline that's hard to cross."[96] With Gershom Scholem's historical account of Sabbatianism, Taubes got new lenses with which to see early Christianity and Paul. Already attracted by the Jewish heretical antinomianism of Sabbatianism, he also becomes engrossed in the Jewish heretical antinomianism of Paul.

Like Sabbatai Zevi, Paul was a heretic. Precisely as heretical, Paul "was better prepared than modern Jewish apologists to define the basic issue dividing Judaism and Christianity."[97] Paul outshone Rosenzweig and Buber in his differentiation between the two faiths. While sharing theological premises with his "Jewish," even his "Pharisaic" tradition, Paul invented two heresies. First, the Messiah had arrived. Second, the law came to an end. The basis of the Jewish religion "since Ezra" was superseded. Like himself, Paul shared the deep familiarity with his tradition and the tendency to transgression. One can find some of the origins of Taubes's strong identification with Paul in the final years of his life already in this text from 1953.

In this article, Taubes discussed attempts at interreligious dialogue between Jewish and Christian scholars (Rosenzweig-Rosenstock, Buber-Schmidt) and emphasized differences. Twenty-six years later Taubes emphasized the opposite in the Jewish-Christian relation when he confronted the stark differentiation of the two faiths by his old master Gershom Scholem. This talk was given at the Jewish World Congress in Jerusalem in 1979 and was preceded by another rejection of Taubes by Scholem in the form of a letter. Taubes insulted or played with Scholem when he proposed a "quasi 'anti-festschrift'" for him at the occasion of his eightieth birthday. "Perhaps you would find it amusing, after so many festschrifts and prizes, to tolerate or even climb aboard a 'critical discussion with Scholem,'"[98] Taubes wrote in his deliberately transgressive manner, beyond any academic code of conduct. The talk in Jerusalem was given upon his return to the Holy Land for the first time since Scholem's banishment of him in the '50s. It was performed as an attack on Scholem's "static oppositions between Jewish and Christian notions of redemption." According to Taubes, for his teacher Christian redemption was private and individual, while Jewish redemption was collective and occurred in history. Therefore, the messianic turn inward in Jewish history resulted for Scholem in a flight and retreat from history and therefore also from the Jewish concept of redemption, as in the case of Sabbatianism or early Christianity. But for Taubes, this retreat from history or interiorization of the messianic idea is not restricted to Jewish heresy or Christianity. "Retreat from history was rather the rabbinic stance," he argues.[99] Therefore, the heavy price of messianism was not only paid by Jews in previous centuries. Both Jewish and Christian messianist movements—for example, the Puritan millenarian colonists in New England—had paid this price. And religious movements were not the only ones to pay it; secular ones did also.[100] The distinction Scholem had posed between a Jewish exteriority and Christian interiority was no less than a "hangover from the classic Jewish-Christian controversy of the Middle ages." Two decades later this argument against Scholem's typology of Jewish and Christian redemption would still hold for a scholar on Jewish mysticism and messianism like Moshe Idel. According to Idel, Scholem's views were "too neat, simplistic and often misleading from a historical point of view."[101]

On the one hand, Taubes transgressed the boundaries separating Judaism and Christianity, emphasizing sameness and deconstructing conventional dualisms, as in the case of his criticism of Scholem. On the other, he transgressed the norms for common understanding in Jewish-Christian relations by intensifying differences, as in the *Commentary* essay from 1953. In both cases, Paul was at the center of the argument. By constructing the Pauline moment as a Jewish one, Taubes could call for a shake-up of established truths.

Thereby he could break a taboo within Judaism. As Taubes recalled in his introduction to the lectures on Paul in 1987, Jesus had in some Jewish circles been adopted as their own son. According to Taubes, there is a consensus in Liberal Judaism that recognizes Jesus and even has "a sort of pride in this son of Israel."[102] As a notorious opponent of liberalism, Taubes is no less in opposition to Liberal Judaism, epitomized by the Jewish philosopher Hermann Cohen. His pamphlet *Germanism and Judaism* is characterized as no less than "shameful" by Taubes. This pamphlet was published in the midst of World War I in an effort to urge Jews worldwide to support Germany against the Allied Powers. If there is an arch-enemy in Taubes's lectures, it is probably Cohen.

Through his father's academic work, Taubes would know plenty about the Jewish estimation of the foundational figure of Christianity. As the father approached Jesus, his son Jacob would go a step further and approach Paul. Taubes mentions briefly how various Jewish thinkers like Leo Baeck and Martin Buber attempt to deal with Paul. But they do not contradict the fundamental fact for Taubes here, that "Paul has not yet really been comprehended by Jewish religious history." By holding unto Judaism's ultimate illegitimate child, Taubes transgresses another fundamental norm: Paul the apostate and law transgressor is not to be embraced. In the act of embracing Paul, the arch-transgressor of the law, Taubes comes dangerously close to a Jewish apostate, a twentieth-century version of Sabbatai Zevi.

Taubes intentionally inscribes Paul within the Jewish history from which the apostle has been excluded, by Christians and Jews alike. For this transgressive rabbi, Paul's antinomianism was not alien or external to Judaism. It was an inner-Jewish moment.

One can consider this antinomianism as a Jewish spiritual way or lifestyle experimented with by Taubes himself. It can become a vocation for a holy man. At the same time, there is something else behind Taubes's search for a love beyond law or a holy antinomianism in the 1940s and '50s. There is something that overshadows everything else. That is "the deluge."

What Was So Seductive about Nazism?

It is in a context where Taubes writes about a love beyond law, leading him to Paul, where he also raises the question about the seductiveness of Nazism. This is done in a letter to Armin Mohler, his one-time Swiss school friend, committed to the extreme political right.[103] It is in connection with a spokesman for the new right in postwar Europe that Taubes confesses his "problem": Why were the thinkers that stand "head and shoulders above all intellectual scribbling" seduced by Nazism? To this question is another added, concerning the possible value of liberalism and humanism:

> What was so "seductive" about National Socialism? Was the breakdown of the liberal-humanist world reason enough to rush into the arms of these lemures?[104]

It is as if Taubes seeks an answer to these questions by turning to his enemies, people like Mohler who once sympathized with the Nazis and still clung to a right-wing point of view. Nonetheless, with regard to liberalism Taubes shared Mohler's skepticism, though from the other side of the political spectrum. The correspondence with his wife, Susan, from these days in February 1952 also bears witness to this discussion, and Susan sees little hope in humanism: "But haven't we seen man create disaster because he suffocates in 'humanism'?"[105] She also responds to "all the Pauline dialectics,"[106] which probably accounts for a Pauline turn in Taubes's letters to her. There seems to be a triangled focus for Taubes in this period: Nazism, humanism, and Paul. Why are these elements juxtaposed in Taubes's writings?

A concern with Nazism surged in Taubes with greater urgency on the heels of the public display in Israel of photographs from concentration camps. This happened as the Israeli government at the time was involved in reparation negotiations with West Germany. One month before the letter to Mohler, Jacob spoke about these public events in a letter to Susan, writing that

> one learns how deep the wound is. I believe we must bear all of that in mind when we move on the "heights" of German philosophy. The events of National Socialism are part of the cross of our age and address us as well. I'm still standing without the shadow of an answer— my entire compass is destroyed, for the rift between "Europe" and my people is a rift straight through myself. Those in the church have it easy![107]

These lines might attest to a new kind of sensibility in the use of German philosophy a few years after the war. In the light of the deep wound that Taubes comes to appreciate at this time in Israel, German philosophy can no longer so easily be appropriated by the young Jewish scholar steeped in German thought. "The events of National Socialism" are troubling Taubes as an intellectual, and what might have appeared as reckless transgressions earlier or later are possibly forever marked by the wound sensed by Taubes and caused by these events. Besides the rift between "Europe" and his "people," Taubes also draws a contrast from his situation as Jew to "those in the church." This also reveals a rift experienced by Taubes between the two religious communities and traditions, between Judaism and Christianity. Four days later he writes to Susan that he wants to demonstrate how "the Christian premises for the concepts of truth, science, etc. . . . were taken away" in the period between Hegel and the Nazi period. He writes as if there are some Christian premises that had to disappear for Nazism to conquer Germany. But why should he as a Jew prove that these premises were taken away? Partly, the answer might be found in the letter to Mohler, when Taubes writes about people that have an "inner connection to Germany":

> Is it only for others (*das Ausland*) to collect "material" on concentration camps and gas chambers, or is it rather a task for those with an inner connection to Germany to confront what has been done in the name of the German people and explain, if at all possible, what happened and why?[108]

Among those who have "an inner connection" is Taubes himself, although this self-understanding is expressed indirectly in the form of a question. This is a task that Taubes connects to the thought of Carl Schmitt, which Taubes still regards as valid in spite of Schmitt's support of the Nazi regime. Schmitt is right that "the doctrine of law still owes an answer for the 'the decisive case,' that is, an answer to the question of the fate of man in the constellation of tyranny,"[109] in Taubes's words. Taubes agreed with Schmitt that the liberal school of law, represented in the person of Hans Kelsen, did not provide law with legitimacy. Liberalism or humanism could not make law just. Therefore, the question of political theology persisted, and the years of Nazi tyranny did not put an end to Schmitt's theses. Nor would the horrors of Nazism mean a simple return to humanism, with its liberal values. In the face of the need for decision, in the persistent modern situation of a crisis of legitimation, political liberalism or secularism was not the answer. Therefore, Taubes had to stick to Heidegger's and Schmitt's insights, which had become a problem because of their former Nazi commitments and memberships. Nonetheless, he, like them, had to question humanism.

> If humanism has run dry (from Plato to Nietzsche, as Heidegger says), that only means that the question of man has to be posed in a more radical fashion than humanism could ever dream of.[110]

How was one to pose the question of man "in a more radical fashion than humanism"? Taubes tells Mohler that he has been occupied with problems of political theology for the last year and a half, while wrestling with

Maimonides. While Christianity has got rid of the whole problem of political theology (including antinomianism and chiliasm) with Augustine, Judaism "is" political theology. In other words, for Taubes the question of political theology, raised in the most enlightening way by none other than Carl Schmitt, is a matter of existence for his Jewish tradition. The redemption of Judaism is by definition public. Precisely because Jewish theology or theology in general is not "exhausted by dividing it up 'politically,'"[111] as happens in modernity's differentiation, there is something beyond law. Religion or even Judaism cannot be reduced to law alone:

> For the law is not the first and the last, because there are "even" relations between man and man that "exceed," "infringe" the law—love, pity, forgiveness (not at all "sentimental," but "real"). I could not go one step further in my poor and often crooked life (and I have no idea how to go one step further) without holding fast to "these three," and that always leads me, against my "will," to St. Paul. Heartfelt greetings, Jacob.[112]

In the Shoah's wake there is a pressing need to question "the powers that be," the powers that seduced millions of Germans to follow Hitler. For Taubes, this involves questioning the certainties of established philosophical systems and religious beliefs/dogmas. In the present postwar crisis of legitimation, which has in Taubes's mind only problematically confirmed Schmitt's theses, the next step for Taubes is "relations between man and man" that transcend law and the political governing of law. It appears to be a new kind of questioning of legality itself in the post-Shoah situation that leads Taubes to possible phenomena that exceed law. Among them is a Christian premise that constitutes the constant critique and delegitimation of this law, epitomized in Paul. More than anything else in Christianity, it is the Pauline premises that have been taken away in the period between Hegel and Nazism. It is therefore Paul's legacy that must be investigated, if we are to judge on the basis of Taubes's conclusions at the end of his life and suggested by the results from the task described in the letter to Mohler. Thirty-five years later it appears that it is this task the Jewish rabbi is still up for solving when he lectures on the legacy of Paul in the Weimar period—the period to which most of the modern philosophers and theologians date whom Taubes relates to Paul. And Taubes, with his "inner connection to Germany," tries to convince his hearers that German liberal Protestantism "in 1933 couldn't stand the test."[113] Nor could all of the German Jews, either, "since they participated just as much" in cultural Protestantism,[114] with Hermann Cohen as Taubes's prime enemy in this context. The view of a certain responsibility on the German Jewry's side is perhaps oriented by Susan, as she expressed it ten days after Jacob wrote about "how deep the wound is" (January 7, 1952).

> I have been re-reading your letters. Again: The center of the "crisis" is not in the "Jewish problem"; the question is not posed, nor can it be solved within Judaism. Retreat into the clan, into national enthusiasm, preoccupation with national problems, is an evasion, because we were not only the "victims" but the accomplices as well of European history.[115]

The Jews were not only victims, and the Catholic Carl Schmitt was not the only perpetrator, with secular liberals (political and philosophical) standing innocently in the middle between the two extreme positions. In his efforts "to confront what has been done in the name of the German people and explain, if at all possible, what happened and why," it is this image Taubes seems to aim at destroying. It was not the illiberals who were to blame. A Protestant theologian like Karl Barth and a Jewish philosopher like Walter Benjamin both criticized modern liberalism and resisted Nazism. And Barth's enemy on the theological field was German liberal Protestantism. Hence, they are considered models to follow in order to guard thinking against the tyranny. By contrast, liberal Protestantism and liberal Judaism have not proved to "stand the test."

It is perhaps on this backdrop that Taubes insists on the problematic and actual compatibility of Nazism and Christianity when he addresses himself in a letter to Schmitt in 1979. He explains that his purpose with the contact is to understand why "the boundary was not thought be there" when Christians like Schmitt joined the Nazi party and its program.

> Although I in no respect take lightly the fact that the Nazi program talked of "positive Christianity" and took this "seriously" with regard both to Catholicism and Protestantism (wanted to take seriously, and could do: Hitler and Goebbels never left the "church," and, if I am right, they paid their church tax right up to the end!), the "race question was introduced and adumbrated according to a political "theozoology." . . . I only wish to learn how to "understand" why the boundary was not thought to be there, despite Romans 13.[116]

"The boundary" should have been thought be there, according to "the Christian premises" that Taubes in the '50s presumed had "been taken away." Taubes admits in this letter that the Nazi tyranny might be palatable to a Christian political theology solely or primarily based on Romans 13. But he implicitly states that there are other texts or legacies within the Christian tradition that clearly draws "the boundary," though Taubes recognizes the ambivalence in these texts in stating that the chapters of Romans 9–11 "were 'at stake' in 1935 (and remains so in 1978)."[117]

In addition to Luther's "two kingdoms" doctrine, theologies of order [ordnungen], and a general revelation, Romans 13 was especially invoked in the Nazi era. This appeared to make the support for Nazism appear a Christian duty, besides being a German and *völkisch* one.[118]

In addition to references to texts, Taubes was also interested in tendencies or elements in Paul, like "Gnostic elements."[119] Taubes detects the operation of one of these elements in Adolf von Harnack's rejection of the Old Testament.[120] This conclusion by "the most important liberal theologian of the Wilhelmine epoch" is a key argument for the view that liberal Protestantism in Germany did not stand the test in 1933. Again, chapters 9–11 from the Letter to the Romans are at stake. In these chapters Paul shows how "Christ and the father of Jesus Christ are cut from the same cloth, namely the God of the Old Testament."[121] With the rejection of traditional Christian doctrines liberal Protestantism paved the way for Nazism.[122] This Christian and Pauline premise was "taken away."

In the effort to find out "what happened and why" in German intellectual culture in the Weimar and the subsequent Nazi period, Taubes comes to Paul. As he states in the introduction to the lectures on Paul's Epistle to the Romans, he comes "as a Jew and not as a professor."

In showing how the Christian premises were taken away, Taubes appears partly as an apologist for an authentic Pauline Christianity. In his letter to Schmitt he directs himself to him in a rather pastoral tone: "You have no better friend than [Erik] Peterson to take you on the path to the Christian Church."[123] Here Taubes is clearly distinguishing "the Christian Church" from the "positive Christianity" of the Nazi program, as if an authentic church exists. Taubes speaks almost like an insider of Christianity who knows what is right theology. He speaks like a Christian to the Christians, as he would speak like a Jew to the Jews.

Another paradox in this is that it is Taubes's enemy, the Third Reich jurist, who commissions him to lecture on Paul. It is Carl Schmitt who sends Taubes from Plettenburg as an emissary to Heidelberg, at least in Taubes's own version: "He said, Taubes, before you die, you must tell some people about this."[124] The event is told by Taubes as if it has been requested by this dubious state law theorist and the transgressive rabbi complies.

The Silence Surrounding Post-Shoah Discourse

Judging from the bibliography in *Occidental Eschatology*, Taubes owed nothing to Schmitt's thought, since Schmitt is simply not listed or even referred to in the whole book. This stands in a remarkable contrast to what Taubes acknowledged in his autobiographical remarks thirty-eight years later in his lecture on Schmitt, published three months after Schmitt's death (April 7, 1985). Here Taubes gives testimony to Schmitt's influence on him as a nineteen-year-old student, and in the letter to Mohler from 1952 Taubes's admiration for Schmitt's thought is also expressed. But no public statement is made of this kind of debt to Schmitt's thought. The former Nazi professor is absent from Taubes's essays through the 1950s, '60s and '70s, with only one exception.[125] A silence surrounds this relationship and confirms the image of Schmitt as *persona non grata* after the war. As a matter of fact, Taubes actively avoided personal contact with Schmitt.

As there is a silence through these three decades (1948–78) about this relationship, there was also silence about Taubes's interest in Paul the Apostle. As several of Taubes's letters from his early academic career reveal,[126] this Christian figure preoccupied him already then, though this peculiar interest is not much reflected in his essays.[127] There seems to be some kind of link between this turn to Paul as well as the open contact with Schmitt. This link appears to have been set up in Taubes's thought already in the '40s and '50s. It is as if the turn to Schmitt as well as the one to Paul constitute two major transgressions that are held back.

This silence is all the more striking since Taubes was a person who deliberately broke the silence in different ways, on a personal as on an academic level. The breaking of silence about personal matters was after all what led Gershom Scholem to denounce Taubes as a *Verräter* and warn Jewish intellectual circles about him for the rest of his life.[128]

However, there may be a silence that in an even more fundamental and existential way conditioned Taubes's intellectual trajectory, including his way to Paul: he was a Jew who survived the Shoah.

In the introduction to his lectures on Paul he briefly touches upon the issue, but he declares at the same time that he does not want to be questioned about it.

> During the war I was a student in Zurich. Don't ask why, how, what: that's just how it is.[129]

This exhortation to the audience is unusual within these lectures and stands out from the text as a whole. Why should not the audience ask questions about this?

The professor of philosophy Babette Babich came to know Taubes as a student in Berlin in the mid-eighties. When she asked where Taubes had been during the war and he replied that he had stayed in Switzerland writing his doctoral thesis, she seems to have noticed a sense of guilt in his answer: "What struck me was that he did not feel altogether sanguine about it, but mocked himself, recalling Scholem's efforts to get him, unsuccessfully, to Israel and to rue a brilliant colleague's death who had been as courageous as he was brilliant."[130] Are these memories written down by Babich traces of a special case of survival guilt?

This category has been used to describe the sense of shame or debt that survivors from the Shoah have felt in years or decades after the horrors, people who were spared when others perished. This sense of guilt lacks a proper foundation, since the people that bear its burden are not able to ground the feeling in any specific event or in anything concrete they themselves have done. They simply feel guilty because they are alive while others have died. It has also been observed how this guilt colored and was connected to episodic or chronic depression. The survivors' experiences and memories naturally affected the second generation of Shoah survivors who were not there.[131] Jacob Taubes does not fit into either of these categories. Taubes was a kind of first-generation survivor *who was not there.*

When Germany annexed Austria in the year 1938 the Germans started immediately to implement anti-Jewish measures that German Jews had already been suffering. The local Viennese population would add its own forms of harassment, as Jews were suddenly beaten on the street and the police put Jews randomly under arrest. Jewish children were expelled from secondary schools.[132] All this took place a couple of years after the Taubes family had left Vienna.

The Shoah would forever alter the self-image of European Jewry. In postwar years this self-image is almost unrecognizable from a prewar standpoint. The Jewish people as a collective were unsettled not only geographically but also psychologically and existentially. The desire to forget could be more pervasive than the call to remember. In fact, a constituent part of this collective memory became the silence. The first generation of survivors and their families, friends, and colleagues were surrounded by silence:

> . . . during the four decades subsequent to their liberation, survivors were mostly silent. Some were silent of their own accord, trying not to dwell on their catastrophic past, fervently wishing to rebuild a new life and move away from the abject vulnerability. Nevertheless, most were shocked and dismayed at the obvious lack of interest in their travails (and the fate of the European Jewry) on the part of their fellow Jews.[133]

The historian Gabrielle Spiegel suggests that what figures as the absent origin of Jacques Derrida's work is the Shoah. "It is my belief that Derrida has alchemized into philosophy a psychology deeply marked by the Holocaust,"[134] Spiegel declares. Without reducing deconstruction to psychology, Derrida was, together with Taubes, one of those Jews "on whose psyche has been indelibly inscribed an event in which it did not participate, but which nonetheless constitutes the underlying narrative of the lives of its members."[135]

Like Taubes, Derrida seldom writes directly about the destruction, but seems, nevertheless, marked by an inescapable consciousness of it.[136] The existence of these Jews would be felt as a sort of exile, as they could not understand the sufferings of their fellow surviving Jews. Their existence and identity were constituted by "the world of Auschwitz," which they could learn of but not possibly know. Or in Taubes's words, from keeping company with Shoah survivors in Israel seven years after the war, "one learns how deep the wound is."

It is this wound and the silence that surrounds it that brought Taubes's endless speculations to an end. It is precisely in the face of the destruction and the great German philosophers' complicity with it that Taubes gets "a problem," as he describes it in the 1952 letter to Armin Mohler. His talk is halted as he becomes disoriented in a world in which his "entire compass is destroyed," since "the rift between 'Europe' and my people is a rift straight through myself."

Since his permanent move to Germany in 1966, Jacob Taubes was a regular guest lecturer at the Maison des Sciences de l'Homme in Paris, where he met Derrida. "Religion drew Taubes to Paris, he confessed: he came to talk to Derrida about God,"[137] writes Babette Babich.

Aleida Assmann has characterized Jacob Taubes's lectures on Paul as a deconstruction of the reception history of the apostle. This reception history may be regarded as a manifestation of "the powers that be." The absent but nonetheless powerful origin of this tirelessly deconstructive effort on Taubes's behalf may be the extermination of Jews in Europe in the twentieth century. In a certain way, in a nearly invisible way, it is the silence from the Shoah that guides Taubes on his way to, and with, Paul.

Paul and Philosophy
Taubes's Contradictory Paul

Given the early Taubes's criticism of historicism, one would expect the scholar to use methods other than the prevailing ones in biblical criticism in his readings of Paul. Although Taubes claims that he comes to Paul as a Jew and not as a professor, he still approaches the ancient apostle with philosophical perspectives. Does this mean that Taubes substitutes historical-critical methods with philosophical ones? Does he have a philosophical system that a consistent Pauline thought fits into or is subsumed under?

Taking into account that philosophy can be etymologically defined as the love of wisdom, a place to start this inquiry could be Taubes's essay on Paul's most extended discussion of wisdom *sophia*, which appears in the Pauline corpus in 1 Corinthians, chapters 1–2. This is an essay that has been neglected by most commentators of Taubes's readings of Paul. How is 1 Corinthians received in Taubes's work and what kind of method could be said to be operative in this reception? If there is some sort of a method to be discerned here, what notions of the historical and the philosophical does it reflect?

Method: The Art of True Disagreement

It will gradually become clear in this chapter that there is a method operative in Taubes's work and that it results in the image of a contradictory Paul, caused by what Taubes regards as Paul's "Gnosticism." This question of Gnosticism is articulated by Taubes in a constant oscillation between the historical and the philosophical, the ancient and the modern.

In chapter 2 a biographical and historical background was given as to why Taubes turns to his enemies in order to find answers to his questions. Taubes does not end his inquiry into German intellectual history with his *Occidental Eschatology*. As testified to in one of his Heidelberg lectures, he really wants to understand his adversaries:

> I have thought about the problem for a very long time and have found something in common—well, take this *cum grano salis*, but it is meant very seriously—something in common between Schmitt, Heidegger, and Hitler. . . . My first thesis is: The German culture of the Weimar Republic and of the Wilhelmine period was of a Protestant and somewhat Jewish coloring.[1]

The "enemies" he refers to are all German names that somehow connect to Nazism: Martin Heidegger, Carl Schmitt, and Friedrich Nietzsche, as will be argued for in this chapter. Of these German figures, Nietzsche is the most decisive for Taubes's interpretation of Paul. Taubes wants to understand why the intellectuals among these enemies welcomed Nazism within this specific intellectual context of "the Weimar Republic and of the Wilhelmine period." Paul, or rather Paul's legacy, provides a key to this longed-for understanding. Here one sees already contours of an approach.

Taubes's approach when it comes to Paul consists mainly in reading the apostle through Taubes's enemies in order to discern a true disagreement. This reflects a peculiar notion of what a text is. The examples here will make it evident that this happens through a close reading of specific texts of Paul as well as through a reading of Pauline legacies that are at work in others' texts. Through Nietzsche, Taubes will do a close reading of 1 Corinthians 1–2, which prepares for his confrontations with Hans Blumenberg as well as his appraisal of Carl Schmitt. By showing how these Pauline legacies are at work in these intellectual discussions, it will be made manifest that a certain reception of Paul in which Taubes's Paulinism plays an important role is part of this wider intellectual history in the twentieth century of Germany.

To Immerse Oneself Talmudically

In spite of his criticism of historicism (see "The Rabbi against Historicism," in Chapter 1) Taubes is nonetheless preoccupied with history in his engagements of Paul. In the Heidelberg lectures he declares how eager he is to know more about what took place before the "turning point,"[2] which occurred shortly after the Second Temple Period when the Jewish Christian congregations were broken between Jews and Gentile Christians.

However, this Taubesian inquiry into what really happened ("was eigentlich gewesen ist") before the Jewish Christian congregations were broken is pursued with tools other than the ordinary historical ones, developed out of the predominantly German Protestant school of modern biblical criticism. The speaker in these Heidelberg lectures is not ready to rely on the strict and logical opposition between synchronic and diachronic readings and to choose one over the other. He can read Paul diachronically and situate the apostle in a reconstructed past where "the balances are different," before "the Jewish Christian congregations are broken by both the Jews and the Gentile Christians," at the same time as he reads Paul synchronically as an author of texts that refer to present realities.

This "method" is also put to work in the best example of a close reading of a Pauline text in all of Jacob Taubes's published works in his interpretation of 1 Corinthians 1–2. In the essay "The Justification of Ugliness in Early Christian Tradition" from 1968 Taubes praises the philosopher Nietzsche for his ability to grasp Paul in a historical sense. Of Nietzsche he writes that "his historical insight still remains unsurpassed by the New Testament exegetes."[3]

This view testifies to a more synchronic approximation of a text. At least it reflects a point of view that does not take for granted that the ambition to make the most accurate historical reconstructions of the past guarantees the greatest historical insights.

"The dialectic of Paul's history of salvation" that Taubes sees operative in Hegel as well as Kierkegaard in *Occidental Eschatology* and in his juxtapositions of Paul and Nietzsche or Paul and Freud in the Heidelberg lectures reflects a peculiar notion of text.[4] This notion is indicated in the Heidelberg lectures when Taubes argues that he can demonstrate the value of a specific reading of a passage in Paul by "immersing oneself—Talmudically, as they say."[5] This is another inspiration for Taubes's modes of reading besides the theological anti-historicism already referred to that also invites Taubes to read texts synchronically rather than diachronically. This inspiration and its implications for Taubes's peculiar hermeneutics are highlighted by Charlotte Elisheva Fonrobert and Amir Engel:

> Taubes reads the sources . . . not as finite texts with finite ideas. They are for him palimpsests, debates, and discussions. The texts that Taubes discusses themselves also try to make a point on the background of an already given argument and in an already given historical moment. Taubes considers the texts primarily as an axis. For

him—in true Talmudic fashion—each primary source is, first and foremost, a moment in time and a position in a debate.[6]

In the Heidelberg lectures Taubes's reading of Nietzsche exemplifies some of this "Talmudic fashion." The claim that Nietzsche's "historical insight still remains unsurpassed by the New Testament exegetes" is argued for by Taubes along two paths. In the 1968 essay he argues for why Nietzsche's insight is unsurpassed through a reading of Paul; in the 1987 lectures he affirms the same point primarily through a reading of Nietzsche.[7]

Taubes provides the listener of the Heidelberg lectures a sign of this when he introduces a Yiddish concept in his reading of Nietzsche:

> I am a level-headed reader. However big an author's mouth, or his pen, I ask after what in Yiddish is called *tachles*. What does he say? Not what does he talk, but what does he say [*Nicht was red'er er, sondern was sagt er*]? That's when it becomes clear to me that Nietzsche actually ties himself up in a very deep contradiction.[8]

With the Yiddish *tachles* Taubes appears to ask for the purpose or the aim of Nietzsche's discourse,[9] as something beyond or underneath Nietzsche's statements. This appears to be Taubes's Talmudic form of a hermeneutics of suspicion. He cannot take for granted that the essential is expressed and spelled out in the statements, since as palimpsests something is always erased partially or completely from texts.[10] As interventions in debates and discussions that transcend time and place, texts necessarily enter into conflicts, and one of the primary tasks for the reader is to discern the true disagreement, which is why Taubes raises the question "what are Nietzsche's countermodels?,"[11] as if this is not given but rather a difficult though crucial question to answer.

In *What Is Talmud?* Sergei Dolgopolski describes the Talmudic "fashion" as the art of disagreement. In a Western philosophical tradition that has privileged an original agreement about truth, which it is the philosopher's task to reflect, it is harder to achieve true disagreement. As Dolgopolski writes, disagreements "are even harder to maintain, for the ghost of agreement constantly haunts and dissipates them."[12] In contrast, when a rational rhetorical disagreement is reached in the Talmudic tradition this outweighs any longing for a final conclusion that would put an end, or cover up, such true disagreements. In a resistance to the historical presence of a text or a biographical presence of an author, the Talmudic reasoning in Dolgopolski's view is reminiscent of Derrida's resistance to Western metaphysical "logocentrism." Within the paradigm or metaphysics of the Talmud the past is only reachable through the process of rational rhetorical reinvention,[13] which perhaps explains why Taubes delves into Nietzsche's anti-Platonic rhetoric in order to understand the past he is "excited" to know more about. This provides for an understanding of Taubes's polemical style, which is not to be simply opposed to a search for historical and philosophical truths. Polemics is rather the pathway to a true disagreement, which is the best basis for further discussion. Talmudic reasoning does not trust the opposition of philosophical truth over against "mere" rhetoric or sophistry.

Nietzsche inhabits a place in opposition to the ideologies of modern historicism on the one hand and the ideologies of Christian metaphysical dogmatics or logocentrism on the other. This is a place where Taubes can breathe and think freely, in resistance to these philosophical and theological ideologies. Although they appear antithetical toward each other, Talmudic reasoning and Nietzchean writing share a common weapon against these ideologies: philology. Accordingly, Taubes states that "philology is an implicit critique of theology and philosophy." Then he quotes from *Daybreak* §84, where he finds "honesty" as a keyword, a word set in opposition to "truth."[14] Taubes has with Nietzsche left a notion of theological or philosophical truth behind and replaced it with "honesty," suspicious of a Christian scholarly interpretation of Paul: "How little Christianity cultivates the sense of honesty can be inferred from the character of the writings of its scholars."[15]

Taubes's Nietzschean task is then already attuned to his Talmudic reasoning. He will replace the dishonest philology of Christianity with a new philology already embedded in Talmudic reasoning in order to achieve honesty, *redlichkeit*, in relation to Paul. Once again, we see how the editors of the written edition of Taubes's oral lectures were right on the mark when they described the lectures as "a deconstruction of the history of the reception of Romans."[16] Taubes reads "Talmudically," with the forerunner to Derridean deconstruction, Nietzsche.[17] His method is deconstructive.

Is Paul a Philosopher?

In his reading of Nietzsche in the Heidelberg lectures Taubes does not depend upon a consistent Nietzsche in order to take him seriously as a philosopher. Taubes is quick to point out that although the critique of rationality is "a pervasive theme" in the German philosopher's thought, Nietzsche "wasn't sharp enough to understand that in the Bible knowledge and the Fall are connected."[18] In his concept of a history of modernity constituted on rational knowledge as decadence, Nietzsche is already more biblical in Taubes's view than the author Nietzsche himself was aware. The history of modernity "is pinned on Paul," although this affirmation is not of any great value to Taubes, since Paul is not a modern figure for Taubes. Paul is rather an "illiberal," "fanatic,"[19] or a kind of an antiphilosopher, like Nietzsche. Although Nietzsche is not willing to admit it, since he has invented the type of the priest as his enemy and Paul (since *Daybreak*) as his arch-enemy, Taubes reads Nietzsche against himself on this matter in order to discern the true disagreement between Paul and Nietzsche. Taubes argues that beneath Nietzsche's declaration of himself as Antichrist there and his opposition to Paul's invention of Christianity, there is no less than "a jealousy with respect Paul"[20] and a "experience with Paul" that "haunts Nietzsche all the way to the deepest intimacies."[21]

What may be thought of as Nietzsche's overall intention with his work, in Taubes's presentation, is the transvaluation of values, though this philosophical project of the return to aristocratic and dionysian values of Greek Antiquity is not what Taubes admires in Nietzsche. What Taubes regards as his unsurpassed historical insight is something that happens unintendedly as Nietzsche "pass[es] through history" with his attempt to overcome the values and "poison of resentment" that he supposes characterize "this most important man" called Paul:[22] Nietzsche sees Paul for what he is, like no other exegete or thinker.

This argument is built upon Taubes's "dogmatic" delineation of the two types of philosophy, a dogmatism for which he excuses himself, but that is also grounded in Rosenzweig's evaluation of the history of philosophy "from Ionia to Jena."[23]

> At the end of the history of philosophy, if one draws the arc from Ionia to Jena, as one of Rosenzweig's formulas goes—that is, from Parmenides to the *Phenomenology of Spirit*—at the end of this arc, then, it breaks open with the antiphilosophers. They include Marx. . . . They include Kierkegaard. . . . Here I'm speaking about Nietzsche.[24]

Along this curved line of philosophers we encounter a thought, according to Rosenzweig, that posits an identification of reasoning and being. This "whole honourable company of philosophers" had established "the unity of the-world-as-totality,"[25] which corresponds roughly to Taubes's first type of philosophy, exemplified by Plato and Aristotle. In this type "truth is difficult to attain, accessible to a few, but always there,"[26] according to Taubes. In the second type "truth is very difficult to attain and has to pass through all of history, but after that truth is for everyone."[27]

The truth that Taubes sees in Nietzsche is obviously very difficult to attain, since in Taubes's view this comes with a high price.[28] With *Zarathustra* as a new Bible, with the transvaluation of all values in which Nietzsche assumed the Pauline (and Mosaic) role of the greatest lawgiver, Nietzsche was not merely reaching a truth that had always been there: "Nietzsche saw quite rightly: Either he fails, or a new age begins with him." A new age, something new could break through with Nietzsche, the completion of philosophy as an antiphilosophical break. But that would require a miracle, since the modern cosmos out of which Nietzsche tried to break was an immanent one, governed by laws. And such a belief or hope for a miracle is already a theology; "theology was everywhere" in these Taubesian reflections on Nietzsche.

What is of great significance in this discussion of Paul is that it appears to Taubes that Nietzsche is preoccupied with the same problem Paul is in the First Letter to the Corinthians: the meaning of suffering and martyrdom.

> I find this absolutely magnificent. And everything speaks for Nietzsche! For in a monistic universe there is no exodus, no transcendence. And then suffering must be explained in an immanent fashion, whether one likes it or not. . . . Modernity is an immanent cosmos. . . . The question is: How can one think about suffering in a transcendent-Christian way? From what vantage, outside, can suffering be described?[29]

Nietzsche makes his attempt, and pursues it "up to the last," when he "tries to penetrate all the way into the Christian mystery, where the paradigm is a giving oneself up, a self-expenditure, and to reinterpret in a Dionysian manner."[30] So it is after this passing through history, "into the Christian mystery" of suffering, that Taubes can discern the true disagreement between Paul and Nietzsche.

Nietzsche's utopia is an aristocratic one, since what he wants to recover of the ancient values is this aspect of the first type of philosophy: truth is for the few. Taubes emphasizes that it is the men of wisdom from 1 Corinthians 1:20, and this minority of wise men is what saves humanity, according to Nietzsche. The aristocratic minority prevents the whole of humanity from being nothing more than a zoological species (merely animals), in Taubes's reading of Nietzsche.

In Taubes's eyes, Nietzsche is quite right to name Paul as his primary enemy, since in Paul's utopia truth is not only for the few, but for everyone, since "they are all in Christ."[31] Nietzsche is right precisely because he discerns the conflict, the true disagreement, between the Dionysian, aristocratic values of Antiquity and the values of Paul. Nietzsche has recognized the transvaluation of all values that has already taken place in Paul with regard to Antiquity. This is the unsurpassed historical insight that

Nietzsche arrives at unintendedly, through his own anti-Christian struggle for a new transvaluation of all values, for his own utopia. This is Taubes's claim already in his 1968 essay:

> Nietzsche's intention to uproot Christian values and to do justice once again to those of antiquity allowed him to focus on the moment when the turnover from ancient to Christian values takes place.[32]

In Heidelberg Taubes reads Nietzsche and encounters Paul. In the 1968 essay he pays attention to the Pauline text against which Nietzsche's attack in *Anti-Christ* is primarily directed, from Corinthians. Since the Heidelberg lectures were to focus on the letter to the Romans, Corinthians was left in the background, though Taubes also pointed out Nietzsche's more explicit use of passages from Corinthians:

> Nietzsche, in the invectives against Paul, in the *Anti-Christ* . . . refers to the Epistle to the Corinthians. That was interesting to me as a professor of philosophy. The passages that he thinks are positively insane, mentally crazy, the delusions of this little people there and so on . . . these passages are from Corinthians.[33]

For Taubes the problem in 1968 is that Nietzsche's historical insight is not recognized because of "the rapid convulsions of his late aphorisms and fragments." In the 1987 lectures Taubes still has this problem, though his strategy to convince his listeners is to highlight Nietzsche's powerful points and to claim that Nietzsche's late and so-called insane writings are not insane at all. While they may be "psychically confused," they are "theoretically coherent."[34] In the 1968 essay the strategy is different: In order to advocate for Nietzsche's stance, Taubes argues through a close reading of 1 Corinthians 1:18–2:5 and through excerpts from some church fathers, building his own historical reconstruction of some aspects of early Christianity.

The overall theme of aesthetics indicated by the title "The Justification of Ugliness in Early Christian Tradition" might be inspired by Nietzsche as well, given that Taubes quotes from *Anti-Christ* §51. Here Nietzsche opposes the beautiful to "the greatest misfortune of humanity," Pauline Christianity, as expressed in 1 Corinthians 1:23:

> Everything that is well-constituted, proud, gallant and, above all, beautiful gives offence to its ears and eyes. Again I remind you of Paul's priceless saying: "And God hath chosen the *weak* things of the world, the *foolish* things of the world, the *base* things of the world, and things which are *despised*":[23] *this* was the formula; *in hoc signo*

the *décadence* triumphed.—*God on the cross*—is man always to miss the frightful inner significance of this symbol?—Everything that suffers, everything that hangs on the cross, is *divine*. . . . We all hang on the cross, consequently *we* are divine. . . . We alone are divine.[35]

Although Nietzsche understood the antithesis between Antiquity and Christianity in terms that were too bold, according to Taubes, he still grasped the unique break carried forward by Paul's teaching of the cross as foolishness in Corinthians, "as only Celsus and Polyphyry before him had done." Again Taubes invokes the polemical counterparts to Pauline Christianity in order to discern its true nature. Taubes, in his usual polemical style, depicts Paul's teaching, manifested in Corinthians, as no less than "a slap in the face of the noble ethos of Antiquity."[36]

Taubes discerns Paul's transvaluation of values without the presumptions of either historicism or dogmatic theology. Through Nietzsche he can see the real Paul. To read Paul through the texts of a philosopher remains constitutive for Taubes's method or optic.

Gnosticism as Contemporary Concern: The Legitimacy of Modernity

The Nietzschean discovery, to be seen in the 1968 essay, of the distinctively new and foreign doctrine does not lead Taubes to whitewash Paulinism with regard to the neutralization of the messianic impulse in early Christianity. On the contrary, this is a revision of the former genealogy, a revision that concludes with a paradox: Paul is at once the most subversive of Christianity with regard to "the noble ethos of Antiquity" and, at the same, or rather in the same letter to the Corinthians, the first expression of the accommodation to the very same "noble ethos." By his own contradiction Paul accommodates and undermines his subversive message. This accommodation is caused by what Taubes considers the infiltration of Gnosticism into Paul's first letter to the Corinthians. Why is Gnosticism chosen as a crucial example of "the noble ethos of Antiquity"?

The question of a "Gnostic infiltration" was obviously important for Taubes to "identify the inner difficulties and external resistances that prevent the 'Christian' impulse from breaking out into the open." But the question of Gnosticism had wide-ranging consequences that went beyond the question of the meaning of Paul's first Letter to the Corinthians.

First, in the academic context where one version of what became the published form of this essay was presented, Gnosticism was already an issue for heated discussion. What was at stake was no less than the status of modernity. Second, for Taubes the question of Gnosticism was also part of the question of the religious and intellectual culture of the Weimar Republic and of the Wilhelmine period that preceded the Nazi period in German history, as brought to the fore in the Heidelberg lectures. The Gnostic, especially in the case of Marcion, was crucial for the understanding of relations between Judaism and Christianity. By reading Marcion as Gnostic Taubes could discern anti-Jewish tendencies that would do away with the Hebrew Bible within "Gnostic" Protestantism.[37] Third, it was not uncommon in New Testament scholarship at the time to suppose the presence of Gnostics in the community that Paul founded in Corinth.

The immediate academic context for "The Justification of Ugliness in Early Christian Tradition" was the 1966 meeting in the research group "Poetik und Hermeneutik." This consisted of a group of young German scholars from mainly philosophy and literary studies with a common commitment to interdisciplinary perspectives as a way of reorienting their studies. With his international network and his experience from this new mode of doing research across the disciplines at Columbia in the United States, Taubes was invited to the group. The research group consisted of renowned scholars, such as Reinhart Koselleck, Hans Robert Jauss, Wolfgang Iser, and Hans Blumenberg. It has been called one of the most significant academic events in the intellectual history of the Federal Republic of Germany.[38]

The same year that Taubes was appointed professor in Jewish Studies in Berlin and moved to West Germany from the United States, he contacted Blumenberg. This contact led to a correspondence for over twenty years, and in the Heidelberg lectures in 1987 Blumenberg is considered by Taubes as "among those who are alive . . . the only philosopher in Germany who interests me."[39] Nonetheless, by seeking contact with Blumenberg, Taubes also sought confrontation. Already in the 1964 meeting in the Poetik und Hermeneutik group Taubes's and Blumenberg's disagreements over the phenomenon of Gnosticism were manifest. While Taubes saw a potential and spirit of revolt in the Gnostics' lawlessness, Blumenberg denied this quality to ancient Gnosticism. The Gnostic protest could not bring any change, in Blumenberg's view.[40]

In his *The Legitimacy of the Modern Age* from 1966 Hans Blumenberg describes modernity as the second overcoming of Gnosticism, assuming like Hans Jonas that Gnosticism is a human mode of relating to the universe that is transcending historical epochs.[41] In existentialism and nihilism Jonas had found analogies to Gnosticism "across ages." Thereby Gnosticism was still present in the modern era and posed a threat to the modern man's reconciliation with the cosmic order or natural laws. In contrast to Blumenberg's notion of secularization as "worldlification" (German: *verweltlichung*) stood the gnostic "deworldlification" (German: *enweltlichung*), a kind of evacuation from the world. Though much less distrustful toward modern science than Jonas, Blumenberg still adhered to the basic scheme of Jonas about the persistent presence of the Gnostic attitude or spirit through the ages. Blumenberg also seemed to accept Gnosticism as a phenomenon that provides some of the most radical answers man can give to the questions raised by his existence.[42]

The Legitimacy of the Modern Age became a milestone in German postwar philosophy. Here Blumenberg launched attacks on several of the philosophers on whom Taubes had based much of his work: Karl Löwith and Carl Schmitt. In order to argue against the continuity that these thinkers saw between premodern Christianity and the presupposed secular modernity, Blumenberg posited modernity as a definitive break with the religious past. Modernity was "neither a renewal of the ancient world nor its continuation by other means."[43] It had a legitimacy of itself. The self-assertion of modern reason and human mastery of nature constituted the second and successful overcoming of Gnosticism for Blumenberg.

The antithesis between Gnosticism and modernity is upheld by Blumenberg in explicit response to Eric Voeglin, who had named modernity "the gnostic age."[44] By framing the question of modernity's legitimacy in terms of an overcoming of Gnosticism,[45] Blumenberg not only relates modernity to this ancient religious phenomenon, he also affirms implicitly that a true understanding of this ancient past is the key to the understanding of the modern present. Although Blumenberg attempts to replace the pessimistic account of modernity in Voegelin and Löwith with an optimistic account of a real progression from this ancient heresy, he still contributes to the inflation in the use of this category in the decades after the First World War.[46]

An important background for this final account is Taubes's confrontation with Hans Blumenberg in the Poetik und Hermeneutik research group, two years after Taubes's essay on "The Justification of Ugliness in Early Christianity." Though published in 1971, this confrontation took place at the 1968 meeting in the group. Two years earlier Blumenberg had published his frontal attack on the theses of secularization and political theology posed by Löwith and Schmitt.

Taking his cue from the very theses posed by Löwith and Schmitt that Blumenberg severely criticized, Taubes would naturally be very suspicious of Blumenberg's attempt. And as a theorist who affirmed a continuous Gnostic tradition that had been "passed down to Hegel and Marx,"[47] Taubes had a position to defend. Two years earlier Taubes had described Blumenberg's tome as "a one-sided interpretation of the process of enlightenment and demythologization."[48] Now Blumenberg was in the process of developing another tome, which was published as *Work on Myth* in 1979.

As Herbert Kopp-Oberstebrink has written, there was "a certain teleological factor" that was "intrinsic to Blumenberg's historical construction."[49] Steeped in the thought of theological anti-historicism, Taubes would also encounter Blumenberg's teleological traits with mistrust. Blumenberg had detected a progression from bondage to freedom in the history of the West through an overcoming of Gnosticism. The modern freedom was manifested in the free play of modern aesthetics, a freedom opposed to the terror of which human myths were expressions and media for establishing distance to a fearful nature. The aesthetic play, by contrast, provided not only distance to nature but also dominion over it, in continuity with the dominion exercised through the modern natural sciences.

The Proto-Gnosticism Hypothesis within New Testament Studies

By the second half of the 1950s what has been known as "the Gnostic hypothesis" was formulated by the German biblical scholars Walter Schmithals and Ulrich Wilckens. The nucleon of this hypothesis consisted in positing that Paul's opponents in Corinth were Jewish Gnostics. This type of Jewish Gnosticism was a result of widespread syncretism around the time of Jesus's birth.

Schmithals argued that a Gnostic Christology could be recognized in the expression "Jesus be cursed" from 1 Corinthians 12:3. For him this was a Gnostic slogan, rooted in the Gnostic view of the body as a prison for the soul, which was used in Corinth against Paul's emphasis on the crucifixion of Jesus. A heavenly Christ could hardly be recognized by such Gnostics in a crucified man, according to this view.

The New Testament scholar Hans Conzelmann moderated Schmithals's view of the existence of Gnosticism in Corinth, claiming that the apostle's opponents were rather "proto-Gnostics" than adherents to the Gnosticism documented in writings from the second century C.E. onward. This proposal did not defy the core of the hypothesis, however, and could not save it from severe criticism within New Testament studies, especially as the knowledge of the Nag Hammadi library increased.

Today only a minority among New Testament scholars are ready to defend the idea of a Gnostic opposition to Paul in Corinth.[50]

Taubes's Objection to Blumenberg's Historical Account

In the 1960s, however, the plausibility of a Gnostic presence within the New Testament could underline the importance of the whole question about Gnosticism, in the past or in the present.

In the Poetik und Hermeneutik group the question of Gnosticism appeared to be important, as the transcription of one of the discussions indicates.[51] Taubes had expressed the disagreement with Blumenberg's historical construction of Gnosticism at the meeting in 1964. Here he had argued for a fruitful comparison between ancient Gnosticism and modern surrealism, in spite of the chronological distance. For him both Gnosticism and surrealism represented revolts against the determinism of the ancient universe on the one hand and of the modern natural sciences on the other. Blumenberg's assertion that the laws of nature constituted a "medium allied with freedom" was not tenable. The law of nature posited by modern science did not simply represent a "solid positive quality of consciousness."[52] Modernity was more contradictory than this, Taubes's argument implied. Gnostic revolts or tendencies could not be that easily overcome, as in Blumenberg's account.

In the 1968 meeting Taubes showed himself to be "the most persistent opponent" of Blumenberg's concept of myth during the latter's academic career.[53] Taubes attacked the fundamental basis of Blumenberg's theory, the sharp distinction between myth and dogma, between the originally oral mythic narratives on the one hand and "theological images that are fixed in written form" on the other.[54] The thesis of a definitive overcoming of the Gnostic myth, inaugurated by Augustine's Christianity, then completed by modernity, relied on such a strict separation between mythic tales and dogmatic theology. As Taubes wrote,

> A line of demarcation is drawn between a dogmatic and mythic tradition that prohibits any transition between the two. The consequences of such an approach are far-reaching. The form of allegorical hermeneutic inaugurated by Greek philosophy and Christian apologetics is repudiated. The judgement about the allegorical form of representation is unambiguous: it has "misunderstood" myth.[55]

For Taubes, this misrepresented the relation between allegory and myth, since allegory should be understood as "a form of translation." This translation of mythic stories into concepts is a kind of demythologization, although the mythic is not simply erased or overcome. The mythic remains fundamental. Using Blumenberg's example of the Gnostic myth, Taubes argues that this myth of late ancient Gnosticism is a new one that consists of mythic and dogmatic as well as aesthetic elements. They "interpenetrate each other," and this observation disqualifies Blumenberg's opposition and makes Taubes's view of the mythical more plausible—namely, that the mythic persists in all ages as the medium for transition and for the advent of the new in history. There was a problem of the question of innovation in Blumenberg's historical construction.[56] Taubes's "solution," with his view of the myth as a response to historical experience, gave in this way an explanation to the problem of innovation and novelty. And he regained a room for the "latent" impulse of Christian ugliness, in opposition to aesthetics. Aesthetics was not to have the final word with the advent of modernity. Modern aesthetics as an expression for human self-empowerment and dominion had not triumphed definitely.

As Herbert Kopp-Oberstebrink underlines, the fundamental opposition between terror and play is present in the work of what he labels "an absent third": Carl Schmitt. For Blumenberg the opposition is viewed as the threatening historical reality of terror and the free self-empowering aesthetic play that overcomes this terror in modernity. In Schmitt's *Hamlet or Hecuba* from 1956 there is a similar opposition, though structured differently: "In fact, Blumenberg's fundamental thesis that myth resorts to aesthetic play in order to banish the terrors of reality rather appears to emerge from a reversal of Schmitt's conception in *Hamlet or Hecuba*."[57]

In other words, Taubes's criticism of the modern triumph of aesthetic play with which he confronted Blumenberg shared an affinity with Carl Schmitt, though Schmitt was never mentioned in Taubes's interventions in the Poetik und Hermeneutik group. Schmitt had, after all, been Blumenberg's primary target in the latter's argument for the illegitimacy of the category of secularization.

The Weimar Marcionism

The list of contributors from German philosophy and theology who contributed to the inflation of the term "Gnosticism" in the intellectual literature of the Weimar period is long: From the Jewish side one may add Gershom Scholem, Walter Benjamin, Franz Rosenzweig, Leo Strauss, and Ernst Bloch, in addition to Taubes. And from the Protestant side one could mention proponents such as Karl Barth and Adolf von Harnack, who were both accused of being Marcionites, a pejorative term within most Protestant circles that was derived from the second-century heretic Marcion.

Marcion had in an early and decisive epoch of Christianity defied what was later held to be the orthodox form of the Christian canon. In the mid- second century Marcion founded his own church in Rome after his excommunication, based on his view on the writings of the Old Testament. According to Marcion there was a sharp divide between the Jewish God of the Old Testament and the God revealed in Jesus Christ. Jesus's Father was essentially a truer and higher God than the God of the Old Testament, who was dismissed as a cruel demiurge.

Derived from this view, Marcion established a canon free of any book from the Hebrew Bible. His Bible consisted of one gospel that was based on Luke and of ten of Paul's letters.

It was first and foremost Adolf von Harnack who sparked a new interest in Marcion in the intellectual debate in the Weimar Republic. According to the liberal Protestant theologian, Paul the apostle "had no more devoted pupil than Marcion,"[58] a view that unavoidably formed a conception of Paul himself. Nonetheless, it was in a new search for a more authentic thought as a reaction to the liberal *Kulturprotestanismus* (including Harnack's ambivalence to Marcion) that a whole range of German intellectuals sought new answers in this revaluation of the ancient Gnostic phenomenon. This required serious consideration not only of the orthodox interpretations of Judaism and Christianity, but also of its heretical counterparts and adversaries, especially in the interest of reconsidering the interreligious relation itself, as in Taubes's case.

This question was also of religious and confessional importance. With more porous borderlines between Judaism and Christianity, the question of Paul's relation to Gnosticism would not only be important in relation to the possible "overcoming" of the heresy in modernity. Paul's relation to Gnosis would also have consequences for the relation between the two religions. Karl Barth had confirmed the image of Paul as an anti-worldly figure, with the result that Harnack accused him of being a "Marcionite," an image Hans Jonas enforced in his 1934 book (later revised and republished as *The Gnostic Religion*). In fact, one of the primary sources for Jonas's view of Gnosticism was Paul's letters, the "locus classicus" of gnostic thought,[59] first and foremost due to Paul's denigration of the flesh.[60] Perhaps Jonas's influential reading of Paul as Gnostic fueled Taubes's interest in the 1968 essay for Paul's relation to Gnosticism, together with Blumenberg's presence.

In *Occidental Eschatology*, Gnosis is not something that exists in a parasitic relation to early Christianity or as simply threatening Judaism from the outside. For Taubes "the boundaries between apocalypticism and Gnosis are, of course, fluid."[61] But the borders between religions with a prehistory from this same geographical area are in Taubes's account always fluid and porous. Besides, these Gnostic and apocalyptic genres or life-modes in the ancient world are not external with regard to Judaism and Christianity, but remain inherent to these religions, always potentially explosive or suppressed by orthodoxies. That is caused by the fact that

> Mandaean, Manicaen, Jewish, Christian, and Islamic religion belong together. They share the same common foundation of apocalypticism. The elements which constitute the foundations of apocalypticism are the symbols of calling and hearing. The nonworldly comes into being through the call. That which is entirely other is audible in the world, but still as that which is entirely other. The call is emitted by "the stranger." All who feel exiled from the here and now of the world and despise the powers of "this" world receive this call with joy.[62]

Motifs like "exile" and "alienation" are no longer limited to Judaism or primarily associated with the Jewish people, but reflected in apocalyptic and gnostic texts that precede the normative delineations of these religions. These sources may then be reread in order to undertake a revaluation of religious history, but the outcome of this revaluation is already marked by a new quest for existential philosophical truth. And here in the early Taubes this religious prehistory is presented in a language that resembles a universally accessible life-mode or human experience, one for "all who feel exiled from the here and now of the world."

This blending of past and present, history and philosophy was, as remarked earlier, not Taubes's invention. Much of Taubes's history of eschatology and its link to Gnosticism is based on Hans Jonas's work, who again read this ancient phenomenon in Heideggerian terms. This is also recognized by the late Taubes in the essay "The Iron Cage and the Exodus from It" (1984):

> Hans Jonas, in *Gnosticism and the Spirit of Late Antiquity* (1934), interpreted the Gnostic teaching by means of Heidegger's Dasein analysis so that the Gnostic form of Heidegger's philosophy itself was brought to the fore.[63]

It is perhaps no wonder that Gnosticism was revived at the same time that Heidegger's philosophy resonated and influenced German intellectuals. Heideggerian "worldhood," "homesickness," or "the call from nowhere" would furnish and inspire their reading of ancient Gnosis, deeming it crucial for the understanding of man's situation in modernity.

This historical situatedness of historical scholarship on Gnosticism is also highlighted by the late Taubes when he wrote that what was at stake in this historically oriented scholarly discussion was also "the legacy of the era" after the First World War:

> The Gnostic hieroglyph of that era after the First World War including the legacy of the era and the debate over it may be clarified through the dispute over Marcion. Scholars part ways over Marcion, but the argument about him clarifies what the intellectual-historical and theo-political significance of the sign "Gnosis" after the First World War might be.[64]

The theopolitical significance of Gnosticism seen by Taubes was made more explicit in his Heidelberg lectures. Here Adolf von Harnack's rejection of the Old Testament and rehabilitation of Marcion is seen as "the secret of German liberal Protestantism, which then in 1933 couldn't pass the test."[65] In other words, this secret Marcionism couldn't stand the test when the Protestant churches should have have defended the legacy of the Old Testament, its Jewish heritage, in loyalty to Paul. This Marcionite spirit of the Wilhelmine epoch was no bulwark against Nazism. It rather seems to have been a symptom of it, in Taubes's perspective. So was Paul in any way culpable of this Weimar Marcionism? Was Marcion Paul's true disciple or his betrayer? What was Paul's relation to Gnosticism?

This question is addressed in Taubes's essay on "The Justification of Ugliness in Early Christianity" in the more immediate context of Taubes's disagreements with Hans Blumenberg and on the broader background of the rise of Nazism. What had been considered by so many German intellectuals in the last years of the Weimar period the highest form of human wisdom in the person of Martin Heidegger had manifested itself as a monstrosity in the form of Nazi collaboration. In this way, Taubes's reading of Paul is a crucial way of getting around Heidegger in order to destroy the wisdom of this supposed wise man. The judgment Taubes makes of Heidegger's Christianity is a trace of this peculiar *Destruktion*:

> I can't here expound on how Heidegger wants to subvert this and wants to neutralize the Christian in Kierkegaard; this is something the theologians never understood, that Heidegger wanted to dig the grave of theology, but I can't go into the Bultmannian naivetés today, who wanted to use the natural man to using Heideggerian categories and Christian man using Pauline categories. And Heidegger played along and managed in this way to make the entire theological Marburg circle into his apostles, which was no small matter.[66]

Taubes's Essay on 1 Corinthians

Taubes's essay on 1 Corinthians from 1968 is the finest example we have left in written form of Taubes's close reading of Pauline passages from the New Testament, and it is crucial for understanding Taubes's refigurations of Paul. It is a reading performed with appraisal as well as rejection of both Nietzsche and Paul. In his search for a true disagreement with them Taubes detects the point in both thinkers where he must stop and no longer follow them.

Taubes opens the essay with bold statements about Nietzsche's "unsurpassed" historical insights in relation to New Testament exegetes. Taubes can read Paul's text as a window to the historical past as the apostle's words allude "to conflicts within the Corinthian community ignited by the understanding of baptism."[67] Though moving from polemics to a more tempered exegetical tone with footnotes to these New Testament scholars along the way,[68] Taubes, however, remains loyal to Nietzsche's historical insight. He never gives up the idea he finds in Nietzsche of "the moment when the turnover from ancient to Christian values takes place." He rather confirms that it is in the exact place that Nietzsche locates, in 1 Corinthians 1:20 and forward, where "the turnover" or revolution is being realized. This is not primarily a social or political revolution, but a textual one. That does not mean that it is safeguarded against a counterrevolution. Far from it, in Taubes's reading this counterrevolution is inherent to the very same text of Paul. The apostle speaks against himself; he speaks with one revolutionary Hebraic tongue and one counterrevolutionary Gnostic tongue.

As stated in the Introduction, this study of the reception of Pauline texts in Taubes's works is undertaken with a genealogical interest in the particular choices made in Taubes's readings. By isolating certain aspects or scenes of reading that can be detected here and linking them to a wider network of historical and philosophical perceptions, new knowledge about Taubes's readings of Paul will be gained. Moreover, to describe how Taubes reads Paul is at the outset not possible without simultaneously producing new readings of Paul. These new intellectual productions that are achieved when Paul's texts are read are always already part of the reception history of these texts. The question is not whether we unavoidably activate layers in this reception history when we read Paul, but how we can do that in a transparent manner that demonstrates some of the immanent potentialities in these texts that are connected to this name. Since this study is guided by an interest in how notions of the historical and philosophical are operative in Taubes's reception of Paul, some readings that are not only philosophically but also historically oriented will be introduced alongside Taubes's readings. Ancient history is part of the intellectual drama that is construed in this study and present as a constant reference for Jacob Taubes's readings of Paul. These carefully chosen readings from recent New Testament scholarship serve to shed light on certain historical presuppositions of Taubes's readings. What is more, they broaden the understanding of Paul's texts that are embedded in Taubes's readings and help to rewrite *our* understanding of the apostle's texts, read through Taubes.[69]

Revolutionary and Counterrevolutionary Christianity

What Taubes advances in this essay in relation to his position in the 1947 book is this specifically Pauline difference with regard to not only the Greek but the Jewish. In *Occidental Eschatology* the cross of Jesus certainly made a difference as well, but it was a political-apocalyptical difference with regard to the Roman Empire. As part of the revolutionary messianism of Israel Jesus is just one among several Jewish historical figures who suffer unjust death for the sake of the Kingdom of God, for the oppressed. The very same apocalypticism is taken up by the Zealot movement as the Jesus movement (including John the Baptist as well as Jesus from Nazareth). "So when someone stirred up the crowds with such a message, he had to be nailed to a cross by the Roman authorities,"[70] writes Taubes about Jesus's fate. The struggle for the oppressed continues after the death and resurrection of Christ in the form an economic communism in the original community. In this way "the early Christian community seeks to anticipate the divine economy of God's kingdom."[71]

The decisive shift occurs with Paul, who solves "the impasse" of "the desperate situation" that confronts the first followers of Christ when God's kingdom is delayed. The apostle teaches that "the new aeon has dawned despite the continued delay of the Parousia. Thereby Paul spiritualizes the political and apocalyptic aspirations of the coming of the Messiah and turns it into 'the mystical, symbolic union of humanity as the Body of Christ.'"[72] Paul introduces the shift that dismantles the explosives of communal, political apocalypticism and reduces eschatology to "the great drama of the soul," to "pure metaphysics."[73] This neutralization culminates in Augustine, who formulates the political theology that will secure the spiritual foundations of the Holy Roman Empire. The conflict between Judea and Rome will not arise in a significant manner before Joachim of Fiore's new historical claim of a "Millennium of Revolution."[74]

In "The Justification of Ugliness in Early Christian Tradition" Taubes traces this genealogy of the explosive messianism in the Jesus movement differently. After all, this is the main purpose of the essay. After referring to Auerbach's analysis of the *sermo humilis*, he sketches out the following:

> Still, our recourse to the first "sermo humilis" of the Apostle Paul is meant to identity the inner difficulties and external resistances that prevent the "Christian" impulse from breaking out into the open.[75]

The "Christian" is not Christian in the ordinary sense. It must be connected to the messianic impulses that led figures like John the Baptist and Jesus to let these impulses break out in the open and "stir up the crowds" in the name of the oppressed and outcasts, as Taubes wrote in *Occiental Eschatology*.[76] But in this essay Paul is no longer the apostle who simply counters the social and political aspirations of the Jesus movement with mysticism. And he is no longer the apostle who, with his words from Romans 13 that each has "to remain in the state in which he was born,"[77] only represses the rebellious origins of Christianity. Taubes has made Paul into a figure who, in 1 Corinthians 1, "Aims high in deploying the plural form of the neuter, in order to bring the derisive judgement of the higher and upper classes before the community's own eyes."[78] Paulinism is socially and politically radical. The election in 1 Corinthians 1:27–28 of the foolish, the weak, and the nameless pariahs enacts God's social judgment, which is turned into a metaphysical judgment on the world as a whole. In contrast to Taubes's tale in *Occidental Eschatology*, the messianic revolution that Jesus proclaimed does not end with Paul. Taubes has discovered Paul's "doctrine of the cross," a doctrine that was absent in his former account. The Jewish professor from the University of Berlin has come to recognize the cross as foolishness against human wisdom as a transvaluation, an inversion of "the noble ethos of Antiquity." Knowing that Nietzsche sides with this noble ethos, Taubes sides with the originary Christian ugliness.

A close reading of Taubes's interpretation of 1 Corinthians will here be followed by attempts to lay bare the potential meanings in the Pauline passages from 1 Corinthians actualized in this particular reading of Taubes, informed by more recent readings from New Testament scholarship.

Taubes's Revolutionary Paulinism in 1 Corinthians 1:17–2:5

Taubes delineates 1 Corinthians 1:17–2:5 into three parts. The discourse of the cross as polemics against Jews and Greeks is unfolded in 1 Corinthians 1:19–25, which then is explained in relation to the standing of the Corinthian *ekklesia* in 1:26–31 and further in relation to the apostle in 2:1–5. Taubes notes how the whole text of 1 Corinthians 1:17–2:5 is referred to in the scholarly tradition of New Testament exegesis as "particularly well-structured" and "rhetorical to the point of theatricality."

> If one reads the text aloud and attempts to imagine it spoken, one would note exact word correspondences, rhyming consonance, symmetrically measured sentences often with homonymic endings, and a series of questions, anaphora, and antitheses.[79]

However, what is regarded in this scholarly tradition as "the finest writing or eloquence" can mislead interpreters, in Taubes's opinion. If one only pays attention to the rhetorical beauty one misses the crucial historical break recognized by Nietzsche: Paul's justification of ugliness, the revolutionary words of the cross:

> In this passage, possibly for the first time in history, the prevalent rhetorical means of expression are put into the service of a cause that revolutionizes ancient perception and experience. For what could be more foreign to the ancient imagination, be it Jewish or Greek, than the doctrine of the cross?[80]

The foreign nature of Paul's cause is indicated already by the opposition in the Corinthian community to which Paul's rhetoric attests. Taubes detects the intention of Paul's opponents in the formula *en sophia logou* in 1:17: "Through *logos* or *sophia* the cross is depleted, robbed of its meaning." Paul "authentically distances himself" from *en sophia logou* with his doctrine of the cross in 1:18, Taubes states. In other words, in these verses we meet an authentic Paul or rather an authentic transvaluation.

In this reading Paul's doctrine of the cross is expressed as a thesis in 1:18 about the members of the community in Corinth: for those in the community who are damned, the word of the cross is foolishness, but for those who are saved the same doctrine is God's power. Then Taubes asks what the word of the cross, *ho logos tou staurou*, actually means here and answers:

> What it means is, as 1:23 and 2:2 demonstrate, the proclamation of Jesus Christ, namely, he who is crucified: he in no other than this form. With equal emphasis Paul stresses the Crucifixion in 2:1, while polemically clarifying here the address toward which and *against* which this proclamation orients itself.[81]

In other words, the Pauline difference or uniqueness is articulated and breaks through in heated polemics. The polemics are no deviation from the message, but the medium for its authentic articulation.

Furthermore, Paul's opponents in Corinth consider the apostle's doctrine of the cross as foolishness since these enthusiasts have rejected Christ *kata sarka*, the fleshly Jesus. For them Christ is *kata pneuma*, which means that for them "the exalted Christ is resurrected in their own knowledge (*gnosis*) or wisdom (*sophia*)."[82] But for Paul there is one crucial belief that separates him from his opponents in Corinth, but that also separates the redemptive Christian mystery from "all other mysteries of redemption," the crucified's body:

> Christ *kata pneuma*, the heavenly Christ, is to be envisioned as the crucified: this piece, the *sarx*, this remainder of the earthly is what has salvific importance to Paul.[83]

In his opponent's Christology Paul does not recognize the necessary unity or coupling of the crucified body of Christ and the heavenly Christ. This argument is sustained by Taubes with appeal to some philological observations on how the name "Jesus" and not only "Christ" is used so often in the second letter to the Corinthians and how the formulation *Christ estauromenos* or "Christ the crucified" is used repeatedly in 1 Corinthians 1:23 and 2:1. The event of Crucifixion is for Taubes the decisive emphasis in Paul's soteriology where he differs from his opponents, and indeed, from other comparable soteriologies in Antiquity as well: "This *servo humilis* distinguishes the Christian mystery of redemption from all other mysteries of redemption. The passion itself is the mystery."[84]

Taubes discerns "the elect" as the keyword in 1:26–31 and states that the pericope outlines the characteristics of this election:

> To ground the thesis that God's foolishness is nonetheless wiser than men and God's weakness stronger (1:25), Paul points to the position of the congregation in the world: not many wise ones according to the flesh, nor the mighty or the noble, are called. *Sophoi* signifies the learned, *dynatoi* the wealthy and therefore mighty, and *eugeneis* the noble born, those of good pedigree and social status.[85]

It is, however, not the low social status of the majority of the Corinthian community that causes Paul's doctrine of the cross or makes the Christian difference vis-à-vis the Jewish and the Greek. It is the other way around: the congregation's low social standing in the eyes of the Corinthian society is a consequence and an expression of God's power in the cross, the doctrine that is disregarded by the enthusiasts from the upper classes. Through this election God transvalues all worldly values, and a revolution takes place.

> From the perspective of Corinthian society the members of the congregations are not considered persons, but rather a *quantité négliable*,

or pariahs who remain nameless, or, as Paul (1:28) most fiercely sums up, *ta me onta*, a nothing, a genus of person regarded as nothing.[86]

By referring to "the first Christians" as "pariahs" Taubes destabilizes the image of Christians and Jews as stable identities in this historical setting. Moreover, Taubes blends the separate constituents of these Pauline "Christians" from the past with the Jews up to the modern epoch. "Pariahs" is, after all, a term Max Weber applied to Jews through the ages and that Hannah Arendt made even more known when she embraced it during the Second World War.[87] For Taubes it is not simply that these Pauline congregations are Jewish and therefore fit the "pariah" category. They are pariahs not because of any ethnic or religious ties with Jewish history, but due to their social status as "nothing."

In 2:1–5 Taubes picks out *keryssomen* as the key word, which he translates as "we preach." Paul focuses here on crucial aspects of his preaching. Paul's words about how he came in weakness, fear, and trembling (2:3) are read by Taubes in conjunction with the apostle's Second Letter to the Corinthians, where he also describes himself as bodily weak and rhetorically awkward. In spite of Paul's testimony Taubes suggests that the apostle's weakness in this regard is his construction of a likeness of Christ, more than a reflection of his appearance. He is far from sure that it was because of Paul's physical weakness that he was rejected in some segments of the Corinthian community. The issue is rather doctrinal, a view informed by Taubes's reading of the Second Letter to the Corinthians:

> The opponents of Paul deny him the pneumatic proof of his proclamation and denounce him as pneumatically weak (II Cor 10:2). Paul returns the reproach and uses it as an objection against the Pneumaticists: it is they who act carnally, which for Paul means sinfully. . . . Additionally, in 2:3 Paul adopts arguments of his opponents and confirms that he had proclaimed his sermon of the cross with "fear and trembling," that is, in fear of Judgment, and had been among the Corinthians "in weakness."[88]

Taubes observes how Paul gradually appropriates the discourse of the other and attempts to use their rhetorical weapons against themselves. Through this pericope Taubes's Paul distinguishes clearly his proclamation, the word of the cross, and the teaching of wisdom. His opponents have co-opted *sophia* and *logos*, while the apostle avoids *sophia*. So far, so good.

But these distinguishing efforts are to come to an end, and this is where the counterrevolution sets in. In the encounter with Greek philosophy, Paul proceeds too far, according to Taubes. For Taubes the Christian impulse does not fully realize its revolutionary potential, not even in Paul. This is not something that Nietzsche saw, nor did Heidegger. Taubes reads Paul with his enemies, but here he approximates a line where he can no longer rely on their wisdom:

> Nietzsche, within a nineteenth-century horizon of understanding, interprets this passage of the First Letter to the Corinthians all too vaguely as a general polemic against Greek wisdom and philosophy (and in this Heidegger follows him in his foreword to the fifth edition of his Inaugural Lecture).[89]

What kind of forces are at work when Taubes reads Paul through his enemies? Can we, through readers like Martin and Welborn, identify and thereby actualize Pauline forces operative in the First Letter to the Corinthians that Taubes uncovers through Nietzsche?

Rewriting the Revolutionary Paulinism in 1 Corinthians 1:17–2:5

Like Taubes, we may delineate the passage in three parts, as conventionally done.[90] Then the first part, 1:18–25, is preceded by verse 17. Verse 17 then concludes the exhortation in 1:10–17. Verse 17 reads, "For Christ did not send me to baptize but to proclaim the gospel, and not with eloquent wisdom, so that the cross of Christ might not be emptied of its power" (1 Cor 1:17). Then follows:

> For the message about the cross is foolishness to those who are perishing, but to us who are being saved it is the power of God. For it is written, "I will destroy the wisdom of the wise, and the discernment of the discerning I will thwart." Where is the one who is wise? Where is the scribe? Where is the debater of this age? Has not God made foolish the wisdom of the world? For since, in the wisdom of God, the world did not know God through wisdom, God decided, through the foolishness of our proclamation, to save those who believe. For Jews demand signs and Greeks desire wisdom, but we proclaim Christ crucified, a stumbling block to Jews and foolishness to Gentiles, but to those who are the called, both Jews and Greeks, Christ the power of God and the wisdom of God. For God's foolishness is wiser than human wisdom, and God's weakness is stronger than human strength. (1 Cor 1:18–25)

Taubes's acknowledgment of "the finest writing or eloquence" in this passage reflects the rhetorical skills demonstrated in the biblical text. It has been argued that Paul's strategy is but one example of a *homonoia* or "concord" speech that was a dominant genre in Hellenism with typical literary patterns as well as an ideology.[91] This genre was used with the aim of attaining unity—for instance, in political affairs,[92] which is also the explicit purpose in Paul's case: "I appeal to you, brothers and sisters, by the name of our Lord Jesus Christ, that all of you be in agreement and that there be no divisions among you" (1:10). Paul's deliberative letter would have been written by a rhetorician with a certain amount of rhetorical training. There is indeed dependence and appropriation of an ancient rhetorical tradition, as Taubes remarks, which marks continuity with Hellenism or "the Greek."

Taubes does not, however, emphasize the continuity with "the Jewish," to which the thanksgiving part (1:4–9) of the first chapter of the letter bears witness as Paul writes, "Christ has been strengthened among you—so that you are not lacking in any spiritual gift as you wait for the revealing of our Lord Jesus Christ. He will also strengthen you to the end, so that you may be blameless on the day of our Lord Jesus Christ" (1:7–8).[93] Here the Pauline text elicits themes familiar to Taubes from Jewish apocalypticism, but here overlooked. There is a revelation or apocalypse of Christ for which the Corinthians should wait until the end, on "the day" or possibly in "the court,"[94] as the apocalyptic event will turn the world upside down in terms of time and space.[95] Proclaiming this apocalyptic worldview, the text constitutes a clear ideological break with the *homonoia* genre in which this ideology has no place traditionally. This, however, is not so much a Pauline break with the Jewish as with the Greek.

So does the Pauline text enact such a break with the Jewish as suggested by its reception in Taubes's essay? Is Nietzsche drawing Taubes closer to or further away from the Pauline forces and potential meanings?

According to Taubes, 1:17 introduces the discourse of the "Word of the cross," which for Taubes constitutes "a doctrine" that "revolutionizes ancient perception and experience." Did this Pauline discourse revolutionize the ancient worldview? While such a question hardly can be answered without recourse to historical hypotheses about Antiquity, investigating the New Testament texts can help to confirm Taubes's thesis of Paul's doctrine of the cross as a foreign element and break with Antiquity on various levels. "Even in the Corinthian community this doctrine encountered resistance,"[96] Taubes upholds.

First, elsewhere within the New Testament the word *stauros* occurs rarely, either as a noun or as the root of a verb. As Taubes himself observes in his essay, the pre-Pauline formulas in Paul's letters, which are derived from an earlier tradition, do not contain the concept of the crucified Christ. These traditions maintain the death of the Messiah, though not the manner of this death. In Paul's earliest epistle, 1 Thessalonians, the noun as well as the verb are absent in the text.[97] From a historical point of view it may very well be the case, as Taubes writes, that in the letter to the Philippians the expression *thanatou de staurou* (2:8) is the insertion of Paul's peculiar expression into a pre-Pauline tradition (2:5–11).[98]

Second, Paul's apocalyptic motifs may not be regarded as a Pauline invention but as a reflection of a broader line of thought within Palestinian and Hellenistic Judaism. With regard to Greco-Roman values and ideology this apocalypticism can be seen as revolutionary, since it proclaimed an alternative world where power positions were envisioned as turned on their head. Paul's move in this passage, however, is not typical of apocalypticism, either, when he makes the crucifixion the central act in the apocalyptic drama. This innovation or discourse must have consisted in a "stumbling block to Jews" (1:22), including apocalyptically oriented Jews. Turning a crucified criminal into a divine agent in this drama must have sounded "foreign," as Taubes claims, even to these Jews. But granted that it was foreign, was it really unique in human history, as implied by Taubes's affirmation?

Third, Cicero admonishes the Roman citizen to not think or speak of the cross, since it is considered shameful.[99] This suggests that the act of crucifixion or even its mention within Roman elite circles was scandalous, in spite of the overwhelming presence of this instrument of torture in a society dependent upon slave labor and in which crucifixion served as slaves' punishment. The author of 1 Corinthians broke the silence[100] and indulged in a shameful use of an otherwise respected high culture of writing when he used the very word *stauros*.[101] When the discourse of the cross was first set in motion in 1 Corinthians it may have been a historical moment. "Possibly for the first time in history," to use Taubes's words, a crucified criminal is put at the center of devotion of the divine through "the prevalent rhetorical means of expression" within Greco-Roman culture.[102] Such a stance or belief runs counter to cultural assumptions, expectations, and intuitions. It sounds nothing less than "foolish."

In fact, Paul's choice of vocabulary in 1:18 might reflect an accusation against his message of salvation through the cross or the role he assumed as rhetorician when he preached it. He may have been accused of "foolishness" or being "a fool," an accusation he could have turned back onto his opponents. Furthermore, he may have turned the accusation into a warning of apocalyptic proportions, since his message of the cross is foolishness "to those who are perishing" (1:18). The warning does not have to be limited to his opponents in the Corinthian *ekklesia*, though Taubes's suggestion that Paul's doctrine of the cross is expressed as a thesis in 1:18 about the members of the community in Corinth can be read into the letter; if those within the community continue to denigrate the message of the cross as an expression of foolishness, then a judgment that can lead to extermination may fall upon them.

The word of the cross (1:18) is not merely a description of the apocalyptic turning point. The Pauline text has a potential, as Taubes affirms, to work as "the proclamation of Jesus Christ, namely, he who is crucified: he in no other than this form." The manner of the death, the form of the salvific body is inseparable from the act of proclamation of Paul's gospel. This act is itself crucial in the apocalyptic drama, as the message of the cross is proclaimed in spite of and against the soteriological views in the community that regard this proclamation as "foolishness." As Taubes observes, this doctrine may have come into being as polemics against these opponents in Corinth. The polemical character of Paul's rhetoric may be no deviation from the matter. It can be inseparable from it. However much it came into being *ad hoc* when confronted by accusations, in these verses is the very place where the transvaluation in Paul's gospel comes clearest into being. In this way, the philosopher Nietzsche pointed in the biblical direction for Taubes, but not to a reading free from historical presuppositions about this text. Nietzsche led Taubes to Paul, but also to a historically probable location of the Pauline difference with regard to Antiquity, the Jewish as well as the Greek, read on the background of Martin's and Welborn's contributions: It was not grace that constituted the difference to ancient perception, not universalism or freedom from law that was the origin or cause of Paul's historical break. It was the ugliness of the cross. Thereby the "noble morality" and "beauty" of Antiquity was negated. "The psychology of every *chandala*-morality" had been born, of resentment and vengefulness.[103] In these ways the philosophical and historical are intertwined in Taubes's Nietzschean reading of 1 Corinthians 1.

> Consider your own call, brothers and sisters: not many of you were wise by human standards, not many were powerful, not many were of noble birth. But God chose what is foolish in the world to shame the wise; God chose what is weak in the world to shame the strong; God chose what is low and despised in the world, things that are not, to reduce to nothing things that are, so that no one might boast in the presence of God. He is the source of your life in Christ Jesus, who became for us wisdom from God, and righteousness and sanctification and redemption, in order that, as it is written, "Let the one who boasts, boast in the Lord." (1 Cor 1:26–31)

In Taubes's reading 1:26–31 is interpreted as an attempt "to ground the thesis that God's foolishness is nonetheless wiser than men and God's weakness stronger (1:25)." This resembles a logic that I choose to read as inherent to Paul's argument as well, following conventional views on the letter's rhtetorical structure: 1 Corinthians 1:26–31 fills the rhetorical function of proof to Paul's argument in 1:18–25, which culminates in his statements about "God's foolishness," which is "wiser than human wisdom," and "God's weakness," which is "stronger" than any worldly power or strength. The apocalyptic dualism established as "those who are perishing" against "us who are being saved" (1:18) corresponds to the oppositional tension between "this age" and "the world" against God. In 1:26 the author of the letter locates the Corinthian addressees more firmly within the apocalyptic scheme in a way that functions "to ground the thesis" in 1:25. "Look at yourself," he tells his addresses. They are the proof or the example of the characteristics of God's salvation, which in 1:26–28 is described in terminology full of status significance and with clear class connotations.[104] Within this apocalyptic drama the social acquires metaphysical dimensions in the argument in the biblical text, as Taubes writes: "The social judgement turns into a metaphysical one."[105]

> When I came to you, brothers and sisters, I did not come proclaiming the mystery of God to you in lofty words or wisdom. For I decided to know nothing among you except Jesus Christ, and him crucified. And I came to you in weakness and in fear and in much trembling. My speech and my proclamation were not with plausible words of wisdom, but with a demonstration of the Spirit and of power, so that your faith might rest not on human wisdom but on the power of God. (1 Cor 2:1–5)

Paul moves from "the low and despised" in Corinth to himself as the proving example of the argument put forward earlier. Taubes doubts whether this account of his own appearance and proclamation is autobiographical on Paul's part, as the apostle's weakness amounts more to a construction of likeness to Christ. The argument for a purely rhetorical construction of the apostle's weakness and foolishness can be sustained with reference to the characterization of the cross of Christ in 1:25, as Taubes suggests. His self-presentation places him on the side of the low and despised in contrast to the wise and powerful. When he declares that he proclaimed Jesus Christ without wisdom and that he decided to know nothing but Christ, he breaks with the model of a Greek intellectual in a way that ends in a sort of caricature. He is well on his way to appropriating the role of the fool, which could have many resonances in the foolish orator in the mime and satire of the time.[106] If Paul's opponents in Corinth have drawn a stark contrast between the eloquent wisdom of Apollo's rhetoric and the foolishness of Paul's proclamations, there may be traces of these accusations in this self-presentation. Taubes observes this possible dynamic between the lines in the Pauline text when he observes how Paul in 2:3 "adopts arguments of his opponents and confirms that he had proclaimed his sermon of the cross with 'fear and trembling.'" A construction of his appearance as such a response seems likely, though the degrading and foolish self-image Paul gives of himself remains a stumbling block for many an interpreter. Nonetheless, having already met his opponents halfway in proclaiming "God's foolishness," it may not only be a digression to sustain the argument with his own exemplary foolishness in the form of "weakness" and "fear and trembling." It could rather represent an exemplary belief in the apocalyptic reversal of state of affairs and hierarchy of values. In Taubes's words, Paul "battles against the 'wisdom of the world' or the 'wisdom of this Aeon.'"[107]

Taubes's opinion of the constructed nature of the apostle's self-presentation also points to another aspect of the apostle's rhetoric in the biblical text. Even when the apostle expresses his disavowal of the "lofty words"—that is, the art of rhetoric—the apostle all the same employs a stylistic device. Even his declarations of weakness have a certain rhetorical strength. This is not simply a manifestation of powerlessness. It is a paradoxical and unpredictable power that results from the supposed abstention from the prevalent forms of rhetorical power. There is a new form of freedom achieved in a Pauline intervention comparable to Socratic self-parody.[108]

Taubes's Gnostic Counterrevolution in 1 Corinthians 2:6–10

Taubes works with the hypothesis that there is a "proto-Gnostic" soteriology in the Corinthian congregation, a common assumption at the time,[109] comparable to the Gnosticism from the second century. Paul's battle against these opponents is gradually softened, according to Taubes, which raises the question: what is specifically the relation between these Gnostics and Paul's theology?

In *Occidental Eschatology* Taubes also connects the Corinthian correspondence to the question of Gnosticism. Here Taubes sees the shift in emphasis that "opens the way from apocalypticism to Gnosis" in the very words of Paul in 1 Corinthians 2:2—that the apostle knows nothing except Christ. Though Paul is not himself a Gnostic, since what this heresy does is to replace "the Pauline *pistis*" with "the knowing *Gnosis*," the apostle opens the way for Gnosis. Gnostic as well as Platonic influences are factors that crush the eschatological hopes of messianism and replace them with "the drama" or "the journey" of the soul. Christian theology is turning inward from the second to the fourth century, in Taubes's story.

> Christian theology comes under the sway of speculative Gnosis. In exactly the same way as early Christianity develops in the climate of Jewish apocalypticism, Christian theology develops in a Gnostic environment.[110]

This view of Paul as one who is not completely heretical or Gnostic but still an agent who paves the way for it is derived in *Occidental Eschatology* from Albert Schweitzer.[111] In "The Justification of Ugliness in Early Christianity" Paul still opens the way for Gnosticism. Taubes finds a confirmation of this in the reason for the opposition against Paul in Corinth: they rejected a Christ *kata sarka*:

> For the enthusiasts in Corinth, Christ is *sophia*, the wisdom of God. The exalted Christ is resurrected in their own knowledge (*gnosis*) or wisdom (*sophia*). It is the exalted, heavenly Christ as "wisdom of God" that a Christian belongs to, not the earthly Jesus.[112]

Taubes recognizes Paul's battle against these "pneumaticists" as he envisioned the heavenly Christ as the crucified that for Taubes is "this piece, the *sarx*, this remainder of the earthly." It is this remainder that "has salvific importance to Paul."[113] But this emphasis of the earthly is in the very same apostle's thought weakened by his more spiritualizing tendency:

> It is known how little he is interested in Jesus' works. Paul is also a pneumaticist who attaches no salvific significance to the earthly "life of Jesus."[114]

There is a distinction in Paul between a Christ *kata sarka* and a Christ *kata pneuma*. This is a distinction he shares with his Gnostic opponents, according to Taubes. This constitutes one major problem. Paul becomes vulnerable to Gnostic appropriation.

Taubes's Paul is no Marcionite, however, since he is not drawing the most radical conclusions from the Gnostic schema, though he shares this feature with the "enthusiasts" in Corinth.

> But he shies away from the radical consequences inherent in such a distinction, and he dismisses them with the reference to the "Word of the cross." Even if in general his Christology blends into the Gnostic schema of the redeemed Redeemer, Paul still draws the line at the event of Crucifixion against the radically spiritualizing tendency of Gnosticism.[115]

In this reading Paul does not simply open up for Gnostic heresies in Christianity, which neutralizes the messianic impulse, as Taubes opined in *Occidental Eschatology*. Here Taubes has discerned a more Jewish Paul who makes the Christian breakthrough in the doctrine of the cross as polemical resistance to the Gnostic spiritualizing elements in his Corinthian opponents,[116] elements that will contribute to the installment of Christendom, along with Platonic elements. Therefore, Taubes sees Paul's combat against the doctrine of the Corinthian Pneumaticists as repeated in Augustine's formula from *Civitate Dei* (*Christus humilies, vos superbi*) against the Platonists. The similarity between Paul and Augustine in this regard, however, does not sidestep the fact for Taubes that Paul does not only combat accommodation to "the noble ethos" of Antiquity. Paul himself also hinders "the doctrine of the cross of prevailing in the Christian community." In other words, he forges "the compromise" with this noble ethos of Antiquity.

With Nietzsche Taubes is recognizing a Pauline transvaluation of ancient values. Through a closer reading of the Pauline text, however, Taubes, in contrast to Nietzsche, also recognizes a Pauline accommodation to the very same values. Revolution is followed by counterrevolution, within the very same letter:

> The difficulties begin with Paul himself. Accommodation of the opponents, first of the Corinthian enthusiasts, and then in general of Gnostic "wisdom," begins in Paul, in fact in the very next paragraph of the First Letter to the Corinthians. If Nietzsche rightfully refers to I Cor 1:20ff. as first-rate evidence for the advancing transvaluation of the active values, we might claim I Cor 2:6ff. as the first-rate evidence for the advancing accommodation by Christian values of the Greek world. The *sophia* Paul fought against in the first passage is now introduced in the second, in fact, as truth, *en tois teleois*, for the perfected.[117]

To Taubes it appears as if Paul wants to outdo his Pneumaticist opponents through their own terminology or rhetorical form in 1 Corinthians 2:6–10. The effect of this strategy is, nonetheless, that Paul's intent ends in an adaption or conformation to "the central motifs of Gnostic doctrine of wisdom," in form as well as in content. Taubes argues that the event of Crucifixion is now interpreted by Paul as revealing a type of wisdom or *sophia* that "bears all the characteristics of a Gnostic myth."

Taubes confirms his conclusions based on philology by referring to the use of precisely this Pauline paragraph in the self-legitimation of second-century Gnostics as Valentinus and Basilides. To the church these characteristics of Paul's discourse represented nothing less than "an embarrassment," according to Taubes, though their presence in Paul implies a Gnostic infiltration of Christianity "already at the beginnings of its history."[118]

It is this spiritualizing tendency in Paul that weakens the force of Paul's doctrine of the cross and prepares for the accommodation of the Christian impulse to "the noble ethos" of Antiquity, a process of accommodation that reaches its climax with Constantine:

> With the Constantinian turn, the cross changes into a Christian symbol of triumph whose memory of Christ's suffering and death is effaced.[119]

Here we notice Taubes's typical interest in turning points in history, to which Paul has become an increasingly important figure. In *Occidental Eschatology* it was first and foremost the apocalyptic revolution of Jesus that was suppressed with the rise of the Constantinian church, while in the 1968 essay it was more than anything else Paul's doctrine of the cross. This was something that "his best teacher on Paul" allowed Taubes to see—namely, Friedrich Nietzsche. Nevertheless, this very best teacher of Taubes was, according to his pupil, all the same wrong in his history of *décadence*. In Taubes view, "it was not *décadence* that triumphed, as Nietzsche believed in the aforementioned fragment, but rather the Imperium Romanum over Christianity."[120] While Nietzsche was right in his discernment of the true disagreement or conflict, he was wrong in his description of the conflict's outcome. It was not Taubes's "power from below" that had won with the Constantinian turn. It was instead Schmitt's "power from above." But Paulinism as doctrine of the cross was not finally defeated. It lay rather "latent" in history.[121] Taubes's reading is therefore not only an appraisal of Nietzsche. It is also a critique of him.

Rewriting the Pauline Counterrevolution in 1 Corinthians 2:6–10

> Yet among the mature we do speak wisdom, though it is not a wisdom of this age or of the rulers of this age, who are doomed to perish. But we speak God's wisdom, secret and hidden, which God decreed before the ages for our glory. None of the rulers of this age understood this; for if they had, they would not have crucified the Lord of glory. But, as it is written, "What no eye has seen, nor ear heard, nor the human heart conceived, what God has prepared for those who love him"—these things God has revealed to us through the Spirit; for the Spirit searches everything, even the depths of God.

Can this biblical text work to reflect and represent a Pauline accommodation to a Gnostic or proto-Gnostic opposition in Corinth?

For Taubes it is "only" with a distinction between a Christ *kata sarka* and a Christ *kata pneuma* that "the conflict between Paul and his opponents gain[s] contour."[122] However, this distinction is from second-century Gnosticism. I suggest that to anachronistically project a second-century Gnostic ideology into the first mid-century Corinth appears unnecessary for explaining this conflict. This is hardly a productive anachronism. As I suggested with reference to Dale B. Martin earlier, Paul's unheard-of misuse of rhetorical conventions in 1:18–2:5 was likely to be enough to cause social division and opposition to Paul within this Corinthian congregation. The ideology embedded in these rhetorical conventions clashed with elements of Paul's Jewish apocalypticism, particularly his emphasis on the crucified savior.

Where Taubes projects Gnosticism, it may be historically more plausible to inject apocalypticism. What Taubes considers to be a Pauline form of the Gnostic myth of God's secret wisdom in 2:7 can be read as a typical apocalyptic motif of a divine mystery that is revealed to a privileged few in an evil age. Operating as channels or instruments of the prevailing evil powers in such an age, these rulers who crucified the Lord are surely "doomed to perish" (2:6–8). Rather than Gnosticism, apocalypticism appears to be at stake in this correspondence. As indicated by Paul's use of irony in 1 Corinthians 4, this conflict appears not only to revolve around the heavenly over the earthly, the exalted over the crucified: "Already you have all you want! Already you have become rich! Quite apart from us you have become kings!" (4:8) It appears also to be a matter of disagreement over the "already" versus the "not yet." The opponents' spiritual self-assurance is based on a false notion of already being fully exalted with the heavenly Christ. For this letter writer, however, their immoral practices reveal that they have not at all come to enjoy the full benefits of God's salvation in Christ. But did the apostle not already in the introduction to the main arguments of his letter write that the Corinthians indeed had been richly benefited by God?

To presume a historical Pauline combat against Gnostics remains anachronistic, since Paul does not appear to polemicize against gnosis in 1 Corinthians.[123] Far from it, the apostle declares in 1:5 that his addressees, the ones called in Corinth, have "been enriched in him, in speech and knowledge of every kind" (*en panti logo kai pase gnosei*). Knowledge is presented as enrichment, as a result of their relation with the gracious God. Does not Paul pave the way for an "enthusiastic" eschatology without reservations already in this verse? Is not this a confirmation of Taubes's remark, which states that "the difficulties begin with Paul himself"? Does he not accommodate his discourse to his opponents' here, compromising his own apocalyptic belief?

There is, of course, a need to emphasize that Christ was raised "bodily" from the dead, a need expressed in chapter 15 of 1 Corinthians. But there is also a need to emphasize that precisely the same evil powers that were responsible for Christ's death are still in charge in this evil age of the world. There are two conflicting worlds, and the hidden and secret one has not yet conquered the other. This emphasis is made in the very same passage (2:6–10) that Taubes considers the source and starting point of Paul's "compromise" with the enthusiasts. Is Taubes no longer attuned to Paul's rhetoric here? Has he lost touch with the "exact word correspondences, rhyming consonance, symmetrically measured sentences" to which he was so attentive earlier in the essay?

Taubes wants to "claim 1 Corinthians 2:6ff as the first-rate evidence for the advancing accommodation by Christian values of the Greek world." Is it? We have seen that the passage functions as a reaffirmation of Paul's Jewish apocalypticism, and in that way it is far from an accommodation to the Greek. On the other hand, there is a shift in Paul's rhetoric embedded in this passage. Having appropriated the role of a fool and identified with the lower and the weak in 2:1–5, there is a changing tone in 2:5. Here the author's pledge is that the Corinthians' faith should not rest solely on foolishness or weakness, but also on divine power.

Although Paul applies the terms within an apocalyptic framework, locating secret and hidden wisdom in the realm to come, which "God has prepared for those who love him" (2:9), they are all the same high-status terms.[124] Hereafter in 1 Corinthians 2 the apostle no longer applies low-status terms to his ministry or to God's salvific work to the same degree. From 2:6 on, the vocabulary is increasingly filled with terms loaded with high status—as Taubes observes when he sees how the wisdom Paul speaks of in 2:6 is a truth "for the perfected."[125] He is aware of the usefulness of this very same passage in second-century Gnosticism and claims that there is a Gnostic infiltration of Christianity "already at the beginnings of its history."

> Valentinus and even Basiledes laid claim to the testimony of the first Corinthian letter for themselves. Not without reason the Valentinians contend that the fundamental concepts of their system can be found in Paul, and they appeal to this paragraph with proclivity.[126]

Taubes discerns the adaptability of 1 Corinthians to Gnostic readings.

The Contradictory Paul

This passage in Paul's letter obviously reflects a certain historical period that has worked well in the hands of Marcionites. And this is not "without reason"—that is, not without a plausible appeal to the biblical text itself. In that sense Taubes's peculiar inquiry into what a text might conceal is illustrative of what he considers the latency of texts. This notion of latency leaves a space open for the widely acknowledged polysemy of meaning that postcolonial theory, for instance, has underlined with the concept of "mimicry."[127]

When Paul appropriates the subaltern fool's role, there is a mimicry of this social role that again gives rise to diversity of associations. These associations and connotations might point in opposite directions. Accordingly, there is no unambiguous ideology channeled or communicated through gestures of mimicry such as Paul's in 1 Corinthians. On one level, there might be a noteworthy shift in the social roles, values, or ideologies that are the object of the mimicry. Paul moves up and down from low-status mimicry to high-status mimicry in his rhetoric. He unavoidably speaks against himself, and even more so at some points in his texts than others, and Taubes rightly points to 2:6 as an instance of this. This is one of the reasons one should listen to Taubes's warnings from the Heidelberg lectures against the danger or the failure involved if one overlooks "latent elements" in Paul:

> It's easy to read the story of Paul one-sidedly and to overlook latent elements in him. No one understood him, one might say, but then no one completely misunderstood him either. It's not a question of showing, pedantically, where Marcion diverges from Paul; that's easily done. The question is where he does capture an intention—and he does take himself to be Paul's true disciple.[128]

Here it is also evident how Taubes's method is connected to an image Taubes produces or reproduces of Paul. Since Taubes supposes that a text is "a moment in time and a position in a debate,"[129] the Pauline texts are considered to be already set in motion and dialogue with later appropriations. These "later appropriations" do not add meaning, but manifest what was in fact in the "primary" text, which already destabilizes an often taken-for-granted privileging of the primary and first over later texts. But Taubes's method also leads one to a variety of meanings in the texts—for example, the contradictory ones he found in 1 Corinthians. Accordingly, he does not find a consistent but a contradictory Paul.

Gnosticism surely provides a very illustrative example of how texts can be appropriated and received in multiple and conflicting ways. Taubes claims that the "Gnostic tendency begins in Paul."[130] But what in the biblical text may reflect a mimicry of a high-status discourse is for Taubes a reflection of the very same Gnosticism that the church fathers polemicized against a century after the Corinthian correspondence. And as remarked earlier, the increasing acknowledgment of the variety of ideas and ideologies in texts, which in Taubes's time were reduced to a much more univocal "Gnostic myth," does make the very idea of a religious movement of Gnosticism with a specified set of ideas much more difficult to defend. Although there may not be a Gnosticism at stake in 1 Corinthians, Taubes's question of "where is that beginning?"[131] (of Gnosticism) does still hold a high degree of validity. Though the question the reader faces with the biblical text is "class," "social status," "apocalypticism," or "Christology" rather than "Gnosticism," answers can be pursued by the lines or in the verses with which Taubes fought in his search for "the first-rate evidence for the advancing accommodation by Christian values." There are immanent possibilities in the text to make a case for an accommodation of some sort.

Furthermore, when Taubes applies his question of this accommodation to the post-Pauline era of the church fathers and the Constantinian church, the use of "Gnostic" texts as historical sources that inform his reading is much more appropriate. This strengthens his case for an originary Pauline ugliness of Christianity against the aesthetics of imperial Christendom, a conflict where Paul's legacy is not unambiguous with regard to the imperial powers that, at one point, were believed or hoped to be perishing.

Demonstrating no desire to present a consistent Paul, Taubes presents instead a contradictory Paul that will nonetheless prepare for the more Jewish Paul that is brought to the fore in the Heidelberg lectures. One cannot help but hear a Jewish call to resist making images of the deity in Taubes's Paul, the Paul who justifies "the Ugliness" in early Christianity against the Antique ethos of beauty and nobility so well known to the Corinthians.

The Originary Ugliness of Christianity: Paul against the Aesthetes

The Christian "impulse" in Paul is suppressed in Taubes's story when the cross is aestheticized as Constantine's imperial symbol of victory. Before the Constantianian turn, "the memory of the Old Testament's struggle against pagan divine images remained for a long time vivid."[132] Gradually this Hebraic memory, alongside the memory of Christ's suffering and death, is erased in the Constantinian era, according to Taubes. The Old Testament's prohibition of images is here linked to the memory of Christ's suffering. In Taubes's words, "Precisely in the transition from the word to the image the Christian experience leaves its own terrain behind."[133] In Taubes's view, images of Christ appear for the first time in "Gnostic circles." This "fact" reinforces the opposition established here by Taubes between a Pauline doctrine of the cross and a Pauline Gnosticism, between a Christian ugliness and a Constantinian aestheticization, between the cross as a meaningless torture instrument and as a meaningful cosmic symbol, an opposition encapsulated in the following formulation:

> In the many martyr acts as well, in which—one would initially assume—the death on the cross should once again become a hard reality, the wooden cross is "inflated" and interpreted cosmically.[134]

It is this opposition and tension that structure Taubes's evaluations almost thirty years later in the Heidelberg lectures. In these lectures we meet this so-called hard reality, contrasted with a modern aestheticization of it. This reading of 1 Corinthians, Gnosticism, and Constantinian Christianity shapes the perspective through which Taubes sees his modern interlocutors.

In Heidelberg Taubes pleads that he is not judging anyone morally, but is only thinking "in terms of intellectual history, of actual history." Nevertheless, one still gets a sense of a final account in Taubes's "last will"—namely, the lectures that he regarded as his "spiritual testament." The works of Blumenberg, Barth, Benjamin, and Adorno are to be inscribed on each side of the opposition from the 1968 essay, between "hard reality" and aesthetics, potentially or actually accommodated to the imperial powers of this world.

As Taubes said in the Heidelberg lectures three decades after his confrontations with Blumenberg's theses:

> Blumenberg discovers in the word "secularization" an illegitimate title; he rejects this concept, says it doesn't hold up. (I still believe it does hold up.) Blumenberg's idea is that the same substance gets passed on into other realms; it oozes, in the way that sludge oozes. . . . [135]

At this point Taubes seems to have moved far away from the Pauline texts he has promised to talk about. Why refer to a modern academic secularization debate in a series of lectures that were supposed to be on the Letter to the Romans? One reason for this can be found in the book by Blumenberg that Taubes calls "ein Knüller" in this lecture.[136] In this "piece of work" (as the English translation has it) the source for both Marcion's Gnosticism, as well as for Augustine's attempts of overcoming it, is Paul's Letter to the Romans. Blumenberg writes:

In the very text that had convinced Marcion of the wickedness of the Old Testament lawgiver, in Paul's Epistle to the Romans, Augustine found the theological means by which to formulate the dogma of man's universal guilt and to conceive of man's "justification" as an absolution that is granted by way of an act of grace and that does not remove from the world the consequences of that guilt. There he also found the doctrine of the absolute predestination, which restricted this grace to the small number of the chosen and thus left the continuing guilt of the all too many to explain the lasting corruption of the world. The Gnostic dualism had been eliminated as far as the metaphysical world principle was concerned, but it lived on in the bosom of mankind and its history as the absolute separation of the elect from the rejected. . . . Gnosticism that had not been overcome but only transposed returns in the form of the "hidden God" and his inconceivable absolute sovereignty. . . . [137]

Thus when Taubes's discussion seems far away from Paul he is discussing issues that are crucial for modern self-understanding but that also originate in Romans, according to Blumenberg. Taubes states that "among those who are alive" Blumenberg "is the only philosopher in Germany" who interests him. Is it Blumenberg who also places the Letter to the Romans at the center of Taubes's attention, as documented in *The Political Theology of Paul*?[138] Both the doctrine of original sin and the doctrine of predestination are discussed in Taubes's lectures, and these themes can be regarded as traces of Blumenberg. Moreover, Taubes feels compelled to take a stand in the debate between Schmitt and Blumenberg:

> The upshot of this is: What Schmitt regards as realities, Blumenberg regards as metaphors. Blumenberg, who among those who are alive is the only philosopher in Germany who interests me, is a metaphorologist. Schmitt asks: What is behind the metaphors? And he shows that there is an autism there, lurking behind the metaphors. An *autos*. You can read up on that. Anyway, that is the meaning of secularization: it's an illegitimate category. That something is secularized implies that it has been transferred from a legitimate place to an illegitimate one.[139]

Taubes reiterates Schmitt's argument from *Political Theology II* (1970) about the "autism," though this perspective from Schmitt is backed up with an opposition between "realities" and "metaphors." Then he states that he is dealing with "actual history," probably another word for Schmittian "realities."

> I don't think theologically. I work with theological materials, but I think in terms of intellectual history, of actual history. I ask after the political potentials in the theological metaphors, just as Schmitt asks after the theological potentials of legal concepts. Nor do I think morally. I'm no Last Judge. I don't have Carl Schmitt before me on the stand, or Karl Barth on the stand. I want to understand what is going on there.[140]

The Jewish rabbi assures his listeners that he does not "think theologically." Is this credible? And why declare that he does not think as a theologian but as a historian dealing with "actual history"?

To think like a theologian could refer to the dishonest Christian interpreters Nietzsche criticized in the passage Taubes had already quoted in the lectures, in §84 of *Daybreak*. Taubes had pointed to the value of the *redlichkeit* of the Nietzschean philology in contrast to Christianity. Reading the Bible should not be a matter of reading so badly that one reduces the philological perplexities to Christian dogmas.[141]

To think "theologically" might also refer to the interests Blumenberg had detected behind the secularization theory in *The Legitimacy of Modern Age*. Here Blumenberg had argued that in crisis theology and dialectical theology the secularization theorem was given its theological justification: "The patterns and schemas of the salvation story were to prove the ciphers and projections of intraworldly problems."[142] Moreover, what strengthened the secularization theory even more in Blumenberg's eyes was "a supplementary theory" in which the secularization thesis served "an argument vindicating the 'meaning,' the 'cultural value' of Christianity within the world."[143] As a response to this Taubes swears he is only thinking in terms of "history." Is he?

"Hard Reality" against Aesthetics

It is as if Taubes has given his final word about Blumenberg, perhaps a sense reinforced by Taubes's assurance that he is "no Last Judge." Blumbenberg deals only with metaphors. That is, he has not grasped the problem, "the realities" behind the metaphors.[144] By contrast, Schmitt has. Schmitt is by no means an aesthete, but an apocalypticist. He puts no trust in the syntheses of Cultural Protestantism that breaks down after the First World War. His attack on legal positivism runs parallel to Barth's Pauline attack on Cultural Protestantism.

After taking Schmitt's side against Blumenberg in the Heidelberg lectures, Taubes turns to Walter Benjamin. In Taubes's view Benjamin was also part of this "attack" or reaction after the First World War, and Taubes associates Benjamin and Paul. The various strategies by which these two figures are tied together indicate that there is something more at stake than just an understanding of the similarities between them.

Taubes affirms that Romans 8 has "its closest parallel" in Walter Benjamin's "Theologico-Political Fragment."[145] Then he includes a remark about how Scholem knew how to place this text correctly within the chronology of Benjamin's works, while Adorno did not. Taubes then performs a long exegesis of Benjamin's text, which serves as an argument for this "astonishing parallel" between Benjamin's view of nature and "the Pauline notion of creation" in Romans 8. Moreover, there is a political nihilism according to Taubes, both in this text of Benjamin and in Romans 13, even in 1 Corinthians 7:29.[146] After the arguments of the "astonishing parallel," Taubes turns once again to Adorno and his shortcomings, now in terms of his supposed messianic "standpoint of redemption" from *Minima Moralia*. The great value for Taubes in Benjamin is that he does not (like Paul supposedly) let the Messiah "drift into a neutrality, which isn't a matter of religious history, but an article of faith." Benjamin's text represents a true belief, an authentic messianism. Ernst Bloch is dismissed as "just wishy-washy" compared to Benjamin's position, and "especially Adorno!"[147]

> Think of *Minima Moralia*, the last part. There you can tell the difference between the substantial and as-if, and you can see how the whole messianic thing becomes a *comme si* affair. That is a wonderful, but finally empty, line, whereas for the young Benjamin it's substantial. It's shaken by experiences, and there are hints in the text that confirm this. These are the experiences that shake Paul through and through and that shake Benjamin through and through after 1918, after the war. That's what I'm talking about. This is not a matter of the ABCs of exegesis, but a question of optics. If someone sums up their whole work on one page, this results in an intensity that has no parallel in Benjamin's work. And now listen to the aesthete's variant.[148]

Already having dismissed Blumenberg's reduction of historical realities to metaphors, Taubes detects what he claims as Adorno's "empty" messianism in contrast to Benjamin's "substantial" messianism. Adorno's text is "wonderful"—that is, aesthetically—but not traumatically as in the young Benjamin's "shaken experiences." And here Taubes's reasons for the parallels between Paul and Benjamin are further explained. This parallel is not based on "the ABC of exegesis," as Taubes seems to be well aware that this sort of reading is not common or even acceptable within the disciplines that have specialized themselves on the exegesis of Paul and biblical studies. To further substantiate his claim about the "astonishing" parallel, Taubes appeals to the notion of "optics" and of "experiences" that "shake Paul . . . and . . . Benjamin through and through."[149] Here is one key to Taubes's peculiar negotiation of typical methodological ideals from the philosophical disciplines on the one hand and the historical on the other. With this argument, Taubes appears to presume that people can be affected by the same sort of experiences regardless of time and place.

Furthermore, Taubes had already argued methodologically for such comparisons across time and space when he justified the comparison of ancient Gnosticism and modern surrealism in the Poetik und Hermeneutik group, defending his project against criticism from scholars like Blumenberg:

> What constitutes method in historiography is to be found among its theoretical tools, which initially damage the phenomenon but also rescue it. No historiography can get around the codification of historical reality: Either our procedure is additive, in which each case history presents itself as an infinite series of equally valid events. While such a chronistic method, which avoids every construction of history, does not run the risk of being theoretically refuted, its epistemological value for insight does not transgress the boundaries of an infinite "and-so-on." Or we base the historiography on a constructive principle, and then different but also comparable constellations crystallize out of the raw material of events. Any constructive principle tends towards abbreviation, without which no progress of insight would be possible.[150]

Though Taubes does not employ the pejorative term "historicism," he all the same refers to an aspect of it—for instance, in the phrase "equally valid events." The comparative perspective through which he sees Paul and Benjamin can make "progress of insight," though not without a price—that is, "abbreviation"—possibly meaning something like "intensification" or "condensation."[151]

Then he quotes the final sentences from *Minima Moralia*, before he repeats his affirmation of the contrast between the "aestheticization" of messianism in Adorno and the "real" messianism in Benjamin. In Adorno, Taubes encounters "the same ideas diverted into the aesthetic." Did not Taubes describe the same process of neutralizing the subversive Messiah through an aestheticization in his 1968 essay on 1 Corinthians, as well? Is not the guiding principle here the very same opposition derived from his reading of the Pauline legacy of 1 Corinthians as the "hard reality" of the cross and the aestheticization of this reality? Is Taubes's resistance to Adorno then, at least partly, of a Pauline origin? In this discussion not only does aestheticization enter the picture, but so does a "hard reality," of which the names "Benjamin" and "Barth" bear traces.

> Benjamin has a hardness similar to that of Karl Barth. There's nothing there having to do with immanence. From that one gets nowhere. The drawbridge comes from the other side. And whether you get fetched or not, as Kafka describes it, is not up to you. One can take the elevators up to the highest rises of spirituality—it won't help. Hence the clear break.[152]

"Benjamin ist von Karl-Bartscher Härte," Taubes insists. Therefore, Benjamin can be understood from Barth's *Epistle to the Romans*, according to Taubes, as "dialectical theology outside the church." At this point Taubes goes a step further and includes himself in the list of these dialectical theologians who "have no church . . . , no bayonets, no state [that] stands behinds it that collects the taxes": "Just like me, just like Schmitt, with more or less understanding."[153] So here Taubes lists himself a Jew, Barth a Protestant, Schmitt a Catholic, and Benjamin another Jew. All stand together against "the aesthete": Adorno. Here Taubes even adds Lukács to his list of people who could see through the prestige of the Frankfurt school and perceive the "empty lines" of Adorno, its saint.[154]

Taubes appeals to "experience," to "hardness," and to "substance." Compared to Adorno the aesthete,

> Benjamin is something different altogether. That's just a different substance. That's what I wanted to point out.[155]

Straight enough, this is what Taubes has been heading toward: the different "substance" between Benjamin and Adorno. The argument ends by once again insisting on the contrast between the two or three (with Barth) or four (with Schmitt), on the one hand and the aesthete on the other. On one hand there are the intellectuals who have the same experiences ("erfahrungen") from the Weimar period, which are Benjamin, Barth, and Schmitt. They would never "go in for such naïve notions" as to consider music as having "a soteriological role," which is the case with Adorno, who is deemed the aesthete by Taubes.[156]

So what about Paul and Benjamin? One might ask whether Taubes could not have made exactly the same point about the contrast between Benjamin and Adorno without Paul. If the contrast between Benjamin (together with Barth and Schmitt) and Adorno was what Taubes wanted to point out, as he said, he could have done so without bringing Paul into the discussion. Furthermore, one could ask whether Taubes would have posited the same affinity between "the zeolots of the absolute"—that is, between the supposed enemies Schmitt and Benjamin—without constructing this "astonishing" parallel. So what does the argument on Paul and Benjamin serve?

One may look at the Heidelberg lectures as a whole. Something is prepared by the whole argument of what in the transcription is labeled "Nihilsm as World Politics and Aestheticized Messianism: Walter Benjamin and Theodor W. Adorno." Jacob Taubes is not done with Adorno yet, because the last lecture that appears in *The Political Theology of Paul* is about Taubes's own relationship with Schmitt. The history of this intellectual companionship between him and Schmitt is introduced by a demonstration of how the "left-right scheme doesn't hold"; in other words, how Taubes can approve of Schmittian ideas without betraying the political Left and how on a certain level he can reconcile Schmitt with Barth and Benjamin. To strengthen his case Taubes tells what Herbert Kopp-Oberstebrink calls "a legend."[157] Taubes relates how the letter from Benjamin to Schmitt from 1930 was discovered and the fact of how it was suppressed:

> When I got hold of this letter, I phoned Adorno and asked him: Aren't there two published volumes of Benjamin's letters: why is this letter not published? A letter like this doesn't exist, was the answer. I say, Teddy, I know the handwriting. I know the typewriter Benjamin wrote with, don't tell me stories. I've got it right here![158]

The effect of the "astonishing" parallel between Paul and Benjamin amounts perhaps to this: It aims at reinforcing the plausibility of a personal link and a shared intellectual commitment between Benjamin and Schmitt, thereby legitimating Taubes's own embrace of Schmittian ideas profiting from Benjamin's unquestioned legacy and canonized texts for the philosophical Left.

Besides, there is another effect of Taubes's identification of a text of Benjamin with one of Paul's. The affiliation Taubes draws serves to further substantiate his former depiction of Benjamin as a modern Marcionite. Having already pointed out the Gnostic-Marcionite tendencies inherent in Paul, Taubes further strengthens this controversial similarity between Benjamin and Paul. One may argue that Taubes's argument for Benjamin being a modern Marcionite is "downright misleading." This would confirm another suspicion about Taubes's motive for such readings, that this "misleading" view is directed against Gershom Scholem's Jewish interpretation of the "Political-Theological Fragment."[159] This would indicate that the "astonishing parallel" Taubes claims to see between Paul and Benjamin in the Heidelberg lectures is not fueled by a precise reading of Benjamin. It is rather fueled by another of his intellectual and personal enemies: his former teacher Scholem. This, however, seems to be an enmity that distorts Taubes's otherwise close readings of Paul. While Nietzsche paved the way for a close reading of Paul, Scholem may have provoked Taubes to mobilize a less attentive reading of the apostle: that of the antinomian Jew. This is further argued for in the chapter about Taubes's Introspective Paul. Taubes constructs a picture of an antinomian apostle in order to make his polemics against Scholem effective in a conference paper published as "The Price of Messianism." The antinomian Paul Taubes constructs in this essay, with references to Romans, will be met with some hesitations in this study (see Chapter 4).

Taubes's Enemies: The Fuel and Method of His Readings of Paul

What did Taubes achieve with all these confrontations and final words on key thinkers in modern German intellectual history? What is the result of a view shaped by a Pauline perspective of a "hard reality" that resists aesthetic neutralization, a scandal that is forever a threat to a harmonious cosmological understanding of God, man and world?

One answer might be that this "occasionalist," as Taubes names himself,[160] came closer to his own truth about Paul's legacy in modernity. Nonetheless, this truth was not attainable without confrontations that would reveal true disagreements. This hypothesis about the direction of Taubes's argument in the Heidelberg lectures goes against another hypothesis recently suggested by Larry L. Welborn:

> We will attempt to demonstrate that the document which fuelled Taubes' interpretation of Paul was not Schmitt's *Political Theology*, but another essay of the Weimar period bearing a similar title, an essay which happens to be the only text cited and expounded by Taubes in its entirety—Walter Benjamin's "Theologico-Political Fragment."[161]

Taubes's reading of Paul is polemical from the very start of his lecture. He works his way through a whole range of authors, works, and views with which he disagrees. Moreover, when he discerns something valuable in others' understandings or findings, it is often in spite of their explicit views or expressed aims. This is not the case with Benjamin, who is an exceptional case within Taubes's great library in these lectures.

Welborn is quite right to highlight Benjamin's influence as unique in this regard, and it is no coincidence that Taubes proclaims Benjamin to be "the truest exegete" of Paul's account of the "subjection of the creation to futility" in Romans 8.[162] However, Welborn's term for the function of this influence is imprecise. When Welborn writes that it was Benjamin's text that "fuelled Taubes' interpretation of Paul," it seems to imply that this particular text was the driving force and the energy in Taubes's readings of Paul. The logic that can be discerned in Taubes's course of argument, however, indicates that it was rather the opponents than the allies of Taubes, rather the disagreements than the agreements he had that "fuelled" his lecturing on Paul, with Carl Schmitt as a sort of end station in his drive. Benjamin obviously informs Taubes's image of messianism and therefore also of Paul as a Jewish apocalyptic. Nevertheless, his fundamental view of messianism, which stayed with him, was formed well before he started to read either Benjamin's "Theses on the Philosophy of History" or the "Theologico-Political Fragment." The many continuities between the messianic logic in *Occidental Eschatology* to *The Political Theology of Paul* account for this, and these include a description of messianism that was not substantially revised upon the influence of either Benjamin or Scholem.[163]

If one compares Schmitt to Benjamin, it was rather the first of the two who fueled Taubes's lectures on Paul. Taubes had his disagreements with Schmitt, not least his katechontic apocalypticism, but these served him to achieve the real disagreements with Blumenberg and leftist intellectuals concerning Schmitt. Why else so many efforts to restore Schmitt to a name alongside Benjamin and Barth? These efforts cannot be compared to Taubes's privileging of Benjamin as a true exegete of Romans 8 or Romans 13 (or 1 Corinthians 7:29). This speaker has less of a hard time installing Benjamin as a name within his pantheon of apocalypticists as he has with Schmitt. Therefore, he begins and ends with Schmitt. In that sense, all the intellectuals who have expressed distaste for the texts of Paul, Barth, and Schmitt "fuel" Taubes's readings. Benjamin is a saint from the hagiographies of the Frankfurt School, and therefore Taubes expresses no need for restoring his name. He only appeals to Benjamin's legacy in order to restore another more controversial figure, a true enemy of the Jewish people. With his letter from 1930 Walter Benjamin opened the door that Taubes went through in relation to Schmitt. As an aesthete, Adorno could not take these steps, however much he belonged to the Jewish people.

In this sense, Schmitt and Blumenberg, opponents to Taubes in their different ways, fueled Taubes's interpretations of Paul more than Benjamin. While Blumenberg was a continuous opponent on a theoretical level, Schmitt was an opponent on a more political and existential one. While Schmitt was certainly not Taubes's best teacher on Paul, he gave Taubes's readings of Paul a sense of urgency, which is explicit in the introduction to the 1987 lectures. There was no such urgency with regard to Benjamin. Quite the opposite: Benjamin's insights were already recognized. The time had come to recognize the insights of Schmitt, according to Taubes.

But unlike Nietzsche, Schmitt was not praised for his readings of Paul. By far the opposite, for Taubes went to Schmitt to convince him how badly he had read Paul's letter to the Romans. While "fuel" may be a meaningful metaphor to apply to Schmitt's function, it can indeed be applied to Nietzsche's role, as well.

In contrast to Schmitt, it appears that Nietzsche has substantially informed Taubes's views on Paul, to a certain decisive point. Taubes was in a certain sense led to the biblical Paul by Nietzsche, as demonstrated in this chapter through a presentation of Taubes's reading of 1 Corinthians 1–2. Thereby Taubes achieved his true disagreement with Nietzsche's views, expressed in philosophical texts about Paul and early Christianity that evidently contained fuel for Taubes's motor or interest in Paul the apostle.

With only Paul and Benjamin as company, Taubes would never have come to Heidelberg. And with only philosophical perspectives Taubes would never have come to this place to seek a true disagreement. Heidelberg represents, after all, some of the finest achievements of historical perspectives on Paul. By claiming that Nietzsche's historical insights about Paul are superior to the insights of New Testament exegetes, Taubes boldly transgresses disciplinary boundaries. In this way, he does not simply replace historical perspectives with philosophical ones, in spite of reading Paul through other philosophers. He rather deconstructs the reception history of Paul from within this history. If Taubes could be said to follow a method, then this method is deconstructive in this sense.

Taubes's reading of 1 Corinthians 1–2 is an argument for why and to what degree the philosopher Nietzsche's historical knowledge of Paul is greater than any historian's. Taubes's best teacher about the apostle is Nietzsche. Accordingly, Nietzsche is his explicit point of departure when he reads 1 Corinthians. Taubes agrees with Nietzsche about "the moment when the turnover from ancient to Christian values takes place," as the rabbi calls it. This textual revolution can, according to Taubes, with Nietzsche, be located in 1 Corinthians 1:20. However, Taubes disagrees with Nietzsche about the historical outcome of Paul's revolution. For Taubes it was not Pauline Christianity that triumphed after Antiquity. Far from it; it was the Roman Empire that triumphed over Christianity. The force that Taubes recognized in the ugliness of the cross, as the counterpart to the human adoration of aesthetics, was not completely eliminated. "The Christian impulse," as Taubes named it, lay latent in history and could therefore resurge nearly twenty centuries later in modern apocalypticists such as Barth and Benjamin. But it could also be suppressed by thinkers who welcomed Nazism—another triumph over Christianity.

Taubes's Paul and Philosophy: Conclusion

In this chapter particular attention has been paid to Jacob Taubes's readings of 1 Corinthians and to these readings' negotiations between the historical and the philosophical.

As stated previously in "To Immerse Oneself Talmudically," Jacob Taubes reads Paul in ways that do not easily fall under the category of either the philosophical or the historical. Taubes uses Paul in his own positioning of himself within twentieth-century intellectual debates in Germany featuring Carl Schmitt, Walter Benjamin, Theodor Adorno, and Hans Blumenberg. In that way he explicitly activates various layers of reception of Paul within his readings of the apostle that do not produce an image of Paul as a consistent apostle. Nor is there a clear delineation between what Paul's texts mean and what Paul's legacy through history is. Taubes's Paul breaks with the Jewish in his devotion to the crucified, but this devotion all the same represents a Jewish resistance against pagan divine images ("The Originary Ugliness of Christianity: Paul against the Aesthetes," in this chapter). Taubes's Paul, with his doctrine of the cross in 1 Corinthians 1:20, is revolutionary with regard to ancient imagination, but, with his wisdom for the perfected in 1 Corinthians 2:6, compromises the scandalous ugliness of the cross with the conventions of his time. Taubes's Paul releases countercultural forces in one moment and prepares for their cultural neutralization in the other, with elements that will contribute to the installment of Christendom. These contradictory tendencies are for Taubes manifest in one and the same letter.

Taubes proclaims Friedrich Nietzsche as his best teacher on Paul. While praising the insights of his days' German New Testament scholars as valuable for further interpretation, Taubes claims that Nietzsche's historical insight still remains unsurpassed by the New Testament exegetes. Taubes includes historical as well as philosophical perspectives on Paul, but privileges and discusses Nietzsche's Paul informed by historical perspectives. Nonetheless, in Nietzsche's scenario of a conflict between the noble aristocratic values of Antiquity and the Christian values of the ugliness of the cross, Taubes the Jew sides with the Christian stance, which is discerned by the help of Nietzsche.

By appropriating aspects of Nietzsche's Paul, Taubes encounters a space for his Talmudic reasoning, where polemic in general and Nietzsche's polemic in particular are cherished rather than devaluated epistemologically. This is a space where Taubes can read Paul critically in relation to both Christian metaphysics and dogmatics as well as to modern historicism. One of Taubes's sources of resistance to the pressure of these ideologies is to be found in Nietzsche's "honest philology" (see "To Immerse Oneself Talmudically"). This resonates with the reading Taubes makes of 1 Corinthians, of the letter's "word correspondences, rhyming consonance, symmetrically measured sentences often with homonymic endings, and a series of questions, anaphora, and antitheses" (quoted in "Rewriting the Revolutionary Paulinism in 1 Corinthians 1:17–2:5," in this chapter). In this way Taubes is attuned to the text's possible ambivalences and ambiguities. With one of the forerunners to Derridean deconstruction, Taubes can contribute to the deconstruction of the reception history of Paul. Through his reliance on Nietzsche, Taubes relocates the fundamental conflict between the values of the cross and the values of the Greco-Roman elite.

Taubes's suspicion of historicism does not in fact result in a rejection of historical perspectives. As demonstrated in his reading of 1 Corinthians (see the section "Taubes's Essay on 1 Corinthians," earlier in this chapter), he can read this text diachronically as a window to a historical past without ceasing to hold onto Nietzsche's thesis that 1 Corinthians 1:20 constitutes or expresses "the moment when the turnover from ancient to Christian values takes place." By speaking of Nietzsche's *historical* insight, Taubes's aim appears primarily to be to understand history, of Paul's days and of his own days. This can also be seen in his use of the category "gnosticism" in relation to Paul, which refers to ancient as well as modern realities within Taubes's thought and twentieth-century German thought.

Taubes deliberately and openly combines historical and philosophical perspectives. He does not claim to use one of the two. In Taubes's reading of 1 Corinthians he is attentive to rhetorical shifts and ambiguities with regard to the meaning of passages. Ambivalences in the letter's meaning are highlighted. In this way, Taubes's method could be said to be a Talmud-inspired form of deconstruction where the combination of diachronic and synchronic approaches to text contributes to the destabilization of meaning.

4

Paul as Predecessor to Psychoanalysis
Taubes's Introspective Paul

Paul has been constructed as the first Christian who abrogated the Jewish law and replaced it with the Christian gospel of grace and freedom from the law. The old covenant between God and his elected Jewish people was substituted with the new covenant that God established with the Christian church through Christ. Thereby Christianity superseded Judaism.

Jacob Taubes highlights his own Jewishness as being an advantage for a scholar who wants to understand Paul. In the introduction to his lectures on Romans, Taubes tells a story about his conversation with the philologist Emil Staiger, who had read Paul's letters and concluded that "it isn't Greek, it's Yiddish!" Taubes then refers to another conversation he had, this time with the historian of religion Kurt Latte, who could not understand the letters with his "Greek ear."[1] In this way Taubes had implicitly stated that one needed a Jewish ear. One would expect a Jewish interpretation of the apostle. But did the rabbi actually overturn the Christian understanding of the apostle, replacing it with a Jewish one, attuned to Jewish ears?

In this chapter further evidence will be given to the claim that Taubes's method is deconstructive, primarily with examples from Taubes's lectures on Romans from 1987 and his essay "The Price of Messianism."[2] In addition, I want to deepen my claim that Taubes's Paul is constructed through engagement with what I have referred to as his "enemies" or "opponents." Some of the evidence for my claims can be found in the various choices Taubes makes in his reading of Paul, which I conclude result in a Jewish introspective Paul. By including elements from a typically Christian understanding of Paul as a figure of introspection and interiority and combining them with aspects such as collectivity, election, and apocalypticism from Jewish messianism, Taubes construes an idiosyncratic image of Paul.

This image is reconcilable neither with the traditional Christian concern of an ahistorical individual salvation nor with the traditional rabbinical observance of the Torah. By going against the traditional image of Paul as a Jew who left Judaism, the apostle is no longer the first Christian or the Jew who has fallen into apostasy. In this way, Taubes is deconstructing the reception of Paul not only in Christianity but also within Judaism.[3] This deconstruction is undertaken by turning to another of his "enemies." In addition to Nietzsche, in his lectures on Romans, Taubes is staging battles against Carl Schmitt and Sigmund Freud. In order to read Paul through these opponents, he promises to make them as strong as possible:

> Now I am of course a Paulinist, not a Christian, but a Paulinist, and I think one must make one's opponent as strong as possible. Otherwise it's uninteresting. With an opponent whom I can demolish straightaway it's not worth talking any further. And this is where Freud enters the game.[4]

This should be considered a gesture whose purpose is to reach a true disagreement within a long chain of viewpoints, opinions, and polemics. It is as if Taubes disseminates this Talmudic spirit within the secular and Protestant academic environment in twentieth-century Germany. In a sense, the anecdotes Taubes tells in his Heidelberg lectures testify to this Talmudic spirit. This spirit is not so much embedded in the logic of weighing carefully the pros and cons of an argument as it is spread with the help of rhetorical moves and polemics. On Taubes's Talmudic textual horizon there is neither an original agreement to return to nor a conclusive consensus that could once and for all eradicate disagreements. The concern is rather with the art of achieving true disagreement.[5]

By reading Romans with Schmitt, the importance of reading Paul as a Jew is highlighted, and by relying on the views of Nietzsche and Freud on Paul, a more Christian view of Paul as an introspective figure comes to the fore in Taubes's thinking. Nevertheless, when Taubes reads Paul, and particularly Romans through these modern thinkers, the Jewish rabbi still reads Paul's texts. What is seen in Taubes is still a reception of Paul. Accordingly, one can ask, What kind of reception? And is that reception making Romans primarily a more Jewish or a more Christian text?

To answer these questions, one should as a reception historian not only delve into the intellectual, political, and religious history of which an interpreter like Taubes is part. In order to investigate the effects of the Bible in these intellectual events of postwar Europe,[6] one should measure the plausibility and credibility of Taubes's readings of Paul, however much they might be filtered through or mirrored from his opponents. In this chapter the legitimacy of Taubes's readings will be discussed by looking more closely into Romans as a "thing" that can generate different readings. Taubes's reading of passages from Romans will not only be isolated and contextualized, but also be placed in a wider reception history of Romans. This might help us to see which potential meanings in this thing called Romans are actualized in Taubes's reading and which are overlooked, but are nevertheless real possibilities with their own legitimate reasons or grounds. Taubes's remarks on Romans appear somewhat dispersed as parts of different arguments in several different academic settings. As a result, my discussion of his readings of Paul's letter to the Romans will primarily take the form of a commentary on his remarks, which will be ordered mostly according to the chronology of Romans, chapter by chapter. By this procedure, I will be writing a new understanding of Romans. I regard the newness of this reading as, in one sense, microscopic in relation to earlier readings. Nevertheless, the act of activating layers of reception that have not been brought together in this specific way before produces something new.

The Introspective Conscience of the West: A Jewish Drama?

One of the anecdotes Jacob Taubes tells in his Heidelberg lectures is about Krister Stendahl, whom Taubes refers to as his friend from Harvard. While visiting Taubes once in New York, Stendahl had confessed to Taubes that his "deepest worry" was whether he belongs to the "commonwealth of Israel." This is a profound fear that Taubes reads back into or, perhaps, out of Paul's letter to the Romans, since in Taubes's view, Paul is appointed to a revolutionary task:

> For Paul, the task at hand is the *establishment and legitimation of a new people of God*. This doesn't seem very dramatic to you, after two thousand years of Christianity. But it is the most dramatic process imaginable in a Jewish soul.[7]

Paul may suffer from a plagued conscience in this interpretation, but its desperation is not a product of experiencing the impossibility of keeping the whole law. The relation to Israel and its law is not at stake in Romans 7, as in many Christian readings of this passage. Taubes points instead to

Romans 9:1–3, where Paul's fear of "being accursed and cut off" is expressed. In this interpretation, it is Romans 9 rather than Romans 7 that is autobiographical, in contrast to the influential Augustinian view.[8] In that sense Taubes confirms Stendahl's view of Romans 9–11 not as the appendix, but the climax of the letter.[9] For a Jewish reader like Taubes, the establishment of a new people is the most dramatic event that can take place in Jewish salvation history, a drama of "the Jewish soul."

Stendahl's essay, "The Apostle Paul and the Introspective Conscience of the West," was groundbreaking. Its refutation of the Augustinian-Lutheran projection of a Western model for "the ruthlessly honest man in his practice of introspection" onto the ancient apostle had an immediate impact. Its rejection of Christian "introspection" into the nature of sin as the center of Paul's preoccupation sparked new readings of Paul in New Testament scholarship that emphasized Paul's Jewishness. With regard to the Jewish law, Paul had a "robust" rather than a "plagued conscience."[10] Stendahl encountered no traces in Paul's letters of an awareness of any personal sins that troubled his conscience. Paul's preoccupation was communal, rather than individual. And the universal character of the desperation that necessarily resulted from an attempt to follow the Jewish law was not Paul's problem but that of his later Christian interpreters. Stendahl claimed this anthropological premise was a Christian invention, not Paul's:

> The question about the Law became the incidental framework around the golden truth of Pauline anthropology. This is what happens when one approaches Paul with the Western question of an introspective conscience. This Western interpretation reaches its climax when it appears that even, or especially, the will of man is the center of depravation. And yet, in Rom. 7 Paul had said about that will: "The will (to do the good) is there." (v. 18)[11]

Paul's words in Romans 7 did not reflect a morally deprived individual but an "acquittal of the ego" and corresponding relegation of responsibility to the real source of sin, the flesh. Paul's primary concern was not the ego or the conscience at all, according to Stendahl, who had given a first version of the essay at the 1961 annual meeting of the American Psychological Association. It was Augustine who should be considered the inventor of the introspective conscience, not Paul. Through his praise of Erik H. Erikson's book *Young Man Luther* (1958), Stendahl seems to encourage psychoanalytical readings of Luther while calling for a sharper divide between Jungian or Freudian psychoanalysis, on the one hand, and Paul, on the other.

Four years before Stendahl's intervention at the annual meeting, Taubes had published an essay that affirmed two tendencies that Stendahl's essay criticized. In the essay "Religion and the Future of Psychoanalysis" (1957), Taubes established an intimate link between Freud's psychoanalysis and Paul's gospel, since both called for a confession of guilt. In addition, Taubes emphasized the continuity between Paul and Augustine, where Stendahl would see discontinuity:

> Never since Paul and Augustine has a theologian taught a more radical doctrine of original guilt than Freud. No one since Paul has so clearly perceived and so strongly emphasized the urgent need to atone for the act of original guilt as has Freud.[12]

This view of continuity between Paul and Augustine was reaffirmed when Taubes, at the World Congress of Jewish Studies in 1981, attacked his old teacher Gershom Scholem shortly before the latter's death. What Taubes criticized succinctly was Scholem's sharp delineation of Judaism and Christianity. In the paper, which is published as "The Price of Messianism," Taubes critiques Scholem's reduction of Christian redemption to what takes place "in the private world of each individual" in contrast to the Jewish one that takes place "on the stage of history and within the community."[13] Taubes argues that the messianic turn inward, which Scholem labels pejoratively as a "flight," is not external to Judaism; the two Jewish heresies of Pauline Christianity and the Sabbatian movement are examples of it. In Taubes's view, interiorization is a consequence of the messianic logic within Judaism. When messianic hopes fail and eschatological visions are negated by historical realities, a crisis inevitably results. "The crisis of eschatology becomes for Paul a crisis of conscience," and this follows from the logic of the messianic idea that is immanent to Judaism; it is a necessary consequence of it. Paul's interiorization of the messianic idea is not a Christian innovation. Here one sees that Taubes posits a Jewish introspection:[14] "Turning the messianic experience inward, Paul opens the door toward the introspective conscience of the West."[15]

It is not the case for Taubes that Augustine and the West have simply misread Paul as an introspective figure. For Taubes, Messianic Judaism, including Paul, leads to a kind of introspective conscience. This introspection is posited by Taubes by means or resources in Paul's Letter to the Romans.

Introspection as a Jewish Remedy against the Catastrophe

Taubes's picture of Paul as an introspective figure was drawn in polemical circumstances. In an attack launched against his older teacher's delineation of Judaism and Christianity, Taubes portrays Paul as a messianic figure who never left Judaism, however much he interiorized or spiritualized the messianic idea.[16]

From Taubes's criticism of Scholem's reduction of Christian redemption to what takes place "in the private world of each individual," we can derive that "the introspective conscience of the West" is no Christian invention reserved for the private spiritual realm. Far from it, this introspective turn of the Messianic idea is crucial in order to not let the "wild apocalyptic fantasy" inherent in the messianic hope invade the political sphere, unmediated by adaptation to the earthly conditions and limitations:

> If the messianic idea in Judaism is not interiorized, it can turn the "landscape of redemption" (p. 35) into a blazing apocalypse. If one is to enter irrevocably into history, it is imperative to beware of the illusion that redemption (even the beginnings of redemption, *athalta de geula!*) happens on the stage of history.[17] For every attempt to bring about the redemption on the level of history without transfiguration of the messianic idea leads straight into the abyss.[18]

When Taubes writes that "the historian can do no more than set the record straight," the implication seems to be that this is precisely what the historian should appreciate in Paul. Paul's introspection historically was a remedy to avoid the most "absurd" and "catastrophic" consequences of the messianic idea.

In this intervention at the World Congress of Jewish Studies in Jerusalem in 1981, Taubes parted from Scholem's own account of the messianic idea in order to inscribe Paul into Judaism. Taubes took the role of the historian and claimed:

> The messianic idea ran its full course in the history of Judaism in two messianic movements only: in early Christianity and in the Sabbatian movement of the seventeenth century. . . . During the sixteen hundred years of the hegemony of rabbinic Judaism, we witness only the sporadic and always ephemeral emergence of Messiahs who leave no traces except in historiography. They rise and die with the Messiahs themselves. . . . The only movements to continue are those where the life of the Messiah is interpreted, where outrage upon normal messianic expectation—death or apostasy—is "interpreted" for the community of "believers."[19]

Paul's Messiah was not "sporadic" or "ephemeral" but has had a lasting impact through a transformation of the "normal messianic expectation" into a form of interiorization. Although Taubes here used the expression "early Christianity" for Paul's messianism, in the Heidelberg lectures six years later he wants to do away with the term "Christian" when speaking of Paul. The word "Christian" does not exist for Paul and constitutes now an unfortunate anachronism for Taubes.[20]

In his exegesis of the letter to the Romans, Taubes's first strategy is to gather "the heretic back into the fold."[21] His explicit aim is to emphasize continuity between the prophets of the Old Testament and the apostle of the New. He does so by affirming that the proper meaning of Paul's self-description in Romans 1:1 as "called to be an apostle" is to be found in the allusion to Jeremiah in Galatians 1:15:

> Whoever looks at what Galatians 1:15 says about what is commonly called the conversion, the Damascus experience, knows that what is being talked about here is not conversion but a calling, and that is being done in the language and the style of Jeremiah.[22]

For Taubes, this prophetic language, as in Jeremiah, reveals Paul's self-understanding. Paul is not just an apostle to the Gentiles. He is an apostle *from the Jews* to the Gentiles. Whatever introspective conscience he passes on to his Gentile audiences, it is one with Jewish roots.

Rewriting the Jewish call in Romans

Taubes comments on the first verse in Romans: "Paul, a servant of Jesus Christ, called to be an apostle, set apart for the gospel of God" (Rom 1:1). Let us consider whether this verse can perform the work of emphasizing the Jewishness of the utterer or of the expression itself, as it does in Taubes's discourse.

The notion of "call," which in Romans 1:1 has the form of the adjective *kletos*, may refer to the "call tradition" embedded in the prophets' sayings in the Old Testament. The word *aphorismenos*, usually translated as "set apart" or "singled out," is possibly a translation of the Hebrew word for this action performed by God upon the called person in Jeremiah 1:5.[23] The utterance can be regarded as indebted to the Jewish prophetic tradition. However, elsewhere in the letter Paul describes his apostolic mission in priestly terms as well (Rom 15:16). That does not, however, weaken the supposed continuity with the Jews, a case that can be further strengthened by associating "set apart" with the group of the Pharisees. It has been argued that the word for "Pharisee," *parush* (פרוש), derives from the same Hebrew root that lies behind the appearances in the LXX of the verb Paul employs here (in the form of *aphorismenos*).[24] Paul proclaims himself to be "set apart," which captures the ideal meaning of the Pharisee, an identity he still in some sense adheres to in Philippians 3:5. He literally says he has been called, while there is no mention of being converted to anything. Taubes's strategy, like Stendahl's,[25] is one of subtracting the extratextual notion of "conversion" and using a notion of calling instead, which undeniably figures in the biblical text.

Paul's identity as a Pharisaic Jew may have been affected drastically by the Christ event, but the verse is singled out by Taubes for good reasons. It contains resources for displacing the notion of conversion, especially in the sense of converting from one established religion to another, from Judaism to Christianity, since the possibility of such a conversion only opens up at a much later stage in history.[26]

The Jewish Soul—a Collective Phenomenon

The door Taubes's Paul opened toward the introspective conscience of the West did not lead to the individualized Lutheranism Stendahl attempted to correct. Luther's "How can I find a gracious God?" is not the first question Taubes's Paul would pose, no matter how introspective his Pauline figure is supposed to be.

> [Conscience] is the "invention" of Paul in the crisis of a messianic redemption that failed to take place publicly in the realm of history but is reflected in the soul of the community of "believers." Conscience is by no means "a nonexistent pure inwardness." It is inward, but exists in constant tension with the world, forcing us to construct casuistries to bridge the gap between it and the realm of the world.[27]

Like Luther's Paul, Taubes's Paul also struggles with a problem of justification. But this is a question of justifying the establishment of a new people and not of forgiving or making righteous a repentant sinner. Unlike the general Christian tendency to limit justification by faith to forgiveness of personal sins, Taubes's Paul has to justify the assumption of a new people with new communal practices.

As noted, the most dramatic event to a Jewish soul is in Taubes's view the installation of a new people of God. Taubes recognizes God's anger or wrath in the words of Romans 1:18 from a "central experience of the Torah." Taubes sets out, by recitations and comments on texts from the Hebrew Bible (Exod 32–34; Num 14–15) and from the Talmud, to make the listener understand "the Jewish experience" that lies under this verse from the Romans. The pattern recognized in Romans 1:18 by Taubes is that God wants to annihilate his people, since it has sinned. God's anger in Romans is "a great fugue" that is repeated through Paul's letter until it ends in what Taubes labels "the great jubilation" in chapter 8. The real legitimation of the new people of God, however, is effectuated in chapters 9–11. In that sense, these constitute the peak in the drama for the Jewish soul.

Taubes is eager to dismiss the "Bultmannian naivités"[28] of making the individual of modern existentialism the primary addressee of Paul's theology.[29] Even when Taubes quotes Rosenzweig at length to explain "the Jewish experience" outlined in Rosenzweig's theology of liturgy, Taubes criticizes Rosenzweig for smuggling "German Protestantism and interiority" back into the Jewish ritual.[30] These are anachronisms that hinder an understanding of the experience that Paul's fear of God's anger presupposes. The question of annihilation poses a threat to a collective, not an individual, in Taubes's opinion. And why this threat, according to Taubes? It is there, in Romans 1:18, since the people of God "has rejected the Messiah that has come to it."[31]

Taubes clearly rejects the possibility that Israel remains unscathed by the wrath and that it only concerns the Gentiles. He considers what might constitute a philosophical forerunner to the two-ways paradigm of the radical new perspective in New Testament scholarship, Rosenzweig's two paths, as an alternative vision to Paul's.[32] In his *Star of Redemption* Rosenzweig envisions Judaism and Christianity as two distinctive ways of anticipating the future redemption of "All." Taubes, however, presents Israel as a people that is deeply affected by the Christ event. Israel runs the risk of annihilation in its salvation history. This version of the salvation history is made possible by Taubes's move of relating the divine wrath to Israel's destiny.

Rewriting Wrath in Romans

The motif of wrath first appears in verse 18: "For the wrath of God is revealed from heaven against all ungodliness and wickedness of those who by their wickedness suppress the truth" (Rom 1:18). Let us look at how the wrath in this verse might have the potential of reaching the people of Israel, as Taubes claims.

In its immediate context those who "suppress the truth" and who consequently are affected by the revealed wrath appear to be Gentiles and not Jews. When in the next verses Paul exemplifies the "ungodliness and wickedness" of those "who deserve to die" (1:32) who therefore can be said to be threatened by this wrath, he gives examples of typical Gentile immorality viewed from a stereotypical Jewish point of view. These people are idolaters and typical of those who cannot control their passions, two Jewish stereotypes of Gentiles a Jew like Paul could perfectly reproduce. The problem here is possibly not the Jews; it is the Gentiles. The wrath may be seen to be reserved for them. The text could then be referring not to a corrupted humanity, but to corrupted Gentiles.[33]

The ongoing process of wrath presented in verse 18 appears in considerable tension to the statement that "the righteousness of God is revealed through faith for faith" (1:17). We could translate *dikaiosune theou* as "the justice of God" at the expense of the cited translation of "the righteousness of God." One possible outcome of such a choice could be the avoidance of the strongest forensic and individualistic connotations of the revealed good news "to the Jew first and also to the Greek" (1:16).[34] With the justice of God contrasting the wrath of God, we might label all human behavior that deserves or provokes divine wrath "injustice." When truth is suppressed, it is imprisoned, held down, or taken captive by injustice. This occurs, it seems, in association with a struggle of force or of war. Human behavior unleashes a war on God's justice.[35] This coheres with a dramatic apocalyptic worldview.

The individualist approach to Paul's version of the gospel has not simply been forced upon the text. The biblical text has indeed demonstrated its power to generate such understandings of God's salvation. The diatribe enacted in the epistle, in 2:1–5 and 2:17–24, that launches an attack on an imaginary interlocutor prepares some of the ground for such interpretations. But as the wrath is effected upon "all wickedness" or on "those who by their wickedness suppress the truth," it has a wider scope than the individual.[36] If we recognize the apocalypticism at work in this process of wrath, we can also recognize the potentially overall collective and cosmological dimensions to this wrath as well as its counterpart, the salvific justice. It may therefore be argued that the rhetorical attacks on the Gentile person in 2:1–5 and the Jewish person in 2:17–24 constitute Pauline critiques of types and therefore collectivities.[37] The text addresses not only individual realities, even when written in the diatribe genre, but first and foremost social totalities—first the Gentile polity in 1:18–2:16 and then the Judaic one in 2:17–3:20.[38] This is a critique of how these polities function with regard to the primary concern of the letter: the justice of God (1:17). So what about the wrath of God? Does it only condemn corrupted Gentiles? What about the corruption detected under the Judaic condition or example of 2:17–3:20?

The interlocutor in 2:1–5 is addressed after the enlisted vices or sinful behavior in 1:23–32, stereotypically tied to Gentiles. Therefore, it can make sense to identify this interlocutor as an arrogant Gentile.[39] This accused representative of what we may regard as a Gentile or pagan polity is, through his attitude or conduct, "storing up wrath for yourself on the day of wrath" (2:5). Though this may be said to happen with a typically arrogant Gentile, the reader is soon warned that "there will be anguish and distress for everyone who does evil, the Jew first and also the Greek" (2:9). Here the theme from 1:16, which characterizes a primary role for the Jew and secondary role for the Greek in relation to God's salvation, is evoked but with the contrasting realities of "anguish and distress." As the gospel comes first to the Jews, so the wrath also affects them first when they sin. The same logic of retribution is operating in the punishment for bad works and reward for good deeds. Paul's God is impartial. All the same, there is a primary role in this scheme for the Jew. The corrupted Jew is far from exempted from "the wrath."[40] This wrath returns in 4:15 within a discussion of law, presumably Mosaic, and Abraham's faith. In this reading, the destiny of the Judaic polity is at stake.

In other words, Taubes has actualized one possible outcome of reading these passages in Romans: The destiny of Israel is central to its author. Moreover, it can be said to be a primary concern for Paul.

Taubes's Paul: The Downright Antinomian

According to Jacob Taubes, the reason for God's wrath in 1:18 is that the people has sinned in a fundamental way: "It has rejected the Messiah that has come to it." Paul's notion in this reading is that "here is a Messiah who is condemned according to the law," which has drastic consequences for the status of the law: "*Tant pis*, so much worse for the law."[41] What kind of Judaism and concept of law does this reflect?

In "The Justification of Ugliness in Early Christian Tradition," Taubes interprets the worldly wisdom that is antithetical to God's wisdom in 1 Corinthians as referring "to the laws of the Jews . . . as well as the wisdom of the Greeks."[42] However, the characteristics of the kind of Judaism Paul supposedly polemicizes against remains unclear from Taubes's exegesis.

In "The Price of Messianism," Paul exemplifies the transgressive tendency inherent in the messianic idea in Judaism. In this Taubesian scheme, the conservative defense of the law stands against messianic hopes and expectations, and therefore the messianic idea is potentially explosive. The conservative Rabbinic preservation of law is threatened when intense expectations of messianic movements are cultivated. This is for Taubes a tension at the heart of Judaism, between static and dynamic forces with regard to the law, a religious law that reflects "the structures of the world."[43] In Taubes's perspective there appears to be no possibility of revelation as challenge to the immanent world from the outside through this conservative rabbinic defense of the Judaic law. The law merely reflects the laws of the world:

In Jewish terms, the reality of the external world is not visible in natural laws (*hilkhot olam*), but is represented by the Torah or divine law (*halakha*). A crisis relating to the validity of the structures of the world therefore translates itself "Jewishly" into the question of the validity of the law.[44]

In the Heidelberg lectures, Taubes is more explicit about the kind of Judaism that could not have imagined what Paul invented with the doctrine of the cross. Taubes describes a Jewish concept of law and a Jewish participation or implication in the overall Roman imperial structures in Paul's days. In this view, there was a tendency to elevate any kind of law to divine status, whether it is Roman law, the Torah, or a cosmological or natural law. Though he excuses himself for lacking expertise on this matter, he all the same concludes that when Paul says "law," he means all of these conceptions of the law in one. "Everything is bound up with everything else," says Taubes. Interestingly, this is "not Paul's mistake, it's due to the aura." In other words, when Paul writes of "law," the range of meanings for this word exceeds what Paul intends. "Due to the aura," Taubes says, he cannot limit its scope, such that the word unavoidably refers to more than he means within the historical circumstances. This reflects a hermeneutics in Taubes that has recognized severe limits in the assumption of a detectable authorial or intentional meaning in a historical text.[45]

What Taubes's Paul protests against when he abrogates the law as a logical outcome of the delayed or deferred Kingdom of God is what Taubes calls "the spirit of this great nomos liberalism." Therefore, there is also a kind of "liberal" Judaism that the illiberal Paul breaks with: the apostle who now is even a zealot, "a Jewish zealot." Hence, there is a shift from *Occidental Eschatology* where zealots were the prime proponents of the very same politically revolutionary apocalypticism that Paul had softened with his mysticism. Paul is still a marginal Jew, but he is now also a zealot with a revolutionary transvaluation of ancient values, including Jewish ones, represented by the liberal "fancy court philosopher" named Philo.[46]

Moving from the reasoning based on the inherent logic in Scholem's concept of messianism in "The Price of Messianism," Taubes has now based his view of Paul's relation to Judaism on a more historical argument, with his historical reconstructions of the ancient past:

> All of these different religious groups, especially the most difficult one, the Jews, who of course did not participate in the cult of the emperor but were nevertheless *religio licita* . . . represented a threat to Roman rule. But there was an aura, a general Hellenistic aura, an apotheosis of nomos. . . . So there was an extensively liberal Judaism,

Alexandrian Judaism with its surrounding villages. . . . After all, this sort of thing brings law and order into the Roman Empire, which, indeed, in the Augustan era experienced an unprecedentedly long period of peace after the battles of the world civil war.[47]

Significant parts of ancient Judaism accommodated itself to the dominant political powers and cultural values, as Christianity would do in Late Antiquity. "The balances are different," as Taubes says, and therefore it seems implied in Taubes's procedure that it is necessary to read the crucial breaks on a religious ideological level (the Pauline doctrine of the cross) alongside the social and political history (the different Jewish groups in relation to the Roman Empire).

In this reading, Paul is not a Christian apostle who breaks with Judaism, since his Messiah is crucified according to the law. The apostle is a Jew who abolishes the Jewish law but stays within Judaism, since (with the words from "The Price of Messianism") this abrogation of the law

> followed strictly from his "immanent logic" after acceptance of a Messiah justly crucified in consequence of the law. *Tant pis* for the law, Paul argues, and he has thus to develop his messianic theology in a "downright antinomian" fashion.[48]

Taubes presents Paul in this history as a primary example of messianic abrogation of the law. With this view of a "downright" antinomian Paul, the apostle becomes the parallel to Nathan of Gaza. Both adhered to Messiahs, Paul to Jesus and Nathan to Sabbatai Zevi. In order to argue that this crisis of Jewish eschatology that leads to Paul's antinomianism remains "an inner Jewish event," Taubes refers to passages from Romans: "The crisis of interiorization also forces Paul to distinguish between a Jew who is 'externally' a Jew and one who is 'internally' a Jew (Rom 2:28)—the term 'Christian' does not yet exist for him."[49]

Besides, for Taubes, Paul's antinomianism "culminates" in Romans 10:4 where the crucified Messiah is "the end of the law." The apostle logically rejects the law because of his faith in the crucified Messiah. The doctrine of the cross remains a foreign element to Judaism, but in this reading the consequences of adherence to it follow logically from Jewish messianism. If the messianic idea cannot be realized on the public stage of history, Taubes argues, then it must be interiorized if its community of believers is not to be led straight into the abyss. Paul's notion of the true Jew, which is internal rather than external, represents such an interiorization of the whole messianic idea—an interiorized messianism beyond law.[50] Any concept of law, Jewish, Roman, or whatever, is being rejected by such interiorization.

Without any outer distinctive traits that could identify this interiorized Jew within the Judaism that was a *religio licita* in the empire, it may be no surprise that this type was met with suspicion and opposition. Presented as an anarchic or antinomian group that rejected the notion of law itself, this Paulinism is potentially revolutionary, notwithstanding the lack of a revolutionary political program.

Rewriting the Crisis of the Law in Romans

The verse that is supposed to substantiate what Taubes regards as Paul's antinomianism is the following: "For a person is not a Jew who is one outwardly, nor is true circumcision something external and physical" (Rom 2:28).

Together with Romans 10:4 this is a passage that has proven its effectiveness for maintaining the view of an antinomian Paul who firmly rejects adherence to any law, especially the Jewish law. Paul's words appear to rule out and cancel out the validity of law itself, a revolutionary potential with regard to tradition's institutions or power. This revolutionary energy is even easier to draw from Paul's letter to the Galatians, while certain passages from Romans do possess an ability to drain this antinomian energy. Even the passage Taubes singles out as an expression of antinomianism from Romans 2:28 is capable of weakening Paul's "downright" antinomian power. In contrast to Galatians, where the text manifests a reaction to the imposition of circumcision, here in Romans, the presumed same author discusses the nature of true circumcision in light of the gospel about divine justice.

If one supposes that Paul is responding to his Jewish imaginary interlocutor in Romans 2:17–24 from a different angle, one can substantiate Taubes's notion of Paul's messianic theology as "an inner Jewish event." This discussion concerns a ceremonial, ritual aspect of law that in this text carries the danger of leading to boasting as a sense of cultural or religious superiority.[51] The author of this letter appears to be investing his rhetorical capital into demolishing any such claims of superiority on the basis of circumcision. The force of the argument, however, does not seem to undermine the value of circumcision.[52] It does not spiritualize Judaism to such a degree that the essentials of Judaism disappear altogether.[53] After accusing this imagined representative of Jewish teaching of betrayal of his own prerogatives and his own moral tradition, the text all the same upholds the usefulness or importance of one of its defining traits: circumcision: "Circumcision indeed is of value if you obey the law" (Rom 2:25a), to which the author quickly adds, "But if you break the law, your circumcision has become uncircumcision" (Rom 2:25b). Is not the underlying logic that a Jew should not break the law, since in the case of transgression the value of circumcision will be nullified?

The argument in Romans continues with a question: "So, if those who are uncircumcised keep the requirements of the law, will not their uncircumcision be regarded as circumcision?" (Rom 2:26). Here the technical terminology of legal conformity in the LXX is employed with regard to "those who are uncircumcised."[54] Such a possibility of a moral fulfilling of the Mosaic law had already been opened up in 2:14: "When Gentiles, who do not possess the law, do instinctively what the law requires, these, though not having the law, are a law to themselves." Moreover, this sentence is followed by a motif from the Hebrew tradition, which in Jeremiah 31:33 is expressed as the law written on the hearts of the Israelites. This divine writing has now expanded to the lives of the Gentiles, in the words of Romans 2:15: "They show that what the law requires is written on their hearts, to which their own conscience also bears witness; and their conflicting thoughts will accuse or perhaps excuse them." This exemplary obedience to the law is based on prophetic tradition. This argument in Romans can hardly call for an abrogation of this tradition's fundamental assumptions that the law was revealed by God to Israel and that its purpose was putting it to practice as justice, whether it be social, economic, or political. The force of this argument is rather based on the assumption that these fundamentals are still valid. The same logic appears to underlie the argument in Romans about circumcision:

> For a person is not a Jew who is one outwardly, nor is true circumcision something external and physical. Rather, a person is a Jew who is one inwardly, and real circumcision is a matter of the heart—it is spiritual and not literal. Such a person receives praise not from others but from God. (Rom 2:29)

Here the text of Romans recalls another motif from the Hebrew Bible, that of "the circumcision of the heart" (Deut 10:16; Jer 4:4, 9:26; Ezra 44:9).[55] Already in this Hebrew tradition we witness a spiritualizing or interiorizing of the outward law and the visible physical mark of circumcision. When the argument goes that "real circumcision is a matter of the heart" it may be said to be an echo or actualization of an already established argument for the realization of the law and not its abrogation.[56] It appears premature and too hasty to label this one who inwardly is a Jew as a Christian, indeed. In this sense, Taubes is right. Nonetheless, his case for a Pauline antinomianism is severely weakened by this reading of Romans. The function of the appeal in Romans to the motif of "the circumcision of the heart" can hardly be said to invalidate the law given to Israel; it rather spiritualizes it for the realization of its purpose: justice among human beings.[57] Recall, that in 3:21 it is stated that the justice revealed in the present "is attested by the law and the prophets." It is not that the law is antithetical to justice, but that justice is revealed "apart from" it. Nonetheless, not only the prophets but also the law attest to, point to, bear witness to justice. The aim and the purpose of law is justice, however much it might be abused, as for instance in boasting of the moral or cultural superiority of the privilege of remaining in the covenant.

Rewriting of Antinomianism in Romans

God's revelation of the gospel through Jesus the Messiah in Romans is characterized as justice,[58] which suggests a renewal of the old divine regime of the law rather than a revolutionary Taubesian overturning of it. It is the misuse of the law as boasting rather than the law itself that is presented in the gospel as the obstacle preventing divine justice from being realized in the human sphere. If the ideal Gentile adherent to Paul's gospel in Galatians is not one who voluntarily undergoes circumcision, the one who inwardly is a Jew in Romans is not one who leaves the outward or public ritual requirements of the Mosaic law behind. He is, rather, the one imagined in the Jesus tradition (Matt 6:1–6) who can observe the law and do good without being registered by anyone other than God, without merit in the form of social prestige or cultural power. Romans surely does critique notions of ethnocentric exclusivism that may be propagated by Jews, but the very same critique is put forward toward Gentiles. A certain type of Gentile is responsible for the same arrogant ethnocentric attitude as the part of Israel referred to by Paul's critique.[59] There is a certain "interiorization" of the messianic hope, but this is not so much an abrogation of law as an interiorization of its purpose, which is justice. Relying on Hebrew scriptural traditions, the Pharisee scribe Paul extends the scope of the gospel to include the Gentiles. Taubes's remark about Paul being an apostle not only to the Gentiles but *from the Jews* to the Gentiles makes a lot of sense within this reading. The kind of critique Paul launches against the arrogance of the Jewish position of moral superiority due to covenantal privilege can hardly be reduced to a critique from outside Judaism. It can easily be recognized as "an inner Jewish event"—that is, a critique of Jewish behavior from within Judaism. Privileging calling over conversion may be one effective way of emphasizing this position from within Judaism. Another is to draw the contrast to older views of the Jew presupposed in Romans as the representative of the worst religious form of boasting and instead posit that the criticism of the Jewish interlocutor in Romans is rather based on the Jew's reputation for practicing what he teaches:[60]

> Paul's appeal to the title of "Jew" is apparently based upon assuming awareness among his readers of a widely held stereotype that Jews by definition served as the model for practicing what one preaches.[61]

Accordingly, the criticism of this Jew was not directed at his boasting, but rather his hypocrisy. The critique, once again, aimed at living according to the teaching, realizing, and effecting of justice.

Moreover, one could argue for Paul's critique of the Judaism of his day as "a piece of Pharisaic propaganda"[62] while emphasizing the continuity with Paul's former position as Pharisee when he persecuted the new communities that were formed in the aftermath of Jesus's crucifixion. It has been argued that conversion language was prevalent in the first century and that the Pauline letters reflect the apostle's self-understanding as a convert.[63] One may talk of a conversion from one Jewish position to another Jewish position. Although it is difficult to make a case for a Paul converted to Christianity, with all the connotations of this word, one can emphasize the newness and radicalism of Paul's critique of Judaisms of his day. One could compare Paul's texts with other contemporary Jewish texts and conclude that his use of typical Hebrew motifs is both new and radical. For instance, it might be argued that Paul's argument about the "advantage" of circumcision, where he makes the value of this external mark dependent upon lawful praxis, is both a way of affirming a Pharisaic view of the law and an innovative critique that makes him a radical Jew compared to Jewish groups of his day.[64] Paul's continuity and discontinuity with regard to these comparable texts of his time can be measured differently according to how one reads both sets of texts.

Taubes's strategy, when referring to Romans, in "The Price of Messianism," was to include only two references to this letter, both of which are classical passages for construing Paul as an antinomian. This strategy could be defeated by the inclusion of passages in the same letter that point in another direction. Hence, such passages are not brought into Taubes's texts or his lectures from 1987.

If we move forward in the argument within Romans, we encounter one of the letter's potentially strongest threats to the view of Paul's gospel as "downright" antinomian. It has great potential to be regarded as one of the text's prime defenses against the allegation of antinomianism: "Do we then overthrow the law by this faith? By no means! On the contrary, we uphold the law" (Rom 3:31).

One way Paul may be said to uphold the law is in his discussion of circumcision. The text does not claim that circumcision "for the Jew" is without value: "Then what advantage has the Jew? Or what is the value of circumcision? Much, in every way" (Rom 3:1–2). In Romans circumcision undoubtedly has a value that excludes a total immersion of the law into an introspective conscience that is totally freed from its constraints. But the value of this external ritual depends on lawful practice. The whole argument of Romans 2:25–29 revolves around the importance of being obedient to and keeping the law, of doing what the law requires, based on the assumption that circumcision is compulsory for the Jew. But this argument of the importance of lawfulness loses much of its force if circumcision is no longer binding for the Jew. Therefore, "to uphold the law" consists of reaffirming both the concrete external commandments and the lawfulness that produces justice.

Rewriting the Critique of Law in Romans

Nonetheless, the letter has put forward such a strong critique of a certain law that the author expresses a need to defend himself in advance, proactively. That law is referred to as "the law of works"—*ergon nomou*. This expression is introduced in Romans 3:19–20, and it is used to characterize the religious or cultural mode of observing the law represented by the boasting Jew in 2:17–24.[65] In Romans the person is made just or empowered to build justice by faithfulness, trust, or loyalty *pistis* in a divine action "apart from works prescribed by the law" (Rom 3:28), which is outside this law. This justice is given or realized independently of any concrete human expression or interpretation of the law.

While "the law of works" or "deeds prescribed by the law" are associated with boasting, there is another law that stops or effectuates an end to this boasting. That is "the law of faith" (Rom 3:27). This double function or aspect of the law had already been established in Galatians as a contrast between "the works of law" (Gal 3:10) and "the law of Christ" (Gal 6:2). In Romans this contrasting relation is further elaborated.

But what kind of law is the model for "the law of faith"? And which law is implicated in "the works of law" from which one is set free in the life in the spirit? Although Paul's rejection of law is not as broad as Taubes claims, the apostle still rejects firmly certain aspects of law, under certain circumstances. The apostle is, for instance, aggressively reacting against any conformity to "the works of law" in the case of the Galatians, however much he is "establishing" the law for the Jews in Romans. For Taubes the concept of the Jewish law was nearly all-encompassing; it was "the reality of the external world," "represented by the Torah or divine law (*halakha*)."⁶⁶ The Jews had no concept of independent natural laws. When Taubes's Paul speaks of law, therefore, it necessarily refers to natural laws and to "the law of the universe" as well. "It's all of these in one," says Taubes. The law is all over. But there is still more to this concept of law, according to Taubes, since Jewish law was accommodated to the Roman political order where a "liberal" interpretation of the Jewish law was recognized as *religio licita*. In this way the very concept of law "is a compromise formula for the Imperium Romanum."⁶⁷

Indeed, there are good reasons for Taubes's concern for an accommodation to the law, whether it might be labeled "liberal" or not. When the Roman Empire is introduced or, perhaps better, recognized as a context for Paul's letters, then Paul's critique of the boasting Jew in Romans cannot be limited to a religious or Jewish matter. The boasting gains political and imperial meaning within the Roman codes of honor and shame.⁶⁸ The apostle must save the true Torah, "the inwardly Jew, for the Jews to avoid the law being 'hijacked' and desecrated by the Roman imperial law and religion."⁶⁹ If we accept the imperial setting as a valid context for reading Paul, we cannot take for granted that "the works of law" are restricted to Jewish works.

Nor can we exclude the possibility that these works are carried out without any influence from "natural laws" or "the law of the universe," in Taubes's words. Far from it. When Galatians is taken into account, we stumble upon a unique expression in the Pauline corpus, which, however, was never mentioned in Taubes's reading of Paul. In the past without Christ, the apostle states that "we were enslaved to the elemental spirits of the world" (Gal 4:3). Here and in 4:9 the apostle mentions *ta stoicheia tou kosmou*, which often is translated as "the elements of the cosmos." Two epochs are presented in the lives of the Galatians: one before Christ, enslaved by these elements, and one in Christ, liberated from the very same elements of the cosmos, "beings that by nature are not gods" (Gal 4:8). Paul's logic in the letter is contrary to common Jewish assumptions about Gentiles' worship as actually honoring elements of nature. In turning to the law of observing ritual times (Gal 4:10, "You are observing special days, and months, and seasons, and years"), the Galatians are returning to the veneration of these elements. While the Galatians are exhorted not to be circumcised according to Jewish law, they are equally warned about keeping this law of following the ritual calendar.⁷⁰ In order to live in the new cosmos, after the end of the cosmos that was crucified with Christ (Gal 6:14), the Galatians are to live without these laws. What perishes with "the present evil age" (Gal 1:4) is therefore the old cosmos with its laws. For Paul, in the new existence, following the law of Christ, there is an existence beyond the old opposite between Jew and Gentile, the lawful circumcised and the lawless uncircumcised: "For neither circumcision nor uncircumcision is anything; but a new creation is everything!" (Gal 6:15). The law Paul criticizes has cosmological dimensions, not only religious or Jewish ones.

On these grounds, it can make good sense to state with Taubes that when Paul criticizes the law, he means "all of these in one"—that is, the natural, the cosmological, and the Jewish concept of the law in one. This affirmation, however, has the disadvantage, at the outset, of excluding the possibility that the law in question at different places in the letters might refer more or less to one than the other. At certain points in the argumentation, the letters might more evidently echo Jewish than Roman meanings of the law. Taubes's intuition, however, could serve as a cautionary warning not to restrict and fix the meaning of these ancient texts.

If Paul is a Jewish zealot, as Taubes labels him, then he must within the frames of the presented reading be a more lawful zealot with regard to the Torah than a "downright antinomian." Surely, with the advent of Christ the law is seen from a new angle. It is in crisis: now, in contrast to before, the justice of God has been revealed. And it has happened apart from the law. Moreover, through chapters 5–7 the relation between law and sin is becoming increasingly problematic. There are surely reasons to speak, as Taubes does, of "the critique of the concept of law" through "various waves in which it [the critique] is set up in Romans; with the 1:18, the *orge theou*, there begins a great fugue, and then 5 and 7."[71]

With these latter two chapters from Romans in mind, Taubes argues for strong connections between Paulinism and Sigmund Freud's psychoanalysis. These connections contribute to Taubes's construction of a Jewish introspective apostle.

Paul as Freud's Predecessor

In the essay "Religion and the Future of Psychoanalysis" (1957), Jacob Taubes affirmed that "it is not a matter of sheer speculation that Freud conceived his work, his theory, and therapy, in analogy to the message Paul preached to the gentiles."[72] Thirty years later the philosopher had not at all moderated this thesis, but confirmed and sharpened it even more: "I want to defend the claim that Freud, who is involved with the basic experience of guilt, is a direct descendant of Paul."[73]

Taubes argues along two lines in order to establish the analogy between Freud and Paul. To a limited extent, he argues on the basis of references to Romans 5 and 7. But more extensively, he establishes this analogy on the basis of philosophical arguments at a metatextual level.

First, he distinguishes Freud from the first type of philosophy where the truth is accessible constantly, though only to a few, and history hardly plays any role. Freud belongs to the second type of philosophy, represented by Christianity, Hegel, and Marxism in Taubes's account. Truth is open to everyone. Nonetheless, it is very difficult to attain, and one has to "pass through history" to conceive of it. This is where Freudian psychoanalysis belongs, according to Taubes:

> What happens in classical analysis? The analyst sits back, doesn't even look at the patient. The patient lies on the couch, and he talks and talks. He can talk for a week, for months, and at some point something is supposed to click. But that's not something one can foresee. The history is not an a priori, one must go through it, one must work through it.[74]

Similar to Taubes's reading of Nietzsche, there is a modern universe with immanent laws in which something exceptional can take place. Something like a miracle can happen, an event one cannot predict in advance.

This possibility of an exceptional event within the rational modern universe is something Taubes detects against Freud himself, so to speak. Already in the essay from 1957 Taubes is critical of Freud's acceptance of atheistic premises for his new science, but even more of the conservatism of psychoanalysis. In Taubes's view, Freud had overdetermined the power of the traces in consciousness from the past and rejected any possibilities for the future other than repetitions of the past. The rationalistic and conservative Freud is surely an opponent of Taubes. Nevertheless, Taubes wishes to discern his true disagreement with this Freud.

This method is more extensively enacted in Taubes's lectures on Romans nearly thirty years later, where he sticks to his dismissal or opposition to "the Enlightenment Freud." Nonetheless, Taubes declares that he wants to make Freud as strong as possible.

Taubes ends his lecture with long quotations from the "important book" by Freud, *Moses and Monotheism*, but even with regard to this Freudian text, Taubes rejects any serious consideration of some fundamental theses put forward in it:

> The book is a provocation. Any whitesnapper, whether Old Testament or Egyptologist, can go to town here: absolute nonsense, Moses as Egyptian, Moses murdered, and so on.[75]

But the value of Freud's book is high, in spite of its erroneous theses, its "nonsense." Freud preaches no messianic redemption from the modern laws of necessity. There is no final deliverance from man's guilt.[76] There is, however, a messianic potential in Freudian psychoanalysis, which is not unrelated to Paul:

> Certainly Freud was concerned with Moses, but not as a figure of identification. This is a subversive program. How is it possible to suspend the law? For the law is not only Mosaic law—though it means that too—but it means civil law, bourgeois custom, which gives human beings all these neuroses, the Victorian world that Freud of course treats in his first cases.[77]

In this Taubesian reading, Freud differs from Paul on one matter. Unlike Paul, Freud did not identify with Moses but made him instead into an Egyptian. But like Paul, Freud confronted a law that was more omnipresent and universal than the Mosaic law. Freud, however, never entered a phase of messianic joy and jubilation, like Paul. He remained a tragic figure without any messianic belief in the abrogation of law. Although he tried to undermine the bourgeois custom, his problem was not how to overcome but how to suspend it, as if he did not expect any more than "something to click," to "go through history," before the bourgeois law once again installed itself. This suspension was hoped for on the basis of a problem of guilt Freud posited as constitutive for all human beings. And dealing with this problem, Freud runs counter to the modern enlightenment to which he confesses adherence. He runs counter to his own intentions:

> If one reads Freud hermeneutically in this fashion, that is, as self-analysis (*The Interpretation of Dreams*), one notices that at its center is a very deep grappling with the problem of guilt. And one notices that Freud, almost against the intentions of his Enlightenment ambiance, to which he owes his education as a disciple of Charcot and Janet in Paris, and that he thus—and this is Freud's genius—overcomes himself, that his insights are greater than his intentions.[78]

In Taubes's account, the problem of guilt in these insights is not only greater than Freud's intentions but also something that appears to exceed the intentions of figures like Nietzsche, Luther, Augustine, and Paul. What is discovered is that "in the I there is a profound powerlessness," an experience that resembles Romans 7:

> For what he [Nietzsche] finds horrifying, and this is a very humane concern, is the cruelty of the pang of conscience. The conscience that can't be evaded. Romans 7, right?[79]

Whereas his friend Krister Stendahl wanted sharper distinctions between Freud, Luther, Augustine, and Paul, Taubes wants his audience to recognize this experience that unifies them. Having interiorized the messianic idea, Paul opens the West for this experience of introspective conscience. None other than Nietzsche has discovered the essence of this experience, a discovery Taubes finds in *Nachlass*:

> All deeper people are of one mind about this—Luther, Augustine, Paul come to mind—that our morality and its events are not congruent with our *conscious will*.[80]

This is where Romans 7 comes into play in Taubes's lecture. In "Religion and the Future of Psychoanalysis" (1957), he had alluded to "the old Adam" from Romans 5, which confirms that Taubes is finding resonance in Nietzsche and Freud with "the great fugue" of Romans 1:18 that according to Taubes goes through chapters 5 and 7 before it ends in chapter 8.

What happens here? Surely, Taubes reads Paul through Nietzsche and Freud. Notwithstanding, he also claims to discern an apostle operating within them. There appear to be some virtual powers of the apostle's letters operative within these modern philosophers that also reflect certain readings of the same apostle.[81]

Original Guilt in Paul?

In "Religion and the Future of Psychoanalysis" (1957) Taubes put forward his thesis in his typical polemical mode: "Never since Paul and Augustine has a theologian taught a more radical doctrine of original guilt than Freud."[82] In his view, theologians who depicted Freud's doctrine as a secular version of the doctrine of original sin were right.

According to Taubes's reading, Freud developed his doctrine of the original guilt in *Totem and Taboo*. Although the murder of the primeval father by the horde of brothers was forgotten, the original guilt for the deed lived in the unconscious of humankind. To sustain the thesis, Taubes quotes Freud's *Moses and Monotheism*:

> Paul, a Roman Jew from Tarsus, seized upon this feeling of guilt and correctly traced it back to its primeval source. This he called original sin; it was a crime against God that could be expiated only through death. Death had come into the world through original sin. In reality this crime, deserving of death, had been the murder of the Father who later was deified. The murderous deed itself, however, was not remembered; in its place stood the phantasy of expiation and that is why this phantasy could be welcomed in the form of a gospel of salvation (evangelium).[83]

Taubes shows no hesitation toward Freud's affirmation that Paul gave the "primeval source" for the "feeling of guilt" the name "original sin." Rather than pointing out that the expression "original sin" does not occur in Paul's letters, Taubes praises Freud: "Freud penetrates deeply into the dialectic of guilt and atonement that is the central motif of Paul's theology."[84]

Taubes has already alluded to Romans 5 in his mention of the "the old Adam possessed by his drives and instincts, unredeemed from his lusts."[85] Do we then encounter something like original sin in Romans?

In Romans, the word for sin (*hamartia*) in the form of a verb or noun occurs when the text appears to underline the universality of sin, as in 2:12, where it is emphasized that Jew and Gentile alike have sinned (with or without the law). In 3:7 it is stated that the sinner (*hamartolos*), who is perhaps a figure for the radically sinful,[86] will be condemned. There is, however, a universal involvement in the reality of sin. Not even participants in the communities founded by Paul can claim exemption from this and the corresponding need for being forgiven and favored by divine justice:

> For there is no distinction, since all have sinned and fall short of the glory of God; they are now justified by his grace as a gift, through the redemption that is in Christ Jesus, whom God put forward as a sacrifice of atonement. (Rom 3:23–25)

As there is no distinction or difference with regard to sin, there is also a redemption that is open to all without distinction. The mention of sin serves to underline God's impartiality toward Gentile and Jew; it highlights the universality of both its destructive reality and the reactive action on God's part that is the redemptive act in Christ. Here we encounter a possible allusion to Adam, since Adam and Eve were supposed to bear the glory of God.[87] They fell short of it through the fall, however. In chapter 5 Adam is brought explicitly into the text:

> Therefore, just as sin came into the world through one man, and death came through sin, and so death spread to all because all have sinned— sin was indeed in the world before the law, but sin is not reckoned when there is no law. Yet death exercised dominion from Adam to Moses, even over those whose sins were not like the transgression of Adam, who is a type of the one who was to come. (Rom 5:12–14)

Death did, indeed, come into the world by this sin of "one man." Here a transgressive and disobedient Adam is present, though hardly the Freudian Adam "possessed by his drives and instincts, unredeemed from his lusts." So how did Taubes's old Adam become possessed in this way? Was it solely by way of Freud's anthropology or perhaps through Augustine's elaborated notion of original sin? The mere mention of the expression "original sin" suggests Augustine's texts among the influencing powers here.

Romans 5:12–21 is one of the passages in the letter where the tragedy of humankind is given a narrative. It further elaborates on the human guilt that was introduced in 1:18 in the form of "ungodliness and wickedness." Sin plays a major antithetical, and perhaps dialectical, role in relation to redemption. Atonement does not play the same major role in Romans. While sin plays such a major role in both the judicial and the participationist models of redemption in the letter, atonement is but one of several categories within the judicial model. Nevertheless, in Romans 3:25, the letter describes God's salvific act "in Christ Jesus, whom God put forward as a sacrifice of atonement by his blood."

One might conclude that in Romans the experience of guilt or sin is more "basic" than the experience of its dialectic with atonement, since the latter category is only one of several metaphors for God's salvific act. When Taubes claims that "Freud penetrates deeply into the dialectic of guilt and atonement that is the central motif of Paul's theology," his view of Paul's central motif reflects later Christian readings more than it reflects Paul's letters, however much Taubes connects this central motif to the Jewish ritual of Yom Kippur. With their emphasis on sacrifice, expiation, and atonement, the two German-speaking Jewish thinkers, Taubes and Freud, appear to be reading a noticeably Christian Paul. One could therefore ask if Taubes's reading of Romans 7 does not leave even more room for these Christian forces, softening the Jewishness of Paul that Taubes had declared to have reclaimed.

The Powerlessness in Romans 7

Taubes praises Nietzsche for understanding that "in Christianity something in the human soul has changed profoundly." Nietzsche is being quoted on his claim that "all deeper people are of one mind about this—Luther, Augustine, Paul come to mind—that our morality and its events are not congruent with our *conscious will*."[88]

Taubes speaks favorably of Nietzsche's conclusion:

> Whoever has understood this has understood more of Paul and of Augustine and Luther than can be found on this subject in normal exegesis. That is, they all understand that the ego doesn't call the shots. That the autonomous human being, the I, doesn't call the shots, but that behind him there are forces at work that undermine the con-

scious will. . . . That is, if you want to express it in a formula, that in the I there is a profound powerlessness . . . Romans 7, right?[89]

Through conflating Paul, Augustine, and Luther into one view or experience of the profoundly powerless ego, Taubes is, with the help of Nietzsche, doing the opposite of what Krister Stendahl calls for: Taubes is hailing Paul "as a hero of the introspective conscience."[90] And Taubes is interpreting Romans 7 as a text that provides deep psychological insights into Nietzsche's discovery of "the cruelty of the pang of conscience," rather than as Stendahl wanted. Stendahl wanted readers to recognize that "Paul here is involved in an argument about the Law; he is not primarily concerned about man's or his own cloven ego or predicament."[91]

Somewhat in contradiction to his exegesis of Romans 9–11 (which will be treated within this chapter), where he emphasized Paul's theology as the result of his efforts to legitimate a new people of God that included Gentiles, here Taubes's Paul is dealing with more timeless matters concerning the subject. In other words, Taubes is reinforcing the line of interpretation that, according to Stendahl, began with Augustine. While Paul's immediate or primary concern was "the possibility for Gentiles to be included" in the messianic community, Augustine applied the theology Paul articulated out of this concern "in a consistent and grand style to a more general and timeless human problem."[92] For Taubes the powerless I in Romans 7 is a universal I.

The identification of the "I" of Romans 7:7–25 is disputed among scholars. The predominantly Augustinian identification of this voice speaking in first person with the unconverted, the pre-Christian, in the form of the universal Adam, has come under attack from different approaches. It has, for instance, been proposed that the fictitious person is in Paul's mind representative of "Gentiles who try to live by works of the law,"[93] an influential interpretation with ambitions to refute the image of Paul as the introspective apostle. This Gentile character is not representative of universal humanity. On the contrary, the character is constructed to warn Gentile converts in Rome against adopting Jewish laws like circumcision and dietary regulations. The Gentiles are Paul's concern here, not Jews, in this perspective. The character is built to confront a temporary problem of regulating the relations between Jews and Gentiles in these communities. It does not describe a permanent problem, even less a universal feature of human nature. In this way, it is supposed to be effective against stereotypes of the Jew suffering from inordinate pride or Paul's desperation face to face with the oppressing and unnecessary burdening of the Jewish law.

What Taubes achieves by linking Romans 7 to Nietzsche and Freud in the way already described is to reinforce the Augustinian paradigm, which is the traditional Christian view established by the late Augustine. As a Jew he is not allying himself with other supposedly Jewish readings of Paul.[94]

Moreover, in quoting Freud's *Moses and Monotheism* so extensively Taubes is, in effect, disseminating the Freudian story on Paulinism's origins. Freud can be said to write a new version of the old Lutheran story of the stagnated and degenerated Judaism of Paul's time:[95] "And yet Christianity marked a progress in the history of religion: that is to say, in regard to the return of the repressed. From now on Jewish religion was, so to speak, a fossil."[96] Furthermore, Freud provides a glimpse into the introspective mind of the apostle:

> He [Paul] was a man with a gift for religion, in the truest sense of the phrase. Dark traces of the past lay in his soul, ready to break through into the regions of consciousness.[97]

With these Freudian insights, readings of Paul can be undertaken "on an entirely different level."[98] Nonetheless, it is not easy to see how this "entirely different level" may take shape. Additionally, by being put up front at the end of this lecture, Freud's strikingly Christian readings are somehow rather enforced than demolished by Taubes, who claimed to approach Paul with Jewish perspectives. Interestingly, Taubes sees the key for establishing a new paradigm for understanding Paul in the father of modern psychoanalysis that, as Ward Blanton has pointed out, provides us a Lutheran lens for looking at Paul:

> For all his shrewd reflections on revolution, institutionalization, and its repressions, Freud still reads Paul like Martin Luther, participating in an aged panoply of a triumphalistically anti-Jewish and implicitly pro-imperial tradition inasmuch as he finds Paul a founder of a new religion, Christianity, which was in essential (read ideal) respects, *not* Jewish.[99]

Freud keeps Paul within Christianity, and Taubes to some extent takes part in this. Nonetheless, Taubes's move deconstructs the Jewish-Christian opposition through his hypothesis of Paul as Freud's predecessor. Taubes does not only call for new readings of Paul. Through his readings of Freud, he also effectively calls for a new understanding of the so-called Jewish science.[100]

Taubes's Reading of Romans 9–11

In the following I will attempt to demonstrate how Taubes's Paul is constructed through a confrontation with Carl Schmitt, but never substantially informed by the former Nazi professor and *persona non grata* in postwar Germany. While Taubes's dialogue with Schmitt gives the Heidelberg lectures a noticeable sense of urgency (as when Schmitt says, "Taubes, before you die, you must tell some people about this,")[101] it is Nietzsche among Taubes's "opponents" who shapes the latter's readings of Romans 9–11. In contrast to the former evaluation of Taubes's antinomian Paul, here Taubes's reading of Romans 9–11 will meet less resistance on my part. Moreover, Taubes's interpretation of Romans 9–11 is a reading that in a significant way dechristianizes Taubes's introspective Paul.

Within the Heidelberg lectures there is no part of Paul's letter that Taubes quotes as extensively as he does Romans 9–11. These chapters address several major concerns for Taubes. First, they are turned into a weapon against Christian anti-Semitism. Second, they serve to emphasize the Jewishness of Taubes's Paul in a dramatic manner. And third, they function to credit Nietzsche for his criticism of Christianity's dishonest interpretation of the Bible.

The Pauline Judaic Drama

Leaving the conclusion of Taubes's close reading of what he considers to be key passages from Romans 9–11, we begin with 11:28: "As regards the gospel they are enemies of God for your sake; but as regards election they are beloved, for the sake of their ancestors." This is "the powerful sentence" that Taubes read and discussed with Schmitt, among others from these chapters:

> And this is the point I challenged Schmitt on, that he doesn't see this dialectic that moves Paul and that the Christian church after 70 has forgotten, that he adopted not a text but a tradition, that is, the folk traditions of church antisemitism, onto which he, in 1933–36, in his uninhibited fashion, went on to graft the racist theozoology.[102]

In Taubes's account, there is nothing to be learned from Schmitt about Paul, except by avoiding his anti-Semitic misunderstandings of the apostle. Schmitt is a figure who functions to underline the importance of "the powerful sentence" from Romans and Taubes's rereading of it. Nevertheless, it appears that Schmitt does not in any way inform Taubes's readings of Paul. While Taubes elsewhere praises Schmitt for his valuable insights and for their similarity in thinking "apocalyptically,"[103] here there are no records of the value of Schmitt's reading of Paul, only of Schmitt's confession, which contrasts with Taubes's own insight on this matter.

Taubes argues that "enemies" in Paul's text refers to "salvation history" and not "private feuds"; the word *inimicus* is not a private concept. Perhaps it refers to "feuds" when Matthew 6 says "Love your enemies," but not in Paul, says Taubes. In other words, "the hardened" (11:7) or those that have rejected the Messiah in Christ are not literally enemies of those who welcomed the same Messiah. The expression "enemies" does not concern interhuman relations. It is a matter of "salvation history" and of "the dialectic" that Schmitt did not see, demonstrating to Taubes how "it is possible to read texts without noticing what their core point is."[104] This is also powerfully expressed through Carl Schmitt's confession about their meaning, which Taubes had revealed to him: "That I didn't know!"

So what is this dialectic Schmitt did not see in the text? It concerns "the inner dialectic" of "bringing in the Gentiles in order to make Israel jealous."[105] He cites two passages from Romans to make it transparent how Paul employs his "notion of Israel's jealousy": 10:20–21 and 11:11. Taubes quotes these passages in order to make it evident that Paul's God could not have repudiated his people. Taubes's Paul is no supersessionist. And Israel is not relegated to the status of an ordinary people. It is rather the case that the Gentiles become God's instrument for the salvation of his Jewish people.

> The whole business about going to the Gentiles turns out in this context to be a scene of jealousy in order to make the Jews, to whom this message is directed, jealous. I didn't invent that; it says so in the text. Because he doesn't want to cast away his people, but to make them jealous.[106]

Taubes argues that in 11:15 Israel appears to be so central in this salvation history of Romans 9–11 that the event of the resurrection of the dead and the event of Israel's entrance into God's kingdom is one and the same matter for Paul: "It is identical for him."[107] Taubes interprets the words from 11:15 as a reiteration of 11:11: "For if their rejection is the reconciliation of the world, what will their acceptance be but life from the dead!" (11:15).

In 11:11 one of Paul's elaborations of the scene of jealousy appears with the word "jealous" itself. It is hard not to admit with Taubes that "it is in the text": "So I ask, have they stumbled so as to fall? By no means! But through their stumbling salvation has come to the Gentiles, so as to make Israel jealous" (11:11).

Taubes's claim about the simultaneousness of the resurrection of the dead and the salvation of Israel is derived from the unfolding of the motif of jealousy, which he sees as introduced in 10:19 with words from the lips of the Moses figure: "Again I ask, did Israel not understand? First Moses says, 'I will make you jealous of those who are not a nation; with a foolish nation I will make you angry'" (10:19).

The motif of jealousy appears three times in this part of the letter (10:19, 11:11, and 14), aptly characterized by Taubes as containing a "dialectic." It is also powerfully imposed on the eschatological scenarios Taubes quotes from 11:15 and 11:25. In this scene of jealousy, there are two entities in tension with each other that are not reconciled. There are the Gentiles or the nations welcoming the Messiah, and there is the part of Israel that has rejected the same Messiah. Salvation has come to the first, but not yet to the second, though there is a hope or purpose in God's plan for the "full inclusion" (11:11) of this part that has "stumbled."

In Taubes's interpretation the logic of retribution that potentially can drive the argument in Romans plays an important role. It begins with God's wrath in 1:18, which corresponds to the logic (expressed, for instance, in 2:7–8) of punishing (even annihilating) or rewarding. At the same time, he recognizes how this logic is in tension with a God who aims at the salvation of "all," especially or primarily "all Israel." Taubes underlines how *pas* and *pan* are key words in Paul. One "ought to think a great deal about it." He believes Paul is a universalist, but with a universalism that includes the election of Israel.[108] It is a salvation for all, but especially through, or for, one people. "As regards election they are beloved" (11:28), the ones who constitute Israel. The same verse reads, "As regards the gospel they are enemies of God," in the sense of being opposed to God's salvation project. Although it runs against common sense or modern universalism, in Taubes's words against "enlightened philanthropy" or "ethics,"[109] Israel has a special role in Paul's interpretation of salvation history. It is there, in the text, however much it is in Taubes's words, "embarrassing for modern Christianity."[110]

Taubes dramatizes how "it is there in the text." On the one hand, he slows down the speed of his argument and reduces his usual digressions to a minimum, while quoting lengthy passages from Romans 9–11 carefully reading them for his audience.[111] This provides the Pauline passages themselves with a sense of weight for Taubes's message, which ends in the refutation of Schmitt's anti-Semitism. On the other hand, he emphasizes over and over how these passages from Romans are overloaded with references to the Hebrew Bible like no other text of Paul.

> Chapters 9–11 are crammed with Bible passages. Far beyond Paul's normal rate of citation which, after all, is high enough. The text is

overloaded in an almost baroque manner. This is tremendously necessary for him, since he wants to prove by means of Holy Scripture that now the moment has come to open up for the Gentiles.[112]

This dramatization is prepared by Taubes's earlier claims that the task Paul has, the legitimation of a new people of God, "is the most dramatic process imaginable in a Jewish soul."[113] Moses is "a problem" for Taubes's Paul, which creates another obstacle for the main character of this drama. Paul has to outbid Moses. But the greatest threat against this character's success is something Taubes detects in Romans 8:35. In this view, there is a "tremendous fear," in Paul's words, regarding "who will separate us from the love of Christ?" (8:35). For Taubes this fear is based on the premise that God has given an oath: He will annihilate the people if it sins, if it breaks the covenant. For Taubes's Paul, the people have sinned by having rejected the messiah. Could there be a more fundamental sin?

According to Taubes, it is in light of the Jewish experience that destruction exists, that God is bound to annihilate, that Paul has a tremendous task. Like Moses, he has to defend and justify his own people, Israel, vis-à-vis God at the same time that he has to legitimize the establishment of a new people of God. By reading the fear that underlies the jubilation at the end of chapter 8 together with the anguish expressed by Paul the Israelite at the beginning of chapter 9, the anguish of being "cut off" from his people and their God is extended into chapter 8. It is the relation between God and his people that is at stake here in the words Taubes quotes from Romans 8:37–39:

> No, in all these things we are more than conquerors through him who loved us. For I am convinced that neither death, nor life, nor angels, nor rulers, nor things present, nor things to come, nor powers, nor height, nor depth, nor anything else in all creation, will be able to separate us from the love of God in Christ Jesus our Lord.

But the tremendous task is based on the premise that God has elected his people, out of divine will. It is, in other words, something that does not appear dramatic to a Christian soul who does not take God's election of Israel seriously, which is why Taubes states to his predominately Protestant audience, "This doesn't seem very dramatic to you after two thousand years of Christianity."[114] Romans 8, however, is one of the texts that contain the ability to redirect us to this drama, in Taubes's view, as it testifies to a conspiracy Paul experiences:

> Who wants to separate him? Where does this tremendous fear come from? What's clear is that all the powers have conspired, both earthly

and heavenly, the high and the low, have conspired to do one thing: to separate him from the love of God in the face of Jesus Christ.[115]

By linking election and fear of separation in Romans 8, Taubes seems to stand on firm ground. While "the love of Christ" could be considered a Pauline rhetorical innovation, the concept of "the love of God" stems from the Old Testament. There it is intimately connected to the idea of election. Separation from that love leads to damnation and falling under God's wrath.[116] The premise of election is inherent in Paul's argument.

The assurance that nothing can separate Christ-believers from the love of Israel's God will be further tested in Romans 9–11. But the premise of election does not appear here in chapter 8 for the first time. This drama, after all, is not merely an effect of Taubes's stylistic devices in his speech. Taubes's dramatization is not unrelated to the one that has up until Romans 8 already been there "in the text." From the beginning of the letter, Paul seems preoccupied with the destiny and role of Israel in this drama of salvation, with the question of the Jews as a priority. It was, after all, a salvation "to the Jew first and also to the Greek" (1:16).

The problem of unfaithful Jews is raised in 3:3. Paul brings their rejection of the Messiah to the fore, rhetorically asking whether their unfaithfulness can nullify the faithfulness of God. The question remains somewhat unanswered in the letter until chapters 9–11. But the question concerns a fundamental problem in this drama: Has God's word failed? Or, as 9:14 has it, "Is there injustice on God's part?"

Taubes considers 9:1–3 another expression for the same fear of separation as he saw in Romans 8, and he quotes the verses about Paul's "great sorrow and unceasing anguish" no less than three times, highlighting its importance.

Taubes speaks as if the fear of separation expressed in 8:35–39 is experienced by Paul himself. Nowhere does he claim that Romans 7 is Paul's autobiographical account. In this way, he displaces the long tradition of an autobiographical emphasis in Romans 7. But is it plausible that the statements of Romans 8–11 are autobiographical, in any sense?

A common argument against Romans 7 as autobiographical is the hypothesis of the rhetorical form of 7:7–25 as a speech-in-character. This was a common literary device in Antiquity, where an imaginary person was allowed to speak in the first person in order to make an effective argument. While 9:1–5 might be considered an introduction (to a broader argument in Romans 9–11) filled with pathos, it is less likely to be the same rhetorical form as 7:7–25. There is no sudden shift to the form of "I," as takes place from 7:6 to 7:7, as the first-person form continues unchanged from 8:38.

One of the effects of Taubes's description of 8:35–39 and 9:1–3 as expressions of the apostle's experience is an implicit confirmation of Krister Stendahl's refutation of Romans 7 as autobiographical. In addition, in Taubes's dramatization of the apostle's fear, in the need for legitimation for a new people and in the eschatological scenario in Romans 11 there is an implicit confirmation of Stendahl's view of Romans 9–11 as the climax of the letter. The chapters are not merely an appendix, but the peak in the drama of the reconstitution of God's people in light of the Christ event. After all, "the Messiah exists for the purpose of redeeming Israel, that's clear."[117]

It is particularly these readings of Romans 9–11 that contribute to the Jewishness of Taubes's Paul. First, by placing the resurrection of the dead and the salvation of all Israel on the same level in his eschatological scenario, the salvation of Israel becomes a primary concern for Taubes's Paul. Second, by emphasizing the Jewish experience of the threat of annihilation as the frame for reading Paul's concern for justification, the Protestant interpretation of this theme is implicitly challenged. Third, by moving the autobiographical center of Romans from chapter 7 to chapter 9, Taubes emphasizes Paul as "Israelite." He is not simply an apostle to the Gentiles. He is an apostle "from the Jews." That said, there is a non-Jewish literary source of inspiration for Taubes's argument that has not been mentioned.

The Bad Philology of Christian Supersessionism

A way of enforcing the sense of drama in the reading presented so far of Romans, which concerns not only Paul but a long tradition of Christian interpretations, is found in a long quote from Nietzsche inserted by Taubes.

The quote is from "The Philology of Christianity," where Nietzsche contrasts honest philology with dishonest dogmatic Protestantism:

> How little Christianity cultivates the sense of honesty can be inferred from the character of the writings of its scholars. They set out their conjectures as audaciously as if they were dogmas and seldom find any difficulty in the interpretation of Scripture . . . even the one horned beast and the Brazen Serpent, even Moses stretching forth his hands in prayer—even the very spits on which the Easter Lambs were roasted: all these were allusions to the Cross and as it were preludes to it! Did anyone who made these assertions ever believe in them?[118]

In what way can this text teach Taubes about Paul, given that it was written by his "best teacher" on the apostle?

Taubes does primarily two things with this text: First, he underscores what he regards as "the key word," which is "honesty." Second, he refers to Nietzsche's question of if anyone who had asserted these claims really believed them and then gives the answer, "And I say: Yes, Paul the Apostle. That is the enterprise of Romans 9–11."[119] Nietzsche never returns during Taubes's lectures on these chapters,[120] as if he only indicated the way for Taubes. The quotation, however, could be said to provide clues for what Taubes is doing when he reads these chapters from Romans.

One could suppose that Taubes accepts Nietzsche's criticism of the dishonest way in which Christianity has reduced perplexities of biblical texts to unequivocal dogmas. In the lecture he has already warned against reading the doctrine of the Trinity into 9:1–5. He seems to praise Nietzsche for his insight into the "attempt to tear the Old Testament from the hands of the Jews under the pretext that it contained only Christian doctrines and belonged to the Christians as the true people of Israel," as if that is a Christian reduction or extermination of Judaism to which Taubes is opposing himself. For him it is a matter of being honest about Christianity's hijacking of the Jewish heritage but also about being honest about early Christianity's Jewish essence in the figure of Paul. Honesty is the key word. Yet, what Taubes seems to accept from Nietzsche is that Christianity has been dishonest in its "attempt to tear the Old Testament from the hands of the Jews" but not in its projections of Christ into this set of Jewish writings. Taubes demonstrates no eagerness to defend the Jewish scholars Nietzsche mentions who protested against the assertions that allusions in the Old Testament to Christ exist intentionally. Rather, Taubes directs the attention toward a figure who did not assert these allusions dishonestly, but who believed that

> even the one horned beast and the Brazen Serpent, even Moses stretching forth his hands in prayer—even the very spits on which the Easter Lambs were roasted: all these were allusions to the Cross and as it were preludes to it![121]

Before and after the quotation, Taubes is discussing allegorical reading, pointing out that Protestantism has denigrated the allegorical method since Luther. When Nietzsche is criticizing Protestantism and Taubes is concluding that Paul engages in a mixture of typological and allegorical reading, he seems to embrace these methods of reading in a way that deconstructs the traditional binary between Jewish literality and Christian allegory, for he emphasizes how Paul the allegorizer is a Jew.[122] And this method constitutes, perhaps, one resource for not reading "the powerful sentence" of 11:28 about the Jews as, literally, enemies of God.

Rewriting Romans as a Legitimate Resource against Anti-Semitism

Taubes avoids reading "the enemies" of 11:28 as a justification for Christian anti-Semitism. He also avoids a nonhistorical allegorization of Israel, although he attempts to rehabilitate the allegorical method and detects a possible problem with the Protestant, and specifically Lutheran, reduction of the fourfold medieval reading to the literal one when one is to understand Paul. He unleashes powerful textual forces against Christian anti-Judaism. Moreover, by emphasizing the dialectic of salvation history within Romans 9–11, where the priority is to redeem Israel, Taubes reads against one of the dominant Christian modes of interpretation: the Augustinian paradigm, with Romans 9–11 as the confirmation of an individualistic doctrine of predestination.[123] He counters powerful Christian forces.

Commenting on Romans 9:6, the interpreter polemicizes against "Bultmann and all this modern exegesis whose thinking is completely beside the point, which thinks in terms of the individual."[124] The dialectic Taubes detects in Romans 9–11 as a weapon of resistance against Schmitt's anti-Semitism is defended with reference to 9:6: "It is not as though the word of God had failed. For not all Israelites truly belong to Israel" (Rom 9:6).

By emphasizing the differentiation in this verse between those who merely descend from Israel and those who truly are or belong to Israel, Taubes argues against a notion of a relegation of all Israel to the flesh. It is not that the Christian church has replaced the Jewish people as the addressee of the divine promises:

> The word of God cannot just go awry! The word of God is after all true and firm, as the prayer of the Jews emphasizes daily. No, it didn't go awry. Because not all who descend from Israel *are* Israel. That is the key sentence. This means: this "all" according to flesh is not identical to the "all" according to promise.[125]

Taubes's Paul still thinks in terms of election and the election of Israel. There is no separation or divorce between the two; it is rather a matter of jealousy. This dialectic, as Taubes calls it, does not downplay the differences between the Jews according to the flesh and the true Jews according to the promise. There is no harmonious coexistence in this Pauline vision but dialectic with only a final divine solution to the marital problem of jealousy. All Israel, including the Israel according to the flesh, is to be saved within the vision of Taubes's Paul. They are in, as they were before the Christ event as well. What is new with Paul is the inclusion of the Gentiles into this Old Testament dialectic of the true Israel and "the gray mass of Israel-according-to-the-flesh."[126]

Such a reading may indeed provide effective weapons against interpretations like the one Taubes probably knew from his teacher Hans Urs von Balthasar. The Swiss Jesuit wrote in 1943 that the Nazi persecution was the ultimate proof that God had broken his original covenant with the Jews, when they refused to accept and were implicated in the execution of Jesus.[127] For Taubes's Paul there was no such break in the original covenant.

What he regards as Paul's "dialectic" in Romans 9–11 partly explains why Taubes is drawn to Paul, since Taubes was opposed to ecumenism and interreligious dialogue that did not acknowledge the conflicts and disagreements between Judaism and Christianity. While such an argument may serve well against any plain anti-Judaism, the idea of this dialectic of salvation history still contains a mystery:

> So that you may not claim to be wiser than you are, brothers and sisters, I want you to understand this mystery: a hardening has come upon part of Israel, until the full number of the Gentiles has come in. (Rom 11:25)

In Taubes's reading, all Israel is saved, but there is no comment upon "a hardening has come upon part of Israel." Taubes interprets the problem Paul faces as a repetition of the one Moses faces, "after the Golden Calf and after the scouts, where God makes the offer to destroy the people and begin a new one with Moses."[128] The emphasis is on God's will rather than human freedom. Taubes's Jewish Paul does not so much solve the problem as he reminds us of theological discussions that Romans appears to raise. The theological difficulties of theodicy, providence, and predestination are not erased from the horizon that appears with Taubes's reading of Romans 9–11. Rather, they lay latent, to use Taubes's term.

Though one cannot with Taubes's Paul claim anti-Semitic persecution as a proof of God's decision to break the covenant with the Jewish people, his Paul nonetheless does not appear immune against a common Christian exploitation of Romans 9–11. It is still possible to infer that Taubes's Paul is the true source of the Christian theodicy that presented Jewish suffering as divine punishment on the way to salvation for all, including all Israel. The problem is still, arguably, "there in the text."

Romans 13 as Covert Freudianism

What strikes the eye of the reception historian with regard to Jacob Taubes's arguments for his hypothesis of Paul as Freud's predecessor is the absence of references to Paul's texts. While Paul's confrontation with Schmitt's anti-Semitism was presented with dense references to Romans 9–11, Freud's connection to Paul is sustained with only a single reference to the apostle's writings. That reference is to what Taubes considers as Paul's reduction of the dual commandment in Romans 13.

Taubes claims that the absence of any reference to God the Father in the love command of Romans 13:8 is due to Paul's polemics against none other than Jesus himself.

> This sounds sentimental and so on, but it really isn't at all. This is a highly polemical text, polemical against Jesus. . . . Paul doesn't issue a dual commandment, but rather makes them equivocal; I almost want to say, following Kojève, that he pulls a Feuerbach here. Forgive me, Feuerbach doesn't deserve to be mentioned in this context, but it is the love not of the Lord, but of the neighbor that is the focus here. No dual commandment, but rather *one* commandment. I regard this as an absolutely revolutionary act.[129]

Like "Feuerbach's evacuation of God from Christianity,"[130] Paul's revolution consists in removing the Lord or the Father from the command. One of few attempts by Taubes to sustain this thesis is by quoting Freud's *Moses and Monotheism*:

> The ambivalence dominating the father-son relationship, however, shows clearly in the final result of the religious innovation. Meant to propitiate the father deity, it ends by his being dethroned and set aside. The Mosaic religion had been a Father religion; Christianity became a Son religion. The old God, the Father, took second place; Christ, the Son, stood in His stead, just as in those dark times every son had longed to do. Paul, by developing the Jewish religion further, became its destroyer.[131]

After this quote, Taubes claims that precisely in these words from Freud "is also a contribution to the problem of the dual commandment and its radicalization in the love command: the focus on the son, on the human being; the father is no longer included."[132] How is this a contribution?

As remarked earlier, Taubes has dismissed Freud's book, *Moses and Monotheism*, as "absolute nonsense." However, he thinks "one must make one's opponent as strong as possible" and states that in Freud there "is a very deep grappling with the problem of guilt."[133] Moreover, Paul and Freud share one fundamental concern: how to suspend the law.

By removing the paternal law in the dual commandment in Romans 13:8, Paul's "revolutionary act" takes on a Freudian character. They both achieve a suspension of the father religion and its law. According to the early Taubes, Freud admires Paul at the same time as he regards the apostle's gospel as illusory:

> What fascinated Freud in the message of Paul was the implicit confession of guilt contained in his good news. The evangel was at the same time a dysangel, the bad news of the original crime of man. . . . Freud considers himself to be the first to break the spell and dare to delineate the secret guilt that haunts man. What Paul could only acknowledge in the illusion of a "good news" was spelled out by Freud without illusion. Guilt cannot be expiated through the sacrificial death of a Son of God; it can only be acknowledged. By the conscious acknowledgement man liberates himself from blind bondage.[134]

There is a sameness in the confession and the vehicle or secret for the cure. However, the content or the object of these confessionary sciences, Paulinism and psychoanalysis, is radically different. By this fascination expressed in *Moses and Monotheism*, Freud is not only attracted to Paul. Taubes claims moreover that Freud "enters into the role of Paul."[135] However much Freud dismissed Paul's method for healing a culture as illusory and ineffective, he unconsciously entered the role of the apostle, in Taubes's view. As Kenneth Reinhard explains,

> For Taubes, both Pauline Christianity and psychoanalysis are "Jewish sciences" that attempt to transform the way we live under the burden of the paternal law. Freud enters into the place of Paul and continues his work by striving to liberate us from the burden imposed by the obscenely cruel paternal agency that we harbor within ourselves.[136]

By claiming that Paul grapples with the same problem of the burden of the paternal law as Freudian psychoanalysis, Taubes enforces his image of an introspective apostle. This is achieved through a reading of Romans 13:8, which is to a high degree informed by Freud's "nonsense," his "historical novel" *Moses and Monotheism*. Once again, we see how Taubes reads Paul through his intellectual opponents.

But Taubes does not construct thereby a Christian introspective apostle, like the one Krister Stendahl attempted to refute. By reading Paul through Freud, new light is cast upon the two. Freud becomes the father of a Jewish science, despite his fascination with the apostle in his controversial *Moses and Monotheism*, because of his similarities with the apostle whom Taubes has gathered back into the Jewish fold. Simultaneously, the Freudian character of Paulinism may serve Taubes's cause of recognizing Paul as truly Jewish. If Freud is the forerunner to the Jewish science of psychoanalysis, then the apostle must surely be treated as one as well.

One of the most famous attempts of "recircumcising Freud," as Jacques Derrida called it,[137] is found in the monologue that ends *Freud's Moses* by Yosef Hayim Yerushalmi.[138] As Derrida remarks, Yerushalmi "wants above all to make him confess" that he is Jewish and comes from a Hebrew culture.

Taubes's attempt may be considered analogous to Yerushalmi's, though it follows a different strategy for recircumcising Freud. While Yerushalmi gave a certain priority to biographical "facts" (like the inscription Jakob Freud places in the Bible of his son Sigmund) over Freud's own commentary in *Moses and Monotheism*, Taubes allowed the quotations from this book nearly to speak for themselves. Taubes reprised, in effect, Freud's "historical truth" from the novel about Moses the Egyptian and proclaimed that "only now can an interpretation of Paul be begun—on an entirely new level."

Since Taubes left such long quotations from Freud's Moses book without commentary, the listener is left to wonder what their purpose is. This, however, could be recognized as another sign of Taubes's Talmudic spirit. Since his aim is not consensus and agreement, but provocation and disagreement, Taubes leaves so many questions open. Within Taubes's textual horizon there appears to be no original agreement to which to return for further discussions on Paul. Instead, Taubes ends with long quotations. Without any summarizing exegesis of Freud's text or any final conclusions, he simply asks the listeners to interpret Paul anew. In a Talmudic spirit he leaves the final word unsaid; he lets his own lecture as discourse remain incomplete, however much he first has exposed violent disagreements with his "opponents."

Taubes's Paul and Psychoanalysis: Conclusion

One of Taubes's declared aims and ambitions is to read Paul from within the Jewish tradition without being precise on the range of this tradition. The philosophically oriented rabbi frames Paul's Jewishness through an engagement with Freudian psychoanalysis. He considers Paul as no less than a predecessor to Freud.

Inspired by Nietzsche and Freud's *Moses and Monotheism*, Taubes draws a line from Paul to Freud, sometimes through Augustine and Luther (see "The Powerlessness in Romans 7," earlier in this chapter). For Taubes these are all figures who have seen that the subject suffers from a powerlessness with regard to the unconscious forces that can invade the subject against the subject's will. For Taubes no one has taught such a radical doctrine of original guilt as Freud since Augustine and Paul. And like Paul, Freud attempts to suspend the force of law on the subject, according to Taubes. In that sense Freud is a Paulinist and Paul a predecessor to Freud's Jewish science.

Taubes's readings of Paul serve as a challenge to the Jewishness of the supposedly Jewish science of Freudian psychoanalysis, given Paul's legacy at work in his views on Freud. Moreover, the readings Taubes does of Romans 7 contains several presuppositions from the Augustinian paradigm of reading detected in Krister Stendahl's article. Taubes even reaffirms the "old" view of this paradigm that Paul is the inventor of the introspective conscience of the West (see "Introspection as a Jewish Remedy against the Catastrophe"). In this way, the philosopher's ambition to read Paul within a Jewish framework is tempered by what to a significant extent appears as a reproduction of Christian readings (see "The Powerlessness in Romans 7"). The Christian, and particularly Protestant, reception of the apostle is also confirmed by the fact that both philosophers consider Paul to be an antinomian (see "Taubes's Paul: The Downright Antinomian"). Furthermore, the chosen preference for Nietzsche ties his reading to a Christian metaphysical tradition, however much Nietzsche is supposed to resist it.

Taubes engages with Romans 9–11 in order to combat an anti-Semitism founded on Paul, in his positioning with regard to the legacy of Carl Schmitt. It is particularly through a reading of these chapters that Taubes's Paul acquires a more Jewish identity, as someone who takes the divine act of election of the Jewish people seriously and as someone who considers the salvation of Israel to be a primary concern for Paul's God (see "Taubes's Reading of Romans 9–11").

5

Paul against Empire
Taubes's Political Paul

Paul and Empire in Present New Testament Scholarship

The 1997 anthology *Paul and Empire* marked the beginning wave of reading Paul as oppositional to the Roman Empire within New Testament scholarship. According to the anthology's editor, Richard A. Horsley, what was on Paul's agenda was "organizing an international anti-imperial alternative society based in local communities."[1] Moreover, what was promised by Horsley in the introduction to the anthology was a revolutionary change with this type of scholarship that would outbid the paradigm shift proclaimed by adherents to the so-called New Perspective. According to Horsley, the scholars of "The New Perspective" still read Paul as primarily preoccupied with religious issues while ignoring the political connotations and implications of the apostle's message.[2] This deficit was indeed no unique feature to "The New Perspective." Horsley affirmed that modern theology and biblical scholarship had allegedly read Paul as concerned exclusively with religious matters that would not interfere with the political.[3] One could sense a new enthusiasm inherent in some of the revolutionary ways of reading the apostle anew as a hitherto unrecognized symbol of political liberation and anti-imperial resistance. Inspired by these new interpretative possibilities, a scholar like Neil Elliott would make powerful proclamations involving associations with modern movements of political liberation, as when he depicted Paul's gospel as an "ideological intifada."[4] The productive enthusiasm encapsulated in this expression would meet considerable academic resistance, which would lead to moderations or reservations about the range and scope of such associations applied to Paul.[5]

The culmination of this wave should perhaps be located in N. T. Wright's affirmations, such as the one that "Paul intended his gospel to subvert not merely paganism in general but the imperial cult in particular."[6] Unlike scholars who would argue for a less direct and more ambiguous anti-imperial script underlying Paul's message, without this being particularly directed against the emperor himself, Wright had claimed that Paul was against Caesar's empire because Caesar had claimed divine status.[7] This image of an apostle who deliberately and particularly targeted the cult devoted to the divinity of the emperor with a coded language has produced heated polemic.[8] Opponents of such readings have claimed that Paul's message was by no means directed against the *Roman* Empire as such, since Paul regarded the imperial cult as erroneous and sinful idolatry as any other pagan cult. The Roman Empire or its imperial cult is never explicitly mentioned in Paul's letters. This is a finding a scholar like John M. G. Barclay uses against Wright's and other scholars' claim that Paul's language is intended as a coded critique of this Roman cult. The absence of explicit mention of the empire testifies to the small significance it has within Paul's apocalyptic theology, according to Barclay. This, however, does not lead back to the "old" apolitical Paul that Horsley was criticizing:

> If Rome is not specifically named from this angle of vision, it does not mean that Paul's theology was apolitical, only that the political is for him enmeshed in an all-encompassing power-struggle which covers every domain of life, including but not limited to the religio-political domain we call "the Roman empire," and not neatly divisible in a battle between forces "for" and "against" Roman rule.[9]

To Barclay, scholars' efforts to prove the presence of hidden references in Paul's epistles (for instance, as "hidden transcripts") to the Roman emperor or Roman Empire have not proved convincing. According to Barclay, the Roman Empire was insignificant to Paul. In that way Barclay criticizes basic assumptions constituting the hypothesis of a revolutionary anti-Roman Paul. With this introduction to the debate between Wright and Barclay, one can perceive that this field of scholarship is marked by some major disagreement about how to read Paul.

The hypothesis of an anti-imperial Paul consists of a nucleon of assumptions proliferated with the anthology edited by Horsley, which is often referred to. But it has older roots. While some of its intuitions can be traced back to the early twentieth-century scholar Adolf Deissmann, the main assumptions of the hypothesis can be found in a work presented within

Jacob Taubes's early 1980s research project on religious theory and political theology. All the same, they mainly originated in Dieter Georgi's essay "Gott auf den Kopf stellen: Überlegungen zu Tendenz und Kontext des Theokratiegedankens in paulinischer Praxis und Theologie."[10] This essay appeared for the first time in 1987 as part of the three-volume anthology Jacob Taubes edited, named *Religionstheorie und Politische Theologie*. Although Taubes refers to another of Georgi's work on Paul, *The Opponents of Paul in Second Corinthians*,[11] it can be assumed that Taubes was familiar with Georgi's essay on theocracy from his work as editor. This is confirmed by the semblance between Taubes's and Georgi's arguments on Paul's political theology, which will be indicated in this chapter. Georgi's essay from Taubes's anthology was translated in his monograph in English on the same theme,[12] and it was reprinted in Horsley's anthology ten years after it appeared in German,[13] the very same year Taubes held his lectures in Heidelberg.

Summed up in his own words, Taubes's thesis is that "the Epistle to the Romans is a political theology, it consists of "a *political* declaration of war on the Caesar."[14] This thesis has not been embraced as particularly illuminating by any of the scholars who argue for an inherent conflict in the relationship between the Roman Empire and the Pauline movement. If Taubes was right, then we should have met a much more straightforward and direct critique of the Roman propaganda than what can be discerned in the letter of Romans, according to Neil Elliott. But there is no easily discernible polemic against Rome in this letter, according to Elliott. He complains that Taubes did not offer any explanation for his thesis.

> Taubes' characterization of Rom. 1:1–4 as "a *political* declaration of war on the Caesar" may seem an inexcusable exaggeration. After all, nothing in these opening verses sounds particularly incendiary.[15]

This disappointment with Taubes's argument is doubled by James R. Harrison. Harrison praises Elliott's work for possessing what Taubes is lacking[16]—namely, "evidence" from the Roman sources of Paul's time:

> However, Taubes' case for Romans being a "war" document does not convince because, in contrast to Georgi, he pays very little attention to the Julio-Claudian literary and documentary sources.[17]

First, Taubes has hailed Friedrich Nietzsche as "his best teacher on Paul." In other words, he has chosen a philosopher as his main guide for reading Paul. Accordingly, one could raise the question of the legitimacy of Harrison's objection against Taubes's reading for the lack of evidence from sources that are commonly held to be historians' field of investigation. At the very least, there is nothing in Harrison's argument that indicates an awareness of the difference between history and philosophy with regard to the kind of evidence that is usually demanded within these disciplines.

Second, these historically oriented scholars, with what has been praised as an admirable familiarity with the classical sources, pay some attention to Taubes's main thesis about the letter. This thesis is put forward by Taubes after his reading of Romans 1:1–7. The quoted scholars, however, do not discuss Taubes's reading of the political theology of Paul in the epistle more broadly. In contrast to the more philosophically oriented readers of Taubes, they ignore Taubes's reading of what he considers the nihilism of Romans 13 and of 1 Corinthians 7:29. A philosopher like Giorgio Agamben, however, pays homage to Taubes as he writes *in memoriam* of him. Agamben embraces and develops Taubes's reading of the *hos me* passage of 1 Corinthians 7:29 as "nihilistic,"[18] a passage Taubes juxtaposes with Romans 13. Hence, the biblical scholars react toward different representations of Paul in Taubes's statements than the philosophers.

The Hypothesis to Be Tested

The hypothesis put forward here is that Taubes constructs a political Paul through a reading of Romans 1 that stands in tension and potentially in contradiction with his reading of Romans 13. In Taubes's reading of Romans 1 we meet an apostle who consciously stresses the kingly attributes of the crucified and proclaims "his Anti-Caesar" as a condemnation of Rome. In Romans 13, the same apostle exhorts his congregation to demonstrate obedience to Rome in order to avoid being viewed as political rebels. In one moment, the writer of this epistle declares nothing less than war against Caesar. In the other moment, he argues that there is no point in taking up arms against the imperial power. As the readings laid together cannot result in a consistent political theology of Paul, they provide further evidence of Taubes's image of a contradictory Paul that, once again, is partly informed by Nietzsche.

The scholar Peter Oakes has helpfully distinguished between two poles in the argumentation for the relation between the Pauline movement and the Roman Empire. The first is parallel terminology, the other a structural relation. While the first furnishes discussions in scholarship about the meaning of the similarities in the vocabulary employed by Paul and Roman imperial discourse, the other question is of a more systematic character. In Peter Oakes's words the linguistic similarities can be explained in four ways:

Four options for the apparent parallels between Christian and Roman terminology are considered: (1) independent use of common sources, (2) Christian imitation of elements of Roman discourse or practice, (3) Christian writing in reaction to conflict stemming from Rome and (4) Christian writing that conflicts with Roman discourse or practice.[19]

Taubes's reading of Romans 1 in the 1987 lectures revolves around the first pole, with Dieter Georgi's work as the most probable guide and source for the reading. In Taubes's earlier works, however, a structural conflict between early Christianity and the Roman Empire is construed, primarily through Nietzsche. The latter philosopher is also one of the crucial influences when Taubes reads Romans 13.

Taubes's Structural Conflict between Paul and Empire

Already in *Occidental Eschatology* Nietzsche's influence on Taubes's historical accounts of the relation between Christianity and the Roman Empire is evident. Taubes inscribes Jesus and his followers within the apocalyptic movement in Israel,[20] in a political messianic struggle against the Roman Empire, an empire that stands against a world revolution of the oppressed.[21] Taubes invokes Nietzsche as his authority on the historical conflict: "Nietzsche thinks that there has hitherto been no greater event than this struggle, this question, this deadly contradiction."[22]

In "The Justification of Ugliness in Early Christian Tradition," Taubes builds further on this antithetical relation between Rome and Christianity. He points to 1 Corinthians 1:20, the place in Paul's writings where Nietzsche localizes the source of this antithesis. Nietzsche emphasizes Paul's doctrine of the cross as this source, and in this doctrine Taubes recognizes "a cause that revolutionizes ancient perception and experience."[23]

Taubes emphasizes that it is in this text that what Nietzsche names the "chandala-morality born of resentment" first appears, the kind of morality described by Nietzsche in his work *Antichrist*. Though not explicitly cited by Taubes, we find a wider description of allegedly Pauline morality in §58 of this work of Nietzsche.

> Then Paul appeared—Paul, the chandala hatred against Rome, against "the world," become flesh, become genius, the Jew, the *eternal* Wandering Jew par excellence. What he guessed was how one could use the little sectarian Christian movement apart from Judaism to kindle a "world fire"; how with the symbol of "God on the cross" one could unite all who lay at the bottom, all who were se-

cretly rebellious, the whole inheritance of anarchistic agitation in the Empire, into a tremendous power.²⁴

Nietzsche's Paul is full of hatred against Rome and unites all at the bottom of society in their common resentment in a great anarchistic power. His Paul unites these people in a secret rebellion against what is noble and beautiful, while adhering to the ugly cross of their God who chose the weak and foolish things of the world. This Nietzschean contradiction between Paul and empire has aesthetic dimensions that meld together with the political. What is beautiful in contrast to the cross is also the politically powerful. And the resentment Paul ingeniously discovers in the people and that he exploits in order to attract the impoverished masses to his doctrines results from the Roman dominion. In Nietzsche's eyes, they have no legitimate or authentically moral reasons for their hatred against Rome's dominance. Their hatred against Rome, translated into Paul's anti-worldly or sin-combating doctrine, was rather the product of the weak human nature of those who could be but jealous spectators to Roman power and domination. As Nietzsche writes in aphorism 71 in *Daybreak*:²⁵

> This unvoiced century—old hatred of the wearied spectators of Rome found wherever Rome's domination extended—was at length vented in Christianity which united Rome "the world" and "sin" into a single concept. The Christians took their revenge on Rome by proclaiming the immediate and sudden destruction of the world; by reinventing the future—for Rome had been able to transform everything into the history of its own past and present—a future in which Rome was no longer the most important factor and by dreaming of the last judgment—while the crucified Jew as the symbol of salvation was the greatest mockery of the superb Roman praetors in the provinces; for now they seemed to be only the symbols of ruin and a "world" ready for destruction.²⁶

For Nietzsche's Christian, Roman power is combated in two ways: First, it is mocked through the devotion to the crucified Jew and the adherence to the doctrine of the cross. Second, the future is reinvented and dreamed of as the destruction of Rome ("the world"), which prepares for the last judgment. Apocalyptic fantasies of Rome's destruction are for Nietzsche a tremendous power, generated by Paul's "slap in the face" (Taubes) of the values of Antiquity. Paul's textual and conceptual revolution consists of a transvaluation of ancient values.

In "The Justification of Ugliness in Early Christian Tradition," Taubes further sustains his argument about the Pauline transvaluation in Antiquity with a thesis from a professor in literary studies. Taubes refers to Erich Auerbach's thesis from his 1944 article "Sermo Humilis" in favorable terms. Here Auerbach posits a break in literary language, which occurs with the Christian genre of *sermo humilis*. This is a literary form Auerbach locates in Augustine and that shapes European intellectual history since. According to Auerbach,[27] the style of the *sermo humilis* was "a radical departure from the rhetorical, and indeed from the entire, literary tradition."[28] This departure constituted a new Christian sublime. If the Christian will pride himself only in weakness, he will have to refer to this strength with a kind of literary or rhetorical modesty. This new sublime modesty or literary style is related to, or perhaps reflected by, a social position, in Auerbach's view, as the incarnation was "a voluntary humiliation illustrated by a life on earth in the lowest social class."[29] In this way the aesthetic and social is connected.

Though not explicitly quoted by Taubes, the element of the social position of the first Christians is also present in the same paragraph that Taubes quotes in the essay from Nietzsche's *Anti-Christ*:

> The Christian movement, as a European movement, was from the start no more than a general uprising of all sorts of outcast and refuse elements (—who now, under cover of Christianity, aspire to power).[30]

Taubes implicitly confirms this view of the Pauline movement when he in his 1968 essay emphasizes how the Corinthian community was constituted by the nameless pariahs, the persons regarded as nothing and therefore elected by Paul's God.[31]

If Nietzsche's historical insight is really unsurpassed by historical criticism, as Taubes claims, and if Nietzsche's polemic is Taubes's window to early Christianity, then it can make perfect sense to read Paul's rhetoric as a confirmation of this. Although Nietzsche is not explicitly invoked in Taubes's readings of Romans 1 in the first part of the Heidelberg lectures, several of the presuppositions from Nietzsche appear: the structural conflict between Paul and Rome, the construction of an oppositional Pauline power, the inversion of ancient values, and the lower-class social position of the Pauline communities.

In contrast to Nietzsche, however, Taubes defends these presuppositions through a close reading of Paul. While he elsewhere confirms some of Nietzsche's readings through an examination of the first passages of Paul's letter to the Corinthians, Taubes now elaborates on Nietzschean themes with a reading of the first verses of Paul's Letter to the Romans. What is new in Taubes's reading of the relation between Paul and empire, compared to his 1968 essay, is an argument around the other pole named by Peter Oakes: the linguistic parallels between Paul's language and Rome's propaganda. These parallels are overtaken, I suggest, from Dieter Georgi.

Taubes's Reading of Romans 1: Paul's Declaration of War

Taubes affirms that the opening of Romans has a particular emphasis that is lacking in Corinthians. According to Taubes, the descent of Christ is not depicted in heavenly, but in earthly terms in Romans 1:3:

> Paul, a servant of Jesus Christ, called to be an apostle, set apart for the gospel of God, which he promised beforehand through his prophets in the holy scriptures, the gospel concerning his Son, who was descended from David according to the flesh and was declared to be Son of God with power according to the spirit of holiness by resurrection from the dead, Jesus Christ our Lord, through whom we have received grace and apostleship to bring about the obedience of faith among all the Gentiles for the sake of his name, including yourselves who are called to belong to Jesus Christ, to all God's beloved in Rome, who are called to be saints: Grace to you and peace from God our Father and the Lord Jesus Christ. (Rom 1:1–7)

Taubes claims that Paul's designation of Christ as son of David in 1:3 is a natural quality tied to the Messiah, while "Son of God" in 1:4 is far from natural; it is ascribed with terms resonant of "the act of enthronement" that Taubes finds in Psalm 2. With this vocabulary Paul is not only alluding to the Hebrew Bible, but also intentionally connoting the semantic field of the Roman political world:

> So we are dealing with a conscious emphasis of those attributes that are imperatorial, kingly, imperial. They are stressed before the congregation in Rome, where the imperator is himself present, and where the center of the cult of the emperor, the emperor religion, is located.[32]

As these observations are made to serve Taubes's main thesis of a Pauline declaration of war on "the Caesar," Paul is said to be consciously using terms loaded with meaning from the ideology of the devotion to the Roman emperor. Taubes assumes that there is an overlap of meaning between the official Roman discourse proliferated and cultivated in the imperial cult on the one hand and the Pauline ideology in the letter to the Romans on the other. There is not only an overlap, but this shared semantic field of the two discourses is strategically exploited by the politically oriented Paul:

> it is Paul's political genius to write, not to any old congregation, but to the congregation of Rome, the seat of the world empire. He had a sense for where to find the power and where to establish an opposing power.³³

In addition, Taubes claims that with the expression "obedience of faith" in 1:5 Paul is writing polemically against the notion of obedience to laws, since "it is laws you obey, and he [Paul] says no, you obey faith." Here Taubes discerns another Pauline expression with a revolutionary political meaning, since the law for Taubes's Paul is, as underlined in chapter 4 ("Taubes's Introspective Paul"), not reducible to the Mosaic Law. For Taubes's Paul "law" includes the Torah as well as "the cosmological law as a compromise formula for the Imperium Romanum."³⁴

When Taubes's Paul in 1:5 is on a mission "to bring about the obedience of faith among all the Gentiles," this is in strict opposition to Roman law, especially in the form of "the great nomos liberalism" of the time. For Taubes this liberalism is represented by figures such as Philo and Josephus who neutralized the messianic revolt of Jewish zealotry, present in figures like Paul whom Taubes regards as "a Jewish zealot." Against this "liberal" tendency to elevate any kind of law into a divine order Paul launches his critique of law, not only of his own Pharisaic group, but of these "liberal" tendencies in his Mediterranean environment in a broad sense.³⁵ Taubes's Paul is antinomian or with Nietzsche's determination a "holy anarchist."³⁶ The faith the congregation in Rome is called to be obedient to is an antinomian faith, and therefore they are called to live in a permanent enmity toward the Roman law and order. They have a new king, a new emperor in Christ, which eventually will conquer and triumph over the Roman emperor. Taubes's Paul is trying to convince his addressees that they are at war against no one else than the Caesar.

> I want to stress that this is a political declaration of war, when a letter introduced using these words, and not others, is sent to the congregation in Rome to be read aloud. One doesn't know into whose hands it will fall, and the censors aren't idiots.³⁷

Taubes is constructing a kind of Pauline conspiracy. The secret, political dimensions in Paul's doctrine of the cross are in the imperially loaded terms Paul employs in the letter he sends to the center of the world empire. Taubes constructs a Nietzschean scenario where Paul is strategically building an oppositional power to Rome, which is not wholly secret either, since "the censors aren't idiots." Paul's message is explosive in the sense that they can potentially cause violent uprising. Otherwise it would not be a danger to lay it in the hands of the censors. Thereby it is assumed in Taubes's reading that there was a Roman institutional control of meaning in the form of censorship of some kind. One hears associations to the machinery of propaganda.

Unlike Nietzsche's Paul, however, Taubes's Paul is not primarily undermining ancient cults as Mithras or Osiris with his new form of belief.[38] The faith preached by Taubes's Paul is rather directed against another cult—namely, the imperial cult. The kingly and imperial attributes to Paul's Messiah in Romans 1:4 are stressed as a critique and attack on this cult, "the emperor religion." Having understood this aspect of Paul's opening of his epistle to the Romans, one can appreciate Bruno Bauer's old insight, in spite of all his flaws, according to Taubes, that "Christian literature is a literature of protest against the flourishing cult of the emperor."[39] This Pauline protest is depicted by Taubes with recognizably Nietzschean terms:

> This is someone [Paul] who answers . . . with a protest, with a transvaluation of values: It isn't *nomos* but rather the one who was nailed to the cross by *nomos* who is the imperator! This is incredible, and compared to this all the little revolutionaries are *nothing*. This transvaluation turns Jewish-Roman-Hellenistic upper-class theology on its head, the whole mishmash of Hellenism.[40]

Paul presents his true king, the real imperator, the one crucified according to law. This concept, first expressed by Paul, is nothing less than a "transvaluation of values," which turns "upper-class theology" on its head. Paul transvalues the widespread Hellenistic deification of law ("the apotheosis of law"), which secured the interests of the elite and brought law and order into the Roman Empire, in Taubes's historical account. Hence, in this reading of Romans 1 the presuppositions from Nietzsche are maintained: the structural conflict between early Christianity and Rome, the inversion of values inherent in Pauline Christianity, and the social position of this new community, gathering outcasts throughout the Roman Empire.

The notion of a Christianity that is far more revolutionary than any other revolution can also be found in Nietzsche:

> The aristocratic attitude of mind has been undermined by the lie of the equality of souls; and if belief in the "privileges of the majority" makes and *will continue to make* revolutions—it is Christianity, let us not doubt, and *Christian* valuations, which convert every revolution into a carnival of blood and crime! Christianity is a revolt of all creatures that creep on the ground against everything that is *lofty*: the gospel of the "lowly" *lowers*.[41]

However, Taubes's notion of the crucified one as the real imperator and the true king appears not to stem from Nietzsche. Nor does the notions' basis in a linguistic parallel. Taubes's assumptions of such parallels should rather be traced back to the contribution by Dieter Georgi to his three-volume anthology:

> Furthermore, every page of the letter contains indications that Paul has very concrete and critical objections to the dominant political theology of the Roman Empire under the principate. By using such loaded terms as *euangélion, pístis, dikaiosýne,* and *eiréne* as central concepts in Romans, he evokes their associations to Roman political theology.[42]

As efforts to derive the Pauline use of the term *euangélion* from the Septuagint has not yielded success, the most probable source or closest parallel is for Georgi its use in Roman propaganda, which is but one aspect of "the Caesar-religion." Taubes's reading of Romans 1:3–4 is nearly doubled by Dieter Georgi's reading of the same passage:

> The exegete must explain why a text like this should be cited in a letter addressed to the seat of Roman power. The formula, which speaks of the origins and significance of the royal messiah Jesus, reflects a two-phase structure of the biblical law of kingship. . . . Paul introduces the figure he considers to be the true king into the kingship debate. The antagonist is not so much the royal messiah of Jewish missionary theology. . . . The adversary is rather a different figure, a power that in fact claims universal dominion in the political and social realm but bases his claim on a religion and a theology: the Roman Caesar.[43]

It is not immediately clear to what degree the anti-imperial meaning of Romans 1:3–4 can be deciphered by insiders or outsiders of the *ekklesia* in Rome, in either Taubes's or in Georgi's reading. Georgi asks whether there is an element of satire when Paul introduces the crucified Jew as the true king in 1:3–4. But who understands the satirical meaning of it? Georgi does not clarify that in this text.

What appears clear to Taubes, however, is that Paul is hostile to Rome and that this "condemnation" poses a risk with regard to the Roman authorities, "the censors."

> I sit there, read the text, and ask myself: Has he gone *meshugge*, to be writing his condemnation to Rome of all places? Why does he proclaim his Anti-Caesar straightaway in the salutation? This is quite a catch for the censors.[44]

Taubes claims that Paul's Messiah is "Anti-Caesar," which implies that his Messiah is competing with or aiming to destroy Caesar in an apocalyptic battle. The Jewish zealots' messianic struggle is in a sense universalized to the whole empire. Paul declares a war in Romans 1, according to Taubes. The implications of such a war launched against the Caesar, his cult, and his political regime are not specified in Taubes's reading of the first chapter. As Elliott emphasized, Taubes's expression of a Pauline "declaration of war" sounds "incendiary," as if Paul were encouraging the messianic community to take up arms against evil rulers. But is Taubes's Paul advocating a violent uprising against the imperator competing with their true Imperator on the cross? Taubes emphasizes that Paul could have opened the letter in a more careful tone, as if to avoid any criticism of the rulers or call for an armed rebellion: "One could have introduced it pietistically, quietistically, neutrally, or however else; but there is none of that here."[45]

Nor is it fully clear whether the conflict Taubes depicts between Paul and Rome stems from the former or the latter. What is clearly implied by Taubes's interpretation of Romans 1:3–4 is that the kingly attributes given to the Messiah are not simply linguistic parallels with nonconflicting independent uses in different or autonomous spheres, as if one could separate the political-imperial from the Pauline-religious domain. They are competing and conflicting parallels. But are they established as Paul's reaction to the Roman crucifixion of his Messiah, or is this crucifixion rather the sign of an altogether evil empire that Paul is called to declare war on first? Is Paul's declaration of war a consequence of Roman persecution of those who proclaim the crucified criminal to be the Messiah? Or is the initiative rather Paul's in the sense that he first launched the polemical attack on the empire and its Augustan propaganda and cult? This remains unclear in Taubes. Accordingly, none of these three questions can be effectively answered.

Taubes presents an author of Romans 1 as one who in Yiddish might have "gone *meshugge*" since he opens his letter with a proclamation that is "Anti-Caesar." When presenting the same apostle writing in Romans 13, however, Taubes reads him as one who is exhorting his community not to draw the authorities' attention. But how could an apostle with a message with "a catch for the censors" not draw such attention with his kingly attributions to the Messiah in Romans 1? Apparently, this apostle is writing a contradictory letter. Or can these readings be reconciled?

Taubes's Reading of Romans 13: Paul's Political Nihilism

As Taubes makes clear, when his exegesis of the epistle arrives to chapter 13, he is "more or less familiar with the hundreds of variants" that exist in exegesis and theology.[46] In other words, he does not hesitate to highlight the famous passage that at first glance seems to contradict his political reading of Paul. He appears to be utterly aware that these verses have been "a notorious exegetical problem and a theological scandal" in Christianity,[47] to use the succinct expression of Neil Elliott.

All the same, there is a specific line of interpretation of Romans 13 that Taubes attempts to target, the one that reads a Lutheran or modern state theory into the text that separates the political from the religious. For Paul there is no such separation or distinction, according to Taubes. Paul does not have a notion of the profane or secular, anticipated by Augustinianism or Lutheranism: "Then, several centuries after Paul, we have the exegesis of the dogma of the two kingdoms."[48]

Another fault Taubes detects in the history of interpretation is the isolation or fixation on the motif of submission in Romans 13:1: "Let every person be subject to the governing authorities; for there is no authority except from God, and those authorities that exist have been instituted by God":

> The mistake that one makes all too easily here, in my view, consists in fixating on the first part. If you stare at the topic of authority as if it were a predator, then it's hard to see how to get out of here. But chapter 13 has three parts. The passage on obedience to authority, which is so difficult to interpret, can only be understood from the point of view of the two other parts.[49]

It is, however, not enough for Taubes to stick to this hermeneutic principle. In order to understand Paul's word in Romans 13 Taubes also introduces three thinkers through whom to read the text: Barth, Benjamin, and Nietzsche.

Taubes claims that chapter 13 consists of three parts, in which the third speaks of the epoch in which Paul and the congregation of Paul is living and from which Taubes quotes:

> Besides this, you know what time it is, how it is now the moment for you to wake from sleep. For salvation is nearer to us now than when we became believers. (Rom 13:11)

This verse and the following verses 12–14 from chapter 13 are for Taubes evidence of Paul's "apocalyptic-eschatological profession of faith." Why is it so crucial for an understanding of the exhortation for submission in 13:1 that Paul's words in 13:11 testify to his apocalypticism?

In order to explain what he means by an "apocalyptic-eschatological profession of faith," Taubes evokes another famous Pauline passage,[50] from 1 Corinthians 7:29, which he names as "the nihilistic passage."[51] The Pauline nihilism is about having "as if one didn't have."[52] By reading Paul through a philosopher like Nietzsche Taubes discovers a potential meaning of this text that a classic historian of Antiquity or an exegete from biblical scholarship would not unfold. At the very best, they would notice a similarity with such a modern or Nietzschean notion, without investigating it further.

Taubes's Paul Constructed with Early Twentieth-Century Thought

Nietzsche

"Nihilism" is a term applied by Nietzsche as well as Benjamin. One of the effects the term has at this point in Taubes's lecture is to reaffirm the connection between Paul's apocalypticism in Romans and 1 Corinthians 7 on one hand and Nietzsche's nihilism on the other. In Nietzsche's tale the first Christians' apocalyptic belief was an expression of their "revenge on Rome," which they took "by proclaiming the immediate and sudden destruction of the world." As lawless anarchists with regard to the Roman Empire these Pauline communities and outcasts sparked the epoch of decadence in Western philosophy and history. Paul had radically repudiated the highest values of Rome and was depicted by Nietzsche as one of the sources of the poisoning nihilistic devaluation of the noble and the beautiful.

Nietzsche, however, had a dual concept of nihilism. Nihilism was not only the name for the Pauline poison and the Western decadent trajectory that lasted up until Nietzsche's lifetime. Nihilism was also the potential cure, as it could be turned against itself in an overcoming of its moral-philosophical limitations as the form of *the last man* or *the innocence of being* or *becoming*.[53] This second type was not Paul's, in Taubes's reading. However much the first type of nihilism was construed by Nietzsche to target Pauline Christianity, Taubes embraced this type in several aspects as describing the nihilism of Paul. But Taubes did not take it for granted that Paul's nihilism grew out of a lust for power, but the opposite: the love of neighbor.

By tying Paul's apocalypticism to Nietzsche's nihilism in his reading of Romans 13, the Jewish rabbi is able to reaffirm the structural conflict between Paul and Rome. By calling Paul's view of the Roman Empire "evil,"

Taubes sets Paul and empire antithetically toward each other in an apocalyptic conflict. Does this mean that Taubes's Paul thinks the *Roman* Empire specifically is the ultimate expression of evil? Does this imply that the new people has to fight actively against this evil, even in the form of violent revolt, as adherents to the message of the apostle Taubes considers a "Jewish zealot"?

> And his business is the same: the establishment of a people. That's what's accomplished by the chapters 9–13; in 9–11 the legitimation of the new people of God is given; in 12 the Christian life is described; and 13—well, we're living in the evil Roman Empire, so how are we living there? What, should we still be rising up against something that's going down anyway? There's no point in raising a finger; it's going to disappear somehow.... Sure it's evil, but—what are you going to do.[54]

Taubes's Paul proclaims an "anti-Caesar" stance with his writings in Romans. This apostle is a nihilist not only because he negates the imperial virtues and values. His nihilism is expressed in a negation of the "Caesar religion" not primarily because it is pagan, but because it is the source of the values that are negated and transvalued by the apostle. The Roman values are the ones that got Paul's Messiah crucified. Precisely through his proclamation of this crucified criminal as the true king and imperator, these Roman values are transvalued by the apostle. Caesar is an idol, of course. Sure, devotion to him is to be avoided for the monotheistic believer. But Caesar is not the devil. In Taubes's reading the imperial cult and its propaganda countered by Paul are rather the very source of the values that represent evil or suppress the truth. This is implied by Taubes's embrace of Nietzsche's pejorative designation of Paulinism as nihilism, since the latter concept does not refer to a mere negation of values, but a radical repudiation of the very source of them. In Nietzsche's view the first Christians' anti-worldly attitude originated in a fear for the unknown of this world and resulted in a deceitful longing for the world beyond.[55] In Taubes's view the Pauline believers' hatred against the world originated in an authentic recognition of the evilness of the empire that had crucified their Messiah, with the love of the neighbor as the guiding principle.

"Sure it's evil," as Taubes says about the empire, but in addition Paul the apocalypticist supposes this evil is "going down anyway." This apocalyptic stance corresponds for Taubes to nihilism, since the nihilistic negation does not destroy its object (values, people, or institutions). Paul the nihilist does not call for an act of revolt that could anticipate the imminent destruction of the empire. Paul's oppositional power is not armed physically, but spiritually as nihilists with regard to the world, not even specifically the Roman world or the Roman empire. Therefore, Taubes's Paul cannot be anti-Roman because of some unique qualities of "the Roman," its power, or discourse. Instead, Taubes's Paul nihilistically repudiates any form of worldly power.

For Taubes's Paul there is no point in "rising up against something that's going down anyway." It is not even "worth mentioning" the evil of the world or the empire, Taubes appears to argue. That's why he allows that "Mr. Troeltsch" [Ernst Troeltsch, German Protestant theologian] is right that Romans 13 is "quietistic." Taubes accepts Troeltsch's point, but still asks, "Quietistic, but out of what depths?" And it is on this issue that Karl Barth "opens our eyes," according to Taubes, when Barth draws the last sentence of chapter 12 into chapter 13.[56] The quietism has a basis. The words about submission are not simply a reflection of Roman orders, a divine legitimation of this imperial power, or even a limited legitimation of a worldly power in the form of a theology of two kingdoms. For Taubes's Paul any worldly power is without legitimation, in principle.

Karl Barth: The True Pauline Negation

Since Taubes's assertions of a Pauline nihilism follow from his appraisal of Barth's reading, one could suppose that a broader view of Barth's argument than what Taubes provides in the lectures could help to clarify of what such a nihilism might consist. Taubes's Nietzschean Paul is at the outset in conflict with the world and its values and therefore with Rome and the Caesar. His Paul has mounted an oppositional power on the apocalyptic supposition that the empire and its world will be destroyed. However much Taubes's Paul is revolutionary when he inverts ancient values through his proclaimed belief in the crucified, he is nonetheless a nihilist who negates without actively destroying his object. He is no revolutionary in the common political sense. Taubes's Paul is not calling for a physical revolt against evil. He is the defender of a certain quietism. If Barth's reading is "ingenious"[57] and Taubes agrees with him, we should expect Taubes's image of Paul as a nihilist and not as a revolutionary in the conventional sense to be confirmed by Barth's reading of the same epistle. Is it?

Barth's "ingenious philological move" in his commentary on the Romans (Taubes refers to the second edition from 1921)[58] consists in treating verse 21 in chapter 12 as the real beginning of chapter 13. Romans 12:21 reads, "Do not be overcome by evil, but overcome evil with good." Immediately following are the words from 13:1 about showing obedience to the authorities, in the same paragraph in Barth's commentary. But what more specifically could Taubes have in mind here?

Under the heading "The Great Negative Possibility" Barth comments upon 12:21–13:7. For Barth's Paul all human possibilities are open to question, as all human action can be interrupted, since humans relate and are answerable to the destructive judgment of God.[59] Negative possibilities, like positive possibilities, are congruous to God's transformation of this world, human history. Unlike positive possibilities, however, negative possibilities consist of things not to be done or enacted, which through their non-doing bear witness and draw the attention to the Coming World, the Kingdom of God. They do not consist in forbidden things to do, as if Romans could provide an absolute ethics for the believer. But they are possibilities that arise out of the deep significance of non-doing, in encounter with and confronted by "the powers" of "the world" (although not represented by a specific empire, such as the Roman). We must all respond to the interrogation or interpellation of these powers:

> These powers demand recognition and obedience, and we have to decide whether we shall or shall not yield to their demand. If we admit their authority, we concede quite clearly the principle of Legitimism; if, on the other hand, we reject it, we are bound to accept the principle of Revolution.[60]

Barth presents two options. To admit to the first implies taking a politically conservative position, while the other is the politically radical and revolutionary one. Although Barth reckons that a reader of the Epistle to the Romans more likely will embrace the revolutionary than the conservative, as he claims that the revolutionary one is closer to the position or stance defended in Romans, Barth does not concede to one or the other. He finds that Paul's Epistle to the Romans consists of a denial and negation of both positions. To him, Pauline Christianity remains committed to the disquiet, the questioning, and the negation. The reason the revolutionary has erred (the Bolshevik exemplifies him here) is that the revolutionary molds or bends this negation into a positive method for how humans should act and behave. In this way the authentic negation is reduced to a means of justification. The revolutionary has chosen the possible possibility of discontent and hatred, of rebellion and demolition.[61] In other words, Barth, like Nietzsche, seeks a negative stand that negates without destroying its object, a negation without demolition. This is probably the kind of attitude that Taubes discerns in Barth's Paul and is in harmony with his Pauline nihilism.

Taubes's Paul is struggling to legitimate the establishment of a new people of God in a world totally devoid of any legitimation vis-à-vis God.

The nihilist has already delegitimized all worldly attempts of legitimation, including divine sorts of this kind. This suspension of the law, of legality itself, that Taubes's Paul enacts does also have resonance in Barth's Paul:

> Is there anywhere legality which is not fundamentally illegal? Is there anywhere authority which is not ultimately based upon tyranny?[62]

Taubes's Paul has no worldly order or laws on which to sustain its mission, since all legalities, including Roman ones, are already delegitimized. If we read this aspect of Taubes's Paul together with Barth, we might get a clearer view of the kind of politics that Taubes's Paul is to carry out: the continuous delegitimation of worldly powers, laws, and orders and an insistence on criticizing these entities while recognizing that the powers possess no righteousness in themselves:

> What more radical action can he perform than the action of turning back to the original root of "not-doing"—and NOT be angry, NOT engage in assault, NOT demolish? This turning back is the ethical factor in the command, *Overcome evil with good*. There is here no word of approval of the existing order; but there is endless disapproval of every enemy of it. It is God who wishes to be recognized as He that *overcometh* the unrighteousness of the existing order. This is the meaning of the commandment; and it is also the meaning of the Thirteenth Chapter of the Epistle to the Romans.[63]

In Barth's view, this Pauline mission can never succumb to the theological legitimation of these powers, since they are already at war in the apocalyptic battle. The declaration of war, postulated by Taubes in Romans 1, may therefore be consistent with Barth's perspective: the believers in Paul's gospel must surely join the battle, not in order to crush the orders of the status quo, but in order to enact "an endless disapproval" of the defender of the order and the revolutionary demolisher alike. This is the meaning of the whole chapter of Romans 13, according to Barth.

> Though subjection may assume from time to time many various concrete forms, as an ethical conception it is here purely negative. It means to withdraw and make way; it means to have no resentment, and not to overthrow. Why, then, does not the rebel turn back and become no more a rebel? Simply because the conflict in which he is immersed cannot be represented as a conflict between him and the *existing ruling powers*; it is, rather a conflict of evil with evil.[64]

To overcome evil with good then amounts, for Barth, to engaging in an incessant negation and questioning of all evils, without legitimating this questioning by any earthly authority, but founding the critique in a worldly *nothing*, an anti-authority or what the world regards as nothing: the crucified on the cross.

Theologically speaking, the Pauline movement has no worldly legitimation, within the frame of Barth. Furthermore, historically speaking, according to Taubes, they had no legitimation either. This is how Taubes summarizes the meaning of his juxtaposition of references to Barth's commentary, Romans 13 and 1 Corinthians 7:29:

> This means: under this time pressure, if tomorrow the whole palaver, the entire swindle were going to be over—in that case there's no point in any revolution! That's absolutely right. I would give the same advice. Demonstrate obedience to state authority, pay taxes, don't do anything bad, don't get involved in conflicts, because otherwise it'll get confused with some revolutionary movement, which, of course, is how it happened. Because after all, these people have no legitimation, as, for instance, the Jews do, as religio licita—weird as they were, they were nevertheless recognized and didn't have to participate in the cult of the emperor. But now here comes a subterranean society, a little bit Jewish, a little bit Gentile, nobody knows, what sort of lowlifes are these anyway—for heaven's sake, don't stand out![65]

The advice Taubes's Paul then provides for the Christ believers in Rome is to strategically avoid being mistaken for violent zealotry or for being revolutionaries. In Taubes's view, this is a strategy from an apostle "who knows where to establish an opposing power." The quietism implied by this strategy, however, is not merely strategic. It is drawn "out of depths," which Barth helps Taubes to understand and to point to.

Therefore, chapter 13 of the letter, sent to the congregation in the heart of the empire, exhorts the believers to obey the legal authorities, since this new religious group is already on the margins of the laws of the empire. It is risky business to establish a new religious group in this political climate, right there in the center of the empire. Accordingly, this new community will have to obey the authorities, if one is to follow Taubes's exegetical reasoning here. But this obedience is of a nihilistic kind. It is a kind of an empty gesture that does not compromise the underlying and declared apocalyptic war.

These are the Barthian depths that have bypassed historically oriented scholars such as Neill Elliott and James Harrison. They have, at least, not demonstrated any will to go into them. Thereby they have missed the characteristics of the declaration of war that Taubes's Paul makes in Romans 1, which perhaps hinders any further interest in Taubes's reading of Paul, and his reading of Romans 13 in particular. Perhaps the apparent contradiction between Romans 1 and 13 was no contradiction at all, and this was understood or at least implied by Agamben's appropriations of the Pauline nihilism of Taubes. The philosophers got it right, somehow.

Benjamin as "Exegete" of Paul

In his search for an understanding that does not compromise the true meaning of Romans 13, Taubes invokes Karl Barth as an authority from the camp of Christian theologians. More surprising, perhaps, but also more in tune with his presumably Jewish reading of the apostle, is Taubes's invocation of Walter Benjamin.[66]

> I see Benjamin as the exegete of the "nature" of Romans 8, of decay, and of Romans 13, nihilism as world politics. And this is something that Nietzsche already saw, and Nietzsche resisted.[67]

As I earlier suggested (in Chapter 3, under "'Hard Reality' against Aesthetics"), Taubes could have made a contrast between Benjamin and Adorno without recourse to Paul. Nonetheless, to draw out this contrast between the messianic thinker and the merely aesthetic thinker does not appear as the only purpose for bringing Walter Benjamin into the readings of Paul. When Taubes declares that he considers Benjamin an exegete, it could imply an existing literary dependence on Paul's epistles in Walter Benjamin's writings, as Giorgio Agamben takes Taubes to mean. But is such a literary dependence in a strict meaning of the word necessary for making sense of Taubes's hypothesis of Benjamin as an exegete of Romans?

We saw earlier that Taubes considered texts distortions or points in debates.[68] It is not necessary to see in Benjamin's texts hidden or covered literary dependence on Paul's epistles. From Taubes's overall work, it is perhaps more reasonable to consider Paul and Benjamin examples of the unfolding of the messianic idea in Judaism. What they share is primarily an experience and not a set of ideas:

> For Benjamin it's important to note, first, that he maintains the Messiah and doesn't let it drift into neutrality, which isn't a matter of religious history but an article of faith. . . . Of course I don't want to say that it's identical with Paul in a strictly exegetical sense. I want to say: This is said out of the same experience, and there are hints in the texts that confirm this. These are the experiences that shake Paul through and through and that shake Benjamin after 1918, after the war.[69]

Paul against Empire ■ 159

The concept of neutrality is a key concept in Taubes's account of the course of the messianic idea in history. The apocalyptic energy originating from the application of this messianic idea to a historical situation may be neutralized or interiorized when the prophesy fails, when the apocalyptic dreams are crushed by historical realities. If Benjamin shares Paul's experience—that is, of failed prophesies that lead to the deferred instead of realized Kingdom of God—Benjamin must interiorize the messianic idea in some way. As an "exegete" of Romans 13, Benjamin must discern, read, and draw out some of the chapter's meaning. This scenario does not necessarily encourage us to imagine Walter Benjamin sitting and opening up the pages of the New Testament in the aftermath of the First World War. We are rather asked to look for hints in the texts that may indicate a common human experience or faith in some kind of introspective messianism. Besides this interiorization expressed by the quietism of Romans 13, Benjamin must be reconcilable with Nietzsche's Paulinism, which Nietzsche resisted. Is this too much to demand of Benjamin, or can Benjamin's texts perform this for us? And what image of Paul is constructed with Benjamin here?

Benjamin Reconcilable with Nietzsche?

The text by Benjamin that is supposed to perform this work is the "Theologico-Politico Fragment." The expression "nihilism as world politics" is taken by Taubes from this short text of Benjamin.

Given that Taubes claims Benjamin as an exegete of the "nihilism as world politics" that is at work in Romans 13 and that "is something that Nietzsche already saw," there must be some similarities between the two philosophers in the way they have approached the Pauline politics enacted by Romans 13.

"Theologico-Politico Fragment" is a text Adorno edited and entitled for the collection of texts by Benjamin and was published in German in 1977 as *Illumination: Ausgewälte Schriften*. One part of the translated English version of the fragment reads:

> The order of the profane should be erected on the idea of happiness. The relation of this order to the Messianic is one of the essential teachings of the philosophy of history. It is the precondition of a mystical conception of history, containing a problem that can be represented figuratively. If one arrow points to the goal toward which the profane dynamic acts, and another marks the direction of Messianic intensity, then certainly the quest of free humanity for happiness runs

counter to the Messianic direction; but just as a force can, through acting, increase another that is acting in the opposite direction, so the order of the profane assists, through being profane, the coming of the Messianic Kingdom. The profane, therefore, although not itself a category of this Kingdom, is a decisive category of its quietest approach. For in happiness all that is earthly seeks its downfall, and only in good fortune is its downfall destined to find it.[70]

Although Taubes sees it as a "compressed" text, it is nevertheless "polemical through and through." In what sense polemical? For Taubes Benjamin's notion of happiness is "just the opposite" of Nietzsche's notion of "all desire wants eternity."[71] This notion is expressed through Nietzsche's literary figure Zarathustra and is analogous to the Nietzschean overcoming of the merely human as the last man or overman. According to other readers of Benjamin, Taubes seems right in this regard. Benjamin's happiness in this text may well be a way of countering Nietzsche's alternative, which was widely discussed in Benjamin's intellectual milieu around 1920.[72] Like Nietzsche, Benjamin is hoping for the growth or the appearance of a new humanity. They both conduct their minds toward the earthly and the worldly as the stage for the creation or proliferation of the new. For Benjamin, however, this new humanity is not to appear through an immanent and innocent becoming, but in constant tension with the transcendent messianic of history. As Benjamin writes in the "Fragment," "Nothing that is historical can relate itself, from its own ground, to anything messianic."[73] As Taubes is aware, it has to come from outside. Besides, it does not come through the will to power or domination, but through a will to happiness in solidarity with the oppressed of history. The happiness, which shall be sought, is defined in marked contrast to hedonistic pleasures and could include suffering. Furthermore, in other works Benjamin connects the kind of happiness that the profane order should be erected upon to technology. Thereby Nietzsche's last man is radically reevaluated,[74] within Benjamin's intellectual environment, which was heavily influenced by Nietzsche.[75] Technology, and not human instincts, provides new possibilities for the new humanity to emerge.

On the other hand, in spite of Benjamin's openness to the realization of human happiness by technological means in the profane sphere, the Jewish German thinker was allergic to the modern idea of progress as something inherent in human history. Benjamin's concept of history in this regard has some affinities with Nietzsche's resistance against historicism. This allergy or resistance in Benjamin is expressed in the first sentences of the "Fragment":

> Only the Messiah himself consummates all history, in the sense that he alone redeems, completes, creates its relation to the Messianic. For this reason nothing historical can relate itself on its own account to anything Messianic. Therefore the Kingdom of God is not the *telos* of the historical dynamic; it cannot be set as a goal. From the standpoint of history it is not the goal, but the end.[76]

Benjamin (although a leftist) shared Nietzsche's mistrust and suspicion of the (socialist) idea of progress, the bourgeois historicism, and the scientific positivism. Modern progress is not simply a secularized messianic kingdom. The Kingdom is still outside human activity or history as something that cannot be objectified by human reason. And there are no predetermined goals (*telos*) that can be established in advance for assuring the realization of happiness or historical laws to follow. Nietzsche and Benjamin de-teleologize the modern concept of history and thus return it to history. As in in Karl Barth, the messianic is no mere negation of the historical (nonrelation), nor is it affirmation of the historical (relation).[77] All three figures rescue it from modern regulative ideas that might limit the range of human freedom, but the purpose of the use of this freedom is very different in the three thinkers. For Benjamin there is no innocent sphere beyond good and evil, where one could realize the new man through domination of the weak part of humanity. Far from it; the evil is all over in a history of legal tyranny and subjugation.[78] History is a catastrophe, seen from the perspective of the defeated and oppressed.

In conclusion, Taubes's assertion that Benjamin's "Fragment" is polemical against Nietzsche can be confirmed and made plausible, at least possible, with these readings of the two. But if the "Fragment" is unfolding the meaning of Romans 13, then Paul's messianism can be interpreted with regard to categories in Benjamin as the profane and the holy, the political and the theocratic. With these categories is Taubes's political Paul construed.

Paul the Theocratic?

Since Paul is at the outset a Jewish apocalypticist in Taubes's view, the apostle's vision for the world is necessarily in principle theocratic. In *Occidental Eschatology* Taubes had posited theocracy as the logical consequence of eschatology:

> Theocracy is built upon the anarchical elements in Israel's soul. It expresses the human desire to be free from all human, earthly ties and to be in covenant with God. The first tremors of eschatology can be traced to this dispute over divine or earthly rule.[79]

The eschatological visions for a renewal of the earthly, communal, national, and political life inevitably promoted the idea of a theocracy. Since the renewal of the earthly was conceptualized in such radical terms as in Jewish eschatology, the concept of theocracy had in Taubes's eyes the potential for generating a passion for revolution. And in modern times, this passion was expressed by many Jewish key figures in the secular revolutionary movements. In that way, the messianic idea was cultivated and adhered to in new forms and new circumstances.

What is inherent in Taubes's apocalyptic Paul therefore is the hope for theocracy. The deferral of the Kingdom, however, leads to a transformation and interiorization of this theocratic dream in the reality of an evil age without divine legitimation. Said otherwise, the age and the empire that have caused the execution of the Messiah have delegitimized themselves.

The theocratic vision, however, is a messianic impulse that for Taubes is far from neutralized in his introspective Paulinism. It rather lies latent and can break out in new historical circumstances. "Viewed in terms of immanence, theocracy is a utopian community,"[80] writes Taubes in *Occidental Eschatology*. It can be regarded from an immanent secular perspective, but also from a transcendent messianic perspective.

With the help of Nietzsche, Taubes can see how Walter Benjamin comes so much closer to a real understanding of Paul, which now profits from a concept Paul himself is lacking: the profane.

In Benjamin's "Fragment" and its messianic conception of history, the Kingdom of God is *not* the goal of history. This does not imply that the messianic and profane are isolated spheres and accordingly that the messianic awaiting or striving has no effect in the profane sphere. This is no call for a retreat from history altogether for messianic believers. The "Fragment" is rather an attempt to think through the interrelatedness of these two domains, of which one "should be erected on the idea of happiness" (the profane), and the realization of the other (the messianic) is not guaranteed by this striving for happiness. But the messianic kingdom can be sought, although it cannot be realized by human action in a direct manner. The messianic may erupt unexpectedly out of the profane striving for happiness, from within this historical endeavor to create happiness, for the individual or society. The "Fragment" calls for a recognition of an a-teleological and messianic striving, tendency, longing within the historical. And it even calls for an openness to the cataclysmic, essential coming of the Kingdom from within the profane history. But here there is no room given for theocracy as an institutionalized form of the messianic kingdom in society. The interrelation appears rather to safeguard against such a reality, since the Kingdom of God is not the goal, but the end of history:

> From the standpoint of history it [the Kingdom of God] is not the goal, but the end. Therefore the order of the profane cannot be built up on the idea of the Divine Kingdom, and therefore theocracy has no political, but only a religious meaning. To have repudiated with utmost vehemence the political significance of theocracy is the cardinal merit of Bloch's *Spirit of Utopia*.[81]

In other words, as theocracy has no political meaning, it is meaningless to build politics on religious goals or assume that such messianic visions can be realized through politics. It would be in vain to act politically as if that were possible, for theological reasons. Therefore the "Fragment" may be said to destroy the ambitions of idealistic and theological objectives in politics. Whenever politics sets its goals, these goals must be restricted to the profane sphere, in Benjamin's view.

However, Taubes is clear on what Benjamin's denial of the political significance of theocracy does not mean:

> It doesn't mean that the concepts of theocracy aren't political. All the Christian concepts I know are highly political and explosive, or become so at a certain point.[82]

As a Jewish apocalyptic ideology Paul's theology cannot but, at some points, become "highly political and explosive." After all, inherent to this ideology is a theocratic dream that is conceptualized as a monarchical structure and the rule of a Davidic kingdom. The importance of these kingly, monarchical concepts in Paul has been, as we have seen, highlighted by Taubes in his reading of Romans 1.

Paul, however, is no ordinary case for Taubes of Jewish zealotry in the line of Jewish warriors in Josephus's accounts of Jewish uprisings against Rome. Paul is a thinker who opened the introspective conscience of the West. He interiorized the outward ambitions of reinstalling the Davidic kingdom, without ever giving up on his theocratic dream but waiting intensively for the coming of the messianic kingdom, the second coming of his Messiah. But Taubes's Paul, unlike Benjamin, saw no distinctions between the political and the religious. For this apostle the political had no autonomy, particularly not in the modern sense of the word. If Paul were to support a revolution it would have been a struggle for Jewish theocracy. Outside of this apocalyptic struggle Taubes's Paul knew no distinctions, as he had already repudiated any kind of worldly source for such distinctions. Paul the nihilist did not care about politics, nor did he care about the Roman Empire as such. But precisely where the Roman power would conflict with his messianic kingdom, there Taubes's Paul would react. Therefore, he had in Romans 1, according to Taubes, "a conscious emphasis of those attributes that are imperatorial, kingly, imperial."[83] All the same, he did not react as a revolutionary in the political sense of the word. He did not take up arms. He delegitimized and mocked the political power through his proclamation of the crucified as the Messiah. He was indeed "establishing an opposing power . . . in the seat of the world empire."[84] But in Taubes's reasoning it is implied that this apostle knew that his theocratic concepts could become explosive at certain points within the political sphere. Accordingly, Taubes's Paul attempted to prevent believers in Rome from getting involved in any conflict with the authorities. In such a way he practiced "nihilism as world politics." Was this really Paul's practice?

Rewriting the Theocracy of Romans 13 with Taubes's Political Paul

Let every person be subject to the governing authorities; for there is no authority except from God, and those authorities that exist have been instituted by God. Therefore whoever resists authority resists what God has appointed, and those who resist will incur judgment. For rulers are not a terror to good conduct, but to bad. Do you wish to have no fear of the authority? Then do what is good, and you will receive its approval; for it is God's servant for your good. But if you do what is wrong, you should be afraid, for the authority does not bear the sword in vain! It is the servant of God to execute wrath on the wrongdoer. Therefore one must be subject, not only because of wrath but also because of conscience. For the same reason you also pay taxes, for the authorities are God's servants, busy with this very thing. Pay to all what is due them—taxes to whom taxes are due, revenue to whom revenue is due, respect to whom respect is due, honor to whom honor is due. Owe no one anything, except to love one another; for the one who loves another has fulfilled the law. The commandments, "You shall not commit adultery; You shall not murder; You shall not steal; You shall not covet"; and any other commandment, are summed up in this word, "Love your neighbor as yourself." Love does no wrong to a neighbor; therefore, love is the fulfilling of the law. Besides this, you know what time it is, how it is now the moment for you to wake from sleep. For salvation is nearer to us now than when we became believers; the night is far gone, the day is near. Let us then lay aside the works of darkness and put on the armor of light; let us live honorably as in the day, not in reveling and drunkenness, not in debauchery and licentiousness, not in quarreling and jealousy. Instead, put on the Lord Jesus Christ, and make no provision for the flesh, to gratify its desires. (Rom 13: 1–14)

Is it really plausible that Romans 13 represents a literature of protest against "the flourishing cult of the emperor," as Taubes argues, when the apostle undeniably exhorts his addresses in Rome to be subjected to the governing authorities—that is, the Roman Empire? How can a text that apparently obliges its listeners, probably mostly illiterate, to surrender themselves to a state authority be an expression of what Taubes claims to be "a *political* declaration of war against the Caesar"? How can one avoid reading Romans 13 as an endorsement of state power without reading the passage dishonestly?

One way to save the political and anti-imperial Paul from the obvious threat of the words of subjection (13:1) and its justification with the description of the imperial authorities as "God's servants" would be to support the hypothesis of 13:1–7 as an interpolation. It has been argued that the transition from 12:21 to 13:8 is less abrupt than the one from 12:21 to 13:1.[85] Taubes, like the majority of interpreters, does not, however, opt for such a solution.

The Genre and Purpose of Romans

The problem, however, is still there if one reads the Letter to the Romans as a theological treatise that communicates timeless religious doctrines. Such doctrines teach the believers how to act in the world, in spite of changing times and political circumstances. Thereby the passage is assimilated into, for instance, a Lutheran doctrine of the two kingdoms, which neutralizes much of the more dynamic and less calculable messianism of "the theologico-political fragment." Such a presupposition would lead one to read this passage as a peaceful, conforming statement and force it into an opposition or contradiction to statements in Paul that reflect a more hostile, nonconforming stance. One could point to 1 Corinthians where Paul writes about "the rulers of this age" (2:6) who had "crucified the Lord of Glory" (2:8) as an obvious contradiction to the apostle's peace agreement with the very same authorities who historically had the mandate to crucify, the Roman imperial authorities. While the apocalyptic tone in 1 Corinthians 2 might be set to express what Taubes called "a declaration of war," the nonapocalyptic tone in Romans 13 could be made to reflect a later peace agreement on Paul's part some years later, with the same authorities. In this way, Paul would indeed come out as a contradictory apostle, an image that to some degree resembles the one Taubes detected in his readings of 1 Corinthians.[86] All the same, such a reading of Romans 13 would transfer this neutralization or softening of the apocalyptic battle against worldly authorities and executioners of the Messiah into the text of Romans itself. It is not at all self-evident that this contradiction represents the best reading of the text. While Paul's apocalyptic thought may be differently expressed in Romans than in his earlier epistles, it is still hard to ignore its presence in Romans as well. For when the apostle in Romans 8:38 speaks of "the rulers" and "the powers," he still presents them as opponents to his own messianic belief.

As we have seen, Taubes is eager to falsify the assumption of a lessening and softening apocalypticism in Romans, compared to other epistles of Paul. For Taubes, Paul is an apocalypticist through and through. He fuels his argument with an appraisal of Barth's reading of 13:1–7 in the light of 12:19–21. As we will see, Barth's move can be further substantiated with readings of these chapters from contemporary research. But the presence of an apocalyptic Paul in 13:1–7 can also be argued for with insights from a kind of criticism that has been given increasing weight in New Testament scholarship during the last decades: rhetorical criticism.

In line with Taubes's suggestion that "philology . . . has a cathartic function vis-à-vis theology and philosophy,"[87] one may affirm that rhetorical criticism within New Testament scholarship can lead to more refined understandings of these ancient texts that challenge traditional theological assumptions about Paul.[88] While it is possible to argue for the value of the traditional thesis of Romans as a treatise or circular letter, the variety of subtypes of rhetorical forms at least modifies the view that there are no situational aspects to the letter at all. Besides, the existence of these subtypes (the paranetic letter, the hortatory letter, and the philosophical diatribe) can also be used to furnish the hypothesis of Romans as *primarily* a situational letter similar to the other letters of Paul. Romans is then treated less as an exception to the temporary character of Paul's concerns in the other letters. In that way the discussion of the meaning of passages in Romans is more receptive to the shifting historical circumstances, especially plausible historical realities, in the location of the letter's receivers. One need not privilege one single purpose as the overall concern of the whole text of Romans in order to appreciate this emphasis on the situational character of Paul's rhetoric in Romans. Instead of singling out the need for support for the mission in Spain or defending the vulnerable position of returned Jews in Rome after the expulsion, one can include a variety of such concerns in the interpretations of the letter. In the case of Romans 13, one may appreciate the apocalyptic and provisional context that Taubes, with Barth, draws out of the text without having chosen one theme or one overall purpose for the rhetorical efforts embodied in the letter.

The Provisional and Apocalyptic Character of Romans

Perhaps it is worth recalling that a scholar like John M. G. Barclay, who polemicizes against N. T. Wright's reading of an anti-imperial Paul, nonetheless emphasizes the apocalyptic and political aspects of Paul's texts. In his essay "Why the Roman Empire Was Insignificant to Paul," Barclay does not relegate this apocalypticism to an apolitical sphere. He is rather framing the political side to Paul's apocalypticism in a different manner:

> For these reasons, Paul's gospel is subversive of Roman imperial claims precisely by not opposing them within their own terms, but by reducing Rome's agency and historical significance to just one more entity in a much greater drama.[89]

In other words, Paul reduces Rome's significance through his apocalyptic drama. For Barclay, Paul manifests no interest in what is *Roman*. When Paul refers to powers within his apocalyptic framework, they are nameless, and there is no reason to link them up to Roman power as such. At the same time, Barclay sees no reason to distinguish between the way Paul speaks about powers in 1 Corinthians 2:8 and Romans 8:35–38 on the one hand and Romans 13:1–7 on the other.[90] They all fit into this larger drama, which has been intensified by the Christ event. Besides, the distinction of good and bad in Romans 13:3 and the concept of wrath in 13:4 also provide thematic bridges to the clearer apocalyptic ideology enacted in 12:19–21.[91] The argument for such a thematic bridge was the effect of Barth's "ingenious philological move," according to Taubes.

Moreover, Taubes's affirmation that Paul's "apocalyptic-eschatological profession of faith is unwavering" in "his great final letter" can be equipped with additional arguments acquired from readings of the wider section of the letter surrounding Romans 13:1–7.[92] Romans 12:1–15:13 may be read,[93] as is commonly done,[94] as the fourth proof of the letter's *propositio* or main thesis that God's justice has been revealed in Christ, first to Jew then to Gentile (1:16–17). This fourth proof is introduced by a description of the new manifestations of God's spirit in the mode of spiritual worship through a bodily sacrifice and a renewal of the conflicted and twisted human mind, which was a theme through chapters 1–8 (12:1–2). Paul appeals to the adherents of the new Christ-belief in Rome to live according to certain moral standards. Nevertheless, this is framed as a nonconformist existence. The believers are not to live according to standards set by this world, as that will be no sign of the transformation they have undergone in Christ:

> Do not be conformed to this world, but be transformed by the renewing of your minds, so that you may discern what is the will of God—what is good and acceptable and perfect. (12:2)

The next verses have a more paranetic character,[95] with focus on moral behavior. Paul appeals to this renewed kind of worship in one body of Christ, empowered by the charismatic gifts (12:3–7). But this renewed existence has been contrasted to the way of the world in 12:2. This contrasting and confrontational language, which resembles apocalyptic ideology, returns in 12:19 with the exhortation to "leave room for the wrath of God" (12:19). The theme of wrath was first introduced in 1:18 as a divine force or sanction against "all ungodliness and wickedness of those who by their wickedness suppress the truth." Thereby its function was primarily retributive, punishing the wrong-doers. The believers are here encouraged to let this divine retributive force operate. Paul does not refrain from using a militaristic language, typical of apocalyptic ideology as well as Roman propaganda about the *Pax Romana*, when employing the verb for conquering and being victorious in 12:21,[96] translated with "overcome" in NRSV: "Do not be overcome by evil, but overcome evil with good." Additionally, 12:20 speaks of how to behave toward enemies, with an ethics of hospitality.[97] In this way, the ethical guidelines put forward by Paul in chapter 12 are summed up eschatologically by the chapter's verses 19–21. In a parallel way, as we will see, 13:1–7 is also filled with eschatological meaning by the summarizing of 13:11–14.

Romans 13 as a Jewish Perspective on Gentile Rulers

Who are "the governing authorities" in Romans 13:1 to whom Paul expected the Christ believers to subject themselves? Taubes assumes that this refers to the Roman imperial authorities. But is Taubes's image of a Jewish apocalypticist who exhorts his followers or coagents in the apocalyptic drama to surrender themselves to "the rulers of this age" credible? And if Taubes is eager to emphasize Paul's Jewishness, would it not be more consistent to read "the authorities" (13:1) and "God's servant" (13:4) as Jewish authorities?

As has been demonstrated by Mark D. Nanos, it is possible to read Romans 13 as calling for submission to authorities within the Jewish diaspora synagogues in Rome. This would make sense in light of the supposed great number of Gentiles adhering to the Christ-believing community in

Rome, Paul's overall apologetic tone and privileged place for the Jew in the letter ("first to the Jew"), and the overall concern in the letter for the restoration of Israel. One could with Nanos suppose that the newly become Gentile believer would need guidance from the synagogue leadership as even the house meetings of the community were taking place under authority of the local synagogue. The "rulers," *archontes*, in 13:3 would then refer to those in charge in the synagogues to collect the Temple tax and ensure that members of the community fulfilled other communal obligations. The "fear" of these men would then reflect the true fear of God. This would provide a reasonable meaning for the expression "God's servant" in 13:4, as any member of the synagogue leadership would be recognized as the servant of God. The term *telos*, translated as "revenue" in the NRSV, may be instead translated with "custom" and rendered with the meaning of Judaic custom. Moreover, the term for "authorities" (*exousia*) in 13:1 is used by Luke in his gospel as well as in Acts to describe the synagogue authorities.[98] To submit to Jewish and not Gentile authorities could make a whole lot more sense to a Jewish Paul, particularly since the obedience has a character of being obligatory: "Let every person be subject."

Nonetheless, in 13:1 the word for "authorities" appears, unlike in Luke-Acts, with an adjectival participle: *hyperechousai*, which could mean "higher" or "governing." In addition, it is emphasized that they have been established or installed *tetagmenai* by God. Would there be the same need to emphasize that the synagogue leadership has authority from God? Would that not be self-evident for Paul's addresses? Or to argue with Taubes: Is it not the case that "these people [i.e., the Christ-believers] have no legitimation," and must therefore carefully negotiate a legitimate place socially and politically? Is it plausible that obedience to the synagogue leadership would have the same effect for legitimating a group proclaiming a crucified criminal as their Messiah?[99]

One could preserve Taubes's interpretation of these authorities as Roman political authorities and still emphasize the apostle's Jewishness in a direction not taken by Taubes himself. One may line up Romans 13 together with other Jewish perspectives from the Old Testament or texts from Second Temple Judaism and see continuity, as the problem of how to behave toward Gentile rulers was not foreign to Paul's Judaism. In Hebrew literature the motif of the rule of Israel's God over the Gentile nations is unfolded in several ways.[100] God gives mandates to human governments. Israelite rulers may face judgment if they are unfaithful to the Mosaic laws, and if Gentile kings persecute Jews the same destiny awaits them. It may be crucial to have in mind that the image of a God who has providential purposes with the Israelite people while this people is under foreign Gentile rule surges in the exilic traditions of this Hebrew literature. This is typical of the prophetic tradition that considers Gentile empires as arrogant but nonetheless as the sovereign God's instruments of wrath. In spite of the empires' arrogance and injustice, they nevertheless can function as God's servants in the sense of awakening the true Israel to return to pious observance of the law and its calls for justice.[101] As emphasized earlier (in chapter 4), some reasoning in the letter aims at explaining Israel's unfaithfulness with regard to Jesus the Messiah, articulated in the frame of a theodicy. Since reasoning reflecting a divine purpose for such a form of rejection of the divine plan is present in Romans 9–11 vis-à-vis Israel, one could also expect the frame to be at work in Romans 13 with regard to the role of the authorities of the empire.

Although there might be a hidden divine purpose with the role of the empire, as there is with the part of Israel that was "hardened" (11:7), this kind of providence should all the same not amount to a timeless doctrine. The reading does not imply that one necessarily has to regard this part of Israel as enemies or the Roman authorities as God's servants forever and in all circumstances. It merely points to an unknown divine plan behind realities that are humanly perceivable in the present. It does not inevitably result in a doctrine of absolute enmity (against Israel) or absolute obedience (toward governments).

Again, the occasional character of the letter can be made to contribute to safeguard against absolutist claims. This situational specificity of the letter also points to the historical situatedness of Paul's admonition. Although Taubes reads Romans 13 through other thinkers, his argument is also dependent upon a reconstruction of history.

Avoid the Danger of Persecution

When Taubes construes Paul as asking the believers in Rome to "demonstrate obedience to state authority" and not to "get involved in conflicts," the apostle asks this of them so they may not be "confused with some revolutionary movement, which, of course, is how it happened."[102] In Taubes's view these believers are even worse off politically than the Jews, since their societal role was at least legitimate as a *religio licita*. Thus the danger Taubes's Paul sees for these Christ believers is more severe. And Taubes finds a confirmation of this danger in the events in the aftermath of Romans; Paul "met his death in Rome under Nero as a result of some persecution."[103] Surely, in the year 64 some of the potential of conflict between the Christ believers and Rome that Taubes reads into Romans was realized. According to the Roman historian Tacitus, the "Christians" expressed a "hatred of the human race" (*odium generis humani*) and were accordingly viewed as enemies of the Neronian regime.[104]

Is this argument wholly dependent on historical findings and reconstructions, or is there something in the text of Romans 13 that could indicate that these words could serve the purpose or have the effect of avoiding armed revolution?

If one takes Romans 13:1–10 to be ethical prescriptions or exhortations to the community in Rome and 13:11–14 to be the eschatological framing of these guidelines for behavior, then one can read the call for submission as concrete and practical. Although this call, like the apocalyptic ideology, is expressed in a militaristic language, as we will see, its militarism refers not to cosmological battle but to concrete behavior in Rome. Paul's exhortation in 13:1 is expressed through the verb *hypotassestho*, which in the NRSV is translated as "be subject to." When applied to matters or conditions outside the Pauline assembly the military aspects of the term can more justifiably be appreciated. With these military connotations, the term meant "to line up under," "to place or rank under," or "to subordinate to."[105] It described the organizing of an effective military force in a battlefield.

A nonmilitary meaning of the term is also possible. In one of the pseudo-Pauline epistles the same verb is used, but for relations within the Christian community: "Be subject to one another out of reverence for Christ" (Eph 5:21). In Romans it deals with external relations for the community. Therefore, one can appreciate other aspects of this word's etymology when considering its meaning. This also strengthens the claim for the relevance of military connotations of another verb in the same passage, which is in 13:2: "Therefore whoever resists authority resists what God has appointed, and those who resist will incur judgment." Here the word for "resist" is *antitassomai*, and it is the only time it is used in the Pauline epistles.[106] It figures in a sentence that functions to reinforce the importance of the act of voluntarily subjecting oneself to the authorities with the threat of divine judgment against the one who disobeys Paul's exhortation. To resist is here the opposite of to subject oneself. The term was commonly applied to military situations of being placed in strategic positions as a soldier or constituting parts of an organized resistance, like an army, often against a supposed superior force.[107] What the passage attempts to avoid can therefore be said to include, at the very least, an armed uprising against "the governing authorities" in 13:1.[108] The etymology confirms Taubes's thesis of Romans 13 as a strategy, however much it failed in the year 64, against being perceived as a politically revolutionary group. Paul wanted them not to stand out, although he himself stood sufficiently out to be imprisoned by some provincial authorities, and the Christ-believers in Rome were perceived as a distinct group based on "a pernicious superstition."[109]

Such an argument is philological, but does not rely on the existence of the parallels in language between the Roman ideology and Pauline texts. Informed by the historical image of persecution of this group of Christ adherents in Rome, this reading of Paul leans itself more on the pole of the structural conflict in Peter Oakes's scheme than on the linguistic parallels. In Taubes's reading, the source of conflict appears to be the illegitimate role of the early Pauline movement, partly caused by the nature of their belief in the crucified and partly from the imperial order of beliefs that constituted a *religio licita* or not. Indeed, Taubes has emphasized Paul's conscious or intentional emphasis on kingly or imperial attributes that constitute an "anti-Caesar" proclamation in the beginning of the letter to the Romans.[110] First, such an approach may at some point be vulnerable or answerable to the objection of a "parallelomania."[111] Second, it does rely on the notion of the intentional meaning of texts, which has been under pressure and criticism in an academic environment where the author is presumed to be dead.[112] Third, it often presupposes a much contested notion of coding.[113] Fourth, Taubes had argued that Paul's texts constituted a protest against the cult of the emperor, but this is also a controversial claim in light of recent research.[114] Fifth, Taubes presupposed the existence of Roman censors.[115]

Taubes's reading of Romans 13, however, avoids all of these controversies, which are embedded in his construction of Pauline conspiracy in Romans 1. This helps to provide further evidence for his contradictory Paul: whereas his reading of Paul in Romans 1 relies on several controversial historical hypotheses, his reading of Paul in Romans 13 does not do so to the same degree. In Romans 13 the message is more straightforward and plain: subject yourselves and demonstrate obedience. There is no need for the hypothetical existence of parallels to Roman ideology, the hermeneutical legitimacy of an authorial intention, the plausibility of coding in the text, or the presence of censors as original auditors or original readers. Taubes's reading rather relies on the historical reconstruction of a community of believers in danger of persecution. And the temporal and provisional character that Taubes's Paul gives the governmental authorities that one should obey is not dependent on the contrast in the depiction of the same authorities in Roman ideology.[116] It can be sustained with emphasis on and reference to Paul's apocalypticism.

Conclusion: Constructive Appraisal of the Nietzshcean-Benjaminian Paul

Taubes's Paul is an apocalypticist who dreams of theocracy and the reinstallment of the Davidic Kingdom on earth in some or other form. In this sense he is a Nietzschean Paul who dreams of the destruction of Rome while construing his own form of oppositional power as nihilism. The doctrine of the cross is a mockery of the highest values, of what has come to be proclaimed as Roman values in the days of the Roman Empire. Such a Nietzschean apostle is not targeting Roman power because it is pagan, as N. T. Wright has argued. He resembles more the kind of indifferent Paul that John M. G. Barclay has posited. Of course, he condemns idolatry as part of his antiworldly nihilism. But if Nietzsche is to be taken as our best teacher and we are to read Paul with Taubes, this nihilism devalues all sources of valuation of any kind, including idolatry.

The strategic basis for the quietism Taubes has discerned in Romans 13 may be to some degree detectable in the Pauline text, as the possible military connotations have been pointed to earlier. But there may be more to the basis than just the pragmatic part of it. The whole basis of such a subjection that Taubes supposes with insights from Nietzsche, Barth, and Benjamin is, of course, not explicit in the text. For instance, Taubes is clear on the issue of the autonomy of the secular he takes from Benjamin—that this is absent in Paul. But Taubes's Paul points in a direction, and Benjamin follows. Paul takes the lead when he presupposes a world in decay, including an empire in decay, and encourages the Christ believers in Rome to give room for the wrath that is targeting all worldly injustice, until it is destroyed:

> I contend that this concept of nihilism, as developed here by Benjamin, is the guiding thread also to the *hōs mē* in Corinthians and Romans. The world decays, the *morphē* of this world has passed. Here, the relationship to the world is, as the young Benjamin understands it, world politics as nihilism. And that is something that Nietzsche understood, that behind all this there is a profound nihilism at work, that it is at work as world politics, toward the destruction of the Roman Empire.[117]

Although Paul is nineteen centuries from developing a notion of the secular as Benjamin's, it appears to be a thought in Romans 12:21, which can serve to make room for a similar messianic attitude toward the secular. In Taubes's words, "let it go down," as if the right posture or "world politics" for a messianic community is to know the moment for when to act and when to remain passive, in order to make no investments in the world as it is.[118] The aptness of Benjamin's "Fragment" to Paul's thought is indicated if one recognizes Paul as a theocratic thinker who knows no distinctions between the secular and religious and is far from developing any doctrine of the two such spheres. The profane is not in itself a category of Paul's messianic Kingdom. Nonetheless, he is an apocalypticist for whom the apocalyptic theocratic dreams are moderated or adjusted in the light of the crucifixion of the Messiah. The world of decay in which the believer is not to intervene immediately, continuously, or zealously "is a decisive category of its quietest approach." The believer has to expect the Kingdom and indeed the Second Coming, and in this quietist expectation it has to leave room for the wrath. For out of this world targeted by the wrath (Paul's profane) is the Kingdom to arise. Through this expectation the believer is to wake from sleep (13:11) and be alert to the mystical messianic understanding of history, as Benjamin teaches. Only through such a mystical awareness can one discern "the direction of the Messianic intensity" in relation to "the quest of free humanity for happiness," in the words of Benjamin. As this quest can run counter to the messianic direction, it can also "increase another that is acting in the opposite direction, so the order of the profane assists, through being profane, the coming of the Messianic Kingdom."[119] In a world where one cannot rely on and trust governmental structures as fixed on the side of the messianic, one must be alert and attentive to the revelation of signs of the coming of the Kingdom.

As suggested, there are resources within chapter 13 of the Letter to the Romans to further strengthen and legitimize Jacob Taubes's reading of the text. His Nietzschean Paul, blended with Barth's quietism and Benjamin's messianism, stands on some biblical grounds. Taubes's reading is not simply a philosophical projection from outside of the Pauline texts. It has roots within them.

Taubes's understanding of the imperial is to a large extent based on the work of Dieter Georgi, a New Testament exegete and classicist. Georgi provides an interpretation of the historical anti-imperial Paul that Taubes tests against and blends with Nietzsche's interpretation of Paul as an apocalypticist who dreams of the destruction of the Roman Empire and founds a community of social outcasts that are disposed toward violations of Roman and Jewish law alike.

This chapter has argued for the strength of Taubes's political reading of Romans, first and foremost with a basis in his reading of Romans 13 and with the extended recourse to the "exegetes" to whom Taubes himself points in his lectures: Nietzsche, Barth, and Benjamin. The possible contradiction between Taubes's reading of Romans 1 and 13 is not eradicated by this appraisal. Taubes's reading of Romans 13 suggests that Paul's epistles were not some kind of unequivocal anti-imperial resistance literature, although Taubes's reading of Romans 1 may have pointed in that direction. The apparent tension between Taubes's readings of the two chapters results in an image of an apostle whose thought is not entirely consistent. Once again, Taubes has constructed an image of a contradictory Paul.

Peter Oakes suggests two poles around which scholars may anchor claims about the linkage between Pauline theology and Roman ideology; either one accounts for such a relation in terms of the similarities of language, or one probes into it through assumptions of a structural relationship.[120] If we return to Peter Oakes's scheme we can conclude that Taubes moves from one pole to the other for making the Nietzschean scenario of a deadly contradiction between Pauline Christianity and the Roman Empire plausible. In reading Romans 1 Taubes primarily revolves around the linguistic parallels for demonstrating the inherent conflict in the relation between the Roman and the Pauline, while in his reading of Romans 13 he argues more historically for a conflict between the two. In his reading of the quietism in chapter 13 as nihilism one can also perceive that this reading resembles the position of John M. G. Barclay rather than N. T. Wright in the heated scholarly discussion about the relation between Paul and empire on the contemporary academic scene. This is where Nietzsche meets Barclay, with Taubes as the intermediary. And here they seem to agree on all three: Paul founded the ideology that came to be known as Christianity.[121] They all have their own attempts of making a case for Paul as the innovator of Christian ideology, which Barclay summarizes in the following way:

> It was a combination of exclusivity with the Christian drive towards homogeneity, and its creation of a totalising ideology (uniting, myth, ritual and philosophy), that created something genuinely new in the Roman world, not just a new cult, competing for adherents on the same term as others, but a "new social and conceptual system, a new ideology of religion." This new ideology did not just challenge Caesar's claims, it offered a radical alternative to the structures of Roman religion and thus Roman civilization as a whole. . . . Paul has a good claim to be the founding ideologue.[122]

Taubes's notion of Paul as an incoherent thinker is once again confirmed with his political readings of Romans 1 and Romans 13, since these readings stand in considerable tension with one another.

Conclusion

This work was guided by inquiries about Jacob Taubes's methodological approaches to Paul in addition to the question about how Paul's texts might be understood through the background of Taubes's readings of them. One of the presuppositions behind this study has been that studies in reception can help us attain a deeper understanding not only of subsequent readings, but also of the received texts. In this way, twentieth-century European critical thought casts light upon an ancient apostle.

The Power of Texts: What Can Paul Do for the Philosopher?

In Jacob Taubes's intellectual engagements Paul becomes a figure through whom the philosopher can discern a true agreement with his enemies. Taubes does so most extensively with Friedrich Nietzsche. As seen in Chapter 3, Taubes uses resources in 1 Corinthians to argue that the revolution Nietzsche perceives in this Pauline letter and fights against is contained in the letter's doctrine of the cross (1 Cor 1:20). This helps us gain a deeper understanding and recognition of the countercultural forces that may be unleashed from this letter, revolving around what Taubes calls "the ugliness of the cross." Unlike Nietzsche, however, Taubes also finds counterforces to this revolution of ancient perception within the same letter, most markedly in 2:6. In this way his reading broadens our understanding of the ambiguities of this letter. All the same, with Nietzsche he cultivates the opposition between this Pauline ugliness of the crucified victim and the noble aesthetic beauty of the aristocracy. This Pauline ugliness is then mobilized to rehabilitate the insights of Carl Schmitt and to devaluate Theodor Adorno's aesthetic redemption and Hans Blumenberg's optimistic account of modern aesthetics. In this way, Paul serves for Taubes to navigate within these contemporary discussions; the Pauline texts have capacities to orient this reader within the twentieth-century German intellectual world that preceded and proceeded the Shoah.

Paul provides a lens for Taubes to reconsider the Christian culture in which his Jewish identity was formed and his people were persecuted and murdered. Paul's Jewish confidence in the election and the centrality of the Hebrew Bible in Paul's letters become important factors for Taubes to discern the type of Christianity that did not "stand the test" when Nazism arrived in Germany: liberal Protestantism. Through Paul, Taubes establishes a more complex relationship between Judaism and Christianity. By considering Paul as a Jewish antinomian, Taubes can use Paul the Jew to deconstruct the opposition between Christian individualistic and ahistorical salvation and Jewish collectivistic and historical messianism: the pattern Taubes had detected in Scholem's account on the messianic idea and thereafter attacked. Nonetheless, as one of the main messianic thinkers in history for Taubes, Paul can be used to effectively disturb the conventional views about the fundamental difference between Judaism and Christianity that Taubes attempts to target.

Taubes appropriates motifs from within the mainly Christian reception history of Paul and uses them to argue for Paul's Jewishness. The potentialities especially of the letter to the Romans to be actualized as motifs (such as the abrogation of the law), the text as autobiographical, and the text as a document of introspective consciousness can each be used to argue for Paul's letters as expressions of a specifically Jewish collective experience in history. Moreover, Paul's letters can be useful for discerning or hypothesizing about Pauline influences in Nietzsche and Freud. Such hypotheses of a Jewish legacy in Christianity and a religious legacy of critical thought in modernity serve Taubes to deconstruct antithetical relationships and oppositions between Judaism and Christianity as well as between premodern religion and modern secularity.

This book has explored Taubes's idiosyncratic readings of Paul. In this exploration, however, other possibilities of reading the same texts of Paul as read by Taubes have been made manifest with the help of other layers in the reception. Taubes has actualized some potentialities in these Pauline texts, while this study has actualized even more of them in order to broaden the picture. Through the demonstration of such diverse capacities of the text of Romans as seen here, it has become clearer how Romans can generate not only diverse but also contradictory meanings in diverse contexts, guided by different purposes and interests. Romans can work to argue for individual as well as collective emphases, and its elements can be used to argue for Paul's antinomianism as well as Paul's lawfulness. In a similar way, Taubes's readings have drawn attention to the anti-Semitic potential of this letter, actualized in the Nazi era. Nonetheless, Taubes's own close reading, which emphasizes Paul's Jewish adherence to the election and the privileges of Israel, provides extensive resources against this very same anti-Semitism.

The political readings of Paul in Taubes manifest the possibility of reading Romans not as an expression of Christian enmity toward Jews, but as a protest from a Jew who stands against the political power that executed his Messiah. Chapter 9 shows how Romans is, once again in Taubes, used to make the Nietzschean conflict between Pauline assemblies and the Roman Empire plausible. Romans 1 and 13 function to reflect on the problem of theocracy and political theology, and with the Nietzschean category of nihilism Romans 13 can be made into an argument for political enmity rather than political submission. Once again, Paul's texts function to protest against the exploitation of his legacy during the Nazi era. Once more Paul is used to come to terms with history, to understand history. This is done by activating various layers of reception, an act that results in unexpected and improbable encounters—for instance, between Paul and Benjamin.

Furthermore, these are texts that readers often encounter with presuppositions about the past, the historical.

History and Philosophy

Jacob Taubes declares that what he is up to when reading Paul through the prism of other thinkers is to understand history. He laments the lack of biblical knowledge within departments of philosophy and calls for a deeper engagement between biblical scholarship and philosophy, which in a way is anticipated by his own readings of Paul. With this interdisciplinary engagement Taubes's readings not only possess the ability to deconstruct some of the reception history of Paul, but also to destabilize stable oppositions between the abstract nature of philosophy and the empirical solidity of historical science. In the competitive play of images of the originary in relation to religion described by Ward Blanton in his *Displacing Christian Origins*,[1] Taubes may be said to wittingly play these images against each other in remarks such as the one where he asserts the unsurpassable historical insight of Nietzsche in his discussion of 1 Corinthians and New Testament exegetes. By reading Paul with a New Testament scholar in one moment and a philosopher in the other, Taubes's readings attack what Blanton calls the "the excessive nature" of the opposition of the disciplines of philosophy and history. Furthermore, by activating layers of reception from both disciplinary orientations, Taubes brings these layers to the fore in a manner that exposes various cultural assumptions about Paul's texts and his legacy. Taubes's readings as a whole, however, are not merely a documentation of the reception history of Paul. His readings constitute efforts to understand Paul's texts themselves. In that way they can potentially defy or be outbid by philosophical, theological, and historical readings alike. They remain vulnerable to charges from various disciplinary angles and perspectives. On the one hand, it has been one of the objectives of this study to make some of the vulnerabilities evident, as for instance by measuring the plausibility of the philosophers' antinomian Paul. On the other, it has been an objective to highlight the original and idiosyncratic in these readings. Although Taubes has hailed Nietzsche as his best teacher on Paul, he only follows Nietzsche halfway. Moreover, in the moments when Nietzsche discerns a conflict between himself and Paul, Taubes sides with Paul. Taubes's selective appraisal of Nietzsche shares a feature with Derrida's deconstructionism. It is not so much about appreciating Nietzsche's philosophical project as it is about reactualizing the deconstructive force of philology and polemics. These are both fundamental components of the Talmudic reasoning that Sergey Dolgopolski, inspired by poststructuralism and deconstruction, has labeled "the art of disagreement." Through Paul, Taubes has reached a truer disagreement with Nietzsche. This constitutes one of his major intellectual achievements.

Religion and Secularity

Ward Blanton has suggested that in the texts of Hegel, Strauss, and Heidegger, "the Pauline legacy was often a secularizing one."[2] This pattern is also seen in some of the recent philosophical engagements with Paul, as in the case of Slavoj Žižek. As a self-declared Hegelian Žižek repeats this pattern in the sense that his readings of Paul are attempts at purifying religion in order to extract and save its revolutionary "kernel" for his Christian atheism and leftist political activism. His readings of Paul consist of efforts to philosophically secure the Pauline legacy for secular practices, such as psychoanalysis and politics. As such they constitute persistent attempts of secularizing Paul through secular formalizations of Paul's religious content. When Žižek proclaims that one has to go through the Christian experience described by Paul in order to become a true materialist, he confirms his confidence in the secular *exodus* out of religion. He confesses his belief in the possibility and benefits from a pure secularization of a religious figure like Paul. According to Žižek, modern reason can make use of the religious passion of Paulinism. Pauline religion can be purified through secularity. Paul may be used to further and persistently save religion from itself. Paul can continue to secularize.

Alain Badiou follows this program when he claims that his reading of Paul allows him to "extract a formal, wholly secularized conception of grace from the mythological core."[3] The premise that such an extraction, purification, or restoration of the religious mythology to a formalized secularity for our days is possible and desirable is also operative in Giorgio Agamben's work on Paul. Since Agamben claims to retrieve a formal logic from the Jewish messianism of Paul, the Italian philosopher also attempts to secularise Paul. Agamben wants Paul's messianism without Paul's Messiah, Jesus Christ.

Jacob Taubes makes no efforts to use Paul in order to explicitly distance himself from religion as such. He depicts himself as a "Paulinist" and an "apocalypticist from below," inverting the Schmittian scenario of a global civil war between friends and enemies. In stark contrast to Badiou and Žižek, Taubes affirms that he has never cared to be "modern" while polemicizing against what he considers to be "Bultmannian naivités."[4]

Rudolf Bultmann's program of demythologization within New Testament studies has had a powerful secularizing effect on readings of the New Testament as a sacred text of Christianity. This program claimed to possess the ability to liberate the biblical texts from their mythological representations of the world and grasp the demythologized content or existentialist message of the very same texts.

Taubes's maneuver goes, in a way, in the opposite direction of Badiou's and Žižek's Bultmannianism.[5] Taubes aims at discerning the religious and apocalyptic influences on modern philosophy that to him seemed neglected. Rather than to secularize Paul, he detects the Pauline in modern thought. In that way he aims at revealing how the mythological or apocalyptic is still at work in modern thinkers, perhaps against what is explicitly expressed in the texts of these thinkers. When Taubes reads Nietzsche and Freud, for instance, he emphasizes their very dependence on the supposedly Christian and religious figure of Paul. The Pauline influences and shadows that these masters of suspicion sometimes displace to the margins, Taubes places at the center, for instance when he declares that Freud is "a direct descendant of Paul."[6] If Freud adheres to the Pauline doctrine of original guilt more radically than anyone else after Augustine, then Freud's Jewish science may not be that Jewish after all.

Daniel Boyarin has described the common sources of Judaism and Christianity as one "territory":

> Rather than a natural-sounding "parting of the ways," such as we usually hear about with respect to these two "religions," I will suggest an imposed partitioning of what was once a territory without border lines, much as India and Pakistan, and Israel and Palestine were artificially partitioned by a colonial power.[7]

With his Jewish introspective Paul, Jacob Taubes is not attempting to purify either Judaism or Christianity of foreign elements. Rather, he is contaminating both by inhabiting the borderlines themselves through idiosyncratic readings of both. For him Judaism is a land that Freudianism and Paulinism cohabit, only superficially partitioned into "science" and "faith" or into "secularity" and "religion." True Christianity—that is, Pauline Christianity—is in Taubes's view a Jewish science.[8]

Taubes adheres to the idea of a continuous messianic tradition in history, with a messianic idea that can be channeled anywhere and break out at any point, without any regard for borders between Judaism and Christianity or between modernity and religion. Time can get dense at any point in history.

The philosopher also contributes to the notion that something is at stake for modernity in relation to the name "Paul." One can with Jacques Derrida be utterly suspicious toward the notion of a simple "return to religion" in today's world,[9] and at the same time observe how many discussions about the presumed "return" take place with reference to the "turn to Paul" within continental philosophy. Philosophers such as Alain Badiou, Giorgio Agamben, Eric Santner, and Simon Critchley do not engage with the gospels, the book of Revelation, the Acts, or the Hebrew Bible.[10] They engage with Paul's epistles. It is as if "Paul" has become a name for "scripture" or, even more broadly, "religion." The questions about the possible relevance of religious thought for philosophy are to a remarkable degree posed through an interrogation of Paul's legacy. Why Paul? Let me suggest one possible explanation.

Taubes considers Paul as an antinomian. One semantic node of Paul's letters may be said to be "freedom from law," which explains some of Taubes's attraction to Paul. Although arguments have been laid out in this book against the reading of Paul as an antinomian, it should also be recognized that this radical antinomian dimension is not simply projected unto the Pauline legacy. There are elements in the texts that can be appropriated and used to generate such readings. In other words, there are multiple meanings that may be generated from these texts, since any reading actualizes some potentialities and leaves others behind.

Readings of Paul that have emphasized the theme of "freedom from law" have contributed to a relativizing and profanation of law in Western thought. When Taubes sees parallels between Paul on one hand and Nietzsche and Freud on the other it is particularly with regard to the law. They all seek ways of suspending the law in his reading. Already in Paul there is a profanation of the law. In the words of Mika Ojakangas, "Paul paves the way for a purely instrumental view of the world in which the category of usefulness replaces the sacred/holy as the measure of value."[11] Within this conception of history Paul becomes one of the founding fathers of modernity in which law has no value in itself but is measured out of humankind's autonomous evaluation of its reasonability. Grappling with modernity, conscious of its Christian and predominantly Protestant prehistory, the philosophers cannot help but inquire into the legacy of Paul. They cannot help but hear the name "Paul" when they address questions of law and of religion.

The Afterlife of Taubes's Paul

The name "Paul" rings clearly in the work of Giorgio Agamben, and the Italian's work manifests the most influential appraisal of Taubes's Paul in the years that have followed the Heidelberg lectures. Although Agamben builds further on Taubes's reading of the *hos me* passage of 1 Corinthians 7:29, he ignores Taubes's call at the end of the 1987 lectures to interpret Paul anew in the light of Freud's *Moses and Monotheism*. One could imagine Slavoj Žižek dwelling on Freud's speculations on Paul in this obscene work of the founder of psychoanalysis, but Žižek never really hears Taubes's call or Freud's words about the apostle. When the Slovenian uses *Moses and Monotheism* it is never with the aim of understanding Paul.[12] While Agamben's work constitutes the most influential reception of Taubes's Paul, Ward Blanton's recent work *A Materialism for the Masses* (2014) can be said to be the most extensive and relevant one. Already in the title Blanton alludes to Nietzsche, and he begins his discussion by quoting *Moses and Monotheism*. If Taubes is the forerunner to the mentioned contemporary philosophers, Blanton is perhaps the first among them to think through the conditions of a philosophy of Paul with Taubes.

Like Taubes's Paul, Blanton's Paul is a figure that has been repressed by the ideological apparatus that Nietzsche termed "Platonism for the masses." In that way, Blanton follows Taubes in tying his reading of Paul to Nietzsche without accepting the Nietzschean premise about Paul as the source and beginning of popularized metaphysical dualisms and supersessionist anti-Judaisms. Like Taubes, Blanton appropriates Nietzsche's readings of Paul but follows the thinker of the will to power only halfway. Beneath the Christendom that sustains itself through a vulgar Christianized Platonism Blanton finds a partisan Jewish apostle identified with the undying life of the crucified:

> Nietzsche mistook Paul's partisanship with the crucified, his siding with that scandalously failed messiah or his refusal to let the suppressed messiah remain dead, as a bid for a metaphysical guarantee.[13]

This perspective indebted to Taubes is further developed when Blanton turns to Freud who, unlike Nietzsche, approaches Paul as an ambivalent figure within reception history potentially able to question Western cultural memory about its Christian origins.[14]

The rereading of Paul on the background of Freud's *Moses and Monotheism* that Agamben fails to perform is powerfully demonstrated in Blanton's strategy of regarding Paul as a type of Freud's Moses. For Blanton the name of Paul that still functions as "the organizational *apparatus* of Western culture" must be interrogated as if this name were the ghostly symptom of a brutal act of repression in the manner of Freud's Moses. Blanton is one of the very few in recent discussions to have actually heard Taubes's call for a paradigmatic shift of understanding of Paul based on dubious Freudian speculations from 1939. Attuned to a kind of deconstructive reasoning inherent in Taubes's works, Blanton demonstrates how we productively can dig into Freud's and Nietzsche's writings about this ancient author and inventor of the doctrine of the cross and, by way of these new genealogies, produce new meanings from within this powerful apparatus of the reception history of Paul. The desire to cultivate aesthetic beauty may be greater than the call to identify with Pauline ugliness. But the call can still be heard.

Acknowledgments

I am profoundly thankful for invaluable help from a number of people during my work with this book. In my first year as a student at the Faculty of Theology at the University of Oslo, the minister and professor Oddbjørn Leirvik established a new paradigm for us as future ministers of the Church of Norway with the then groundbreaking practice and study of interreligious dialogue in a North European context marked by increasing religious pluralism. More than anyone else at the time, Leirvik inspired us to actively engage with religious otherness, and in that way he led me to concerns about Jewish-Christian relations, which I came to explore through the philosophy of Emmanuel Levinas.

I am still filled with everlasting gratitude for the existential meditations on Levinas's philosophy that Asbjørn Aarnes (1923–2013) led us through at his seminars at our faculty. When I arrived in Brazil as a student at Faculdade Jesuíta de Filosofia e Teologia in Belo Horizonte, I felt privileged to pursue my interest in Levinas enlightened by stimulating conversations with Nilo Ribeiro Jr., and was sparked into a deeper engagement with modern Jewish thought.

When I approached Halvor Moxnes some years later with an idea of approaching and reflecting upon the turn to Paul within continental philosophy from the angle of biblical studies, I was immediately met with the generosity and enthusiasm I already knew from the time I stood on the shoulder of this giant of New Testament studies as a young student of his seminars at the Faculty of Theology in Oslo. His initial support was crucial for making this interdisciplinary Ph.D. project possible and led me to the outstanding reader and supervisor Jorunn Økland. I had already been impressed by her work on critical theorists as a New Testament scholar, and her unique skills and academic model still serve as a deep inspiration for me, comparable only to the inspirational influence that the interdisciplinary biblical scholar Ward Blanton still has on my work in this field.

When it comes to Jacob Taubes, Blanton gave me vital encouragement and some indispensable keys to Taubes's peculiar intellectual world. The eminent speakers at the international conference on Jacob and Susan Taubes at the University of California (UCLA) in 2013. I am filled with gratitude for being invited by Kenneth Reinhard to this unique conference; its speakers proved to be indispensable for a deeper understanding of these intellectual figures, Jacob and Susan Taubes.

Finally, I want to thank Marianne Bjelland Kartzow for confronting me with the right questions about biblical reception at just the right time, Vemund Blomkvist for wise suggestions during the writing process, and Gitte Buch-Hansen for carefully and critically evaluating parts of the work present in this book. Thanks to Marius Timmann Mjaaland for raising key issues in political theology during these years, to Hugo Lundhaug for expertise on early Christian literature, to Karin Neutel for considering parts of this text with Dutch honesty, to Karmen MacKendrick for reading the whole manuscript in such a critical and enlightening manner, and to Jayne Svenungsson for pushing me further with her well-founded interventions and interrogations concerning normativity in my academic work.

I would also like to express my gratitude to the constructive peer reviewer who helped me broaden the scope of and improve this text. You have all contributed to this book on Jacob Taubes's readings of Paul in ways that you could not foresee, and for which I am therefore wholly responsible.

Notes

Introduction

1. Originally Jacob Taubes, *Die Politische Theologie des Paulus* (Munich: Wilhelm Fink, 1993); translated into English as *The Political Theology of Paul* (Stanford, Calif.: Stanford University Press, 2004).

2. To these four we could add names such as Eric Santner and Simon Critchley, to name a few widely read thinkers whose philosophizing was spurred by this turn to Paul.

3. Giorgio Agamben, *The Time That Remains: A Commentary on the Letter to the Romans* (Stanford, Calif.: Stanford University Press, 2005), 3.

4. Žižek declares Taubes's Heidelberg lectures to be "outstanding"; Slavoj Žižek, *Revolution at the Gates: A Selection of Writings from February to October 1917* (2002; repr. London: Verso, 2004), 316.

5. Hent de Vries, *Philosophy and the Turn to Religion* (Baltimore: Johns Hopkins University Press, 1999), 187–88, n. 28.

6. English translation in Jacob Taubes, *From Cult to Culture: Fragments Towards a Critique of Historical Reason* (Stanford, Calif.: Stanford University Press, 2010), 76–97.

7. Through his whole career Taubes published only one book, *Occidental Eschatology*. That was his doctoral thesis. He wrote some essays, most of which are published in the compilation *From Cult to Culture*. But what he wrote the most were letters.

8. Taubes, *Political Theology of Paul*, 5.

9. Michel Foucault, "The Order of Discourse," in *Untying the Text: A Post-Structuralist Reader*, ed. Robert Young (Boston: Routledge & Kegan Paul, 1981), 52–56.

10. Ibid., 56.

11. As Foucault underlines, there is no stable relation and absolute limit between the primary and secondary texts in commentaries; ibid., 57.

12. "One must *accentuate* the 'naivité' of a breakthrough which cannot attempt a step outside of metaphysics, which cannot *criticize* metaphysics radically without still utilizing in a certain way, in a certain type or a certain style of *text*, propositions that, read within the philosophical corpus, that is to say according to Nietzsche ill-read or unread, have always been and will always be 'naivités,' incoherent signs of an absolute appurtenance"; Jacques Derrida, *Of Grammatology* (1976; repr. Baltimore: Johns Hopkins University Press, 1997), 19.

13. Foucault, *The Essential Works of Michel Foucault, 1954–1984* (London: Penguin, 2000), 2:369.

14. As Derrida cannot accept the premise that there is a horizon of meaning as thought or representation that precedes language and governs communication, he confesses that "I am not convinced that we ever really have this experience that professor Gadamer describes, of knowing in dialogue that one has been perfectly understood or experiencing the success of confirmation"; Derrida, "Three Questions to Hans-Georg Gadamer," in *Dialogue and Deconstruction: The Gadamer-Derrida Encounter*, ed. Diane P. Michelfelder and Richard E. Palmer (Albany: State University of New York Press, 1989), 54.

15. Gadamer's principle of *wirkungsgeshichte* has been of central importance for the turn to reception in biblical studies inaugurated by Ulrich Luz, among others; Timothy Beal, "Reception History and Beyond: Toward the Cultural History of Scriptures," *Biblical Interpretation* 19, no. 4 (2011): 363; Mark Knight, "Wirkungsgeschichte, Reception History, Reception Theory," *Journal for the Study of the New Testament* 33, no. 2 (2010): 138.

16. Ward Blanton, *Displacing Christian Origins: Philosophy, Secularity, and the New Testament* (Chicago: University of Chicago Press, 2007), 18.

17. Brennan W. Breed, *Nomadic Text: A Theory of Biblical Reception History* (Bloomington: Indiana University Press, 2014), 3.

18. Ibid., 4.

19. Ibid., 100.

20. Ibid.

21. Jorunn Økland, "Setting the Scene: The End of the Bible, the End of the World," in *The Way the World Ends: The Apocalypse of John in Culture and Ideology*, ed. William John Lyons and Jorunn Økland (Sheffield: Sheffield Phoenix Press, 2009), 25.

22. Breed, *Nomadic Text*, 142.

23. Taubes, *Die Politische Theologie des Paulus*; Taubes, *Political Theology of Paul*.

24. Susan Taubes, *Die Korrespondenz mit Jacob Taubes 1950–1951: Herausgegeben und Kommentiert von Christina Pareigis* (Paderborn: Wilhelm Fink, 2011); *Die Korrespondenz mit Jacob Taubes 1952: Herausgegeben und Kommentiert von Christina Pareigis* (Paderborn: Fink, 2013).

25. Breed, *Nomadic Text*, 141.

26. Heikki Räisänen, "The 'Effective History' of the Bible," in *Challenges to Biblical Interpretation: Collected Essays, 1991–2000*, ed. Heikki Räisänen (Leiden: E. J. Brill, 2001), 276–79.

1. The Historical and the Philosophical: A Contemporary Scene

1. Brennan W. Breed, *Nomadic Text: A Theory of Biblical Reception History* (Bloomington: Indiana University Press, 2014), 100.

2. In the words of Roland Boer in the afterword to Negri's commentary on the book of Job, "Eisegesis and exegesis are inseparable: the heuristic framework with which one begins reading invariably wobbles and changes shape in the face of the text's own words and sentences"; Antonio Negri, *The Labor of Job: The Biblical Text as a Parable of Human Labor*, trans. Michael Hardt (Durham, N.C.: Duke University Press, 2009), 113.

3. Paula Fredriksen, "Historical Integrity, Interpretative Freedom: The Philosopher's Paul and the Problem of Anachronism," in *St. Paul among the Philosophers*, ed. John D. Caputo and Linda Martín Alcoff (Bloomington: Indiana University Press, 2009), 61.

4. "Consider the remarkable awkwardness of one of the earliest of the extraordinarily important recent encounters between Pauline scholars and Continental philosophers, that staged by John D. Caputo as *St. Paul among the Philosophers*"; Ward Blanton, "Mad with the Love of Undead Life," in *Paul in the Grip of the Philosophers: The Apostle and Contemporary Continental Philosophy* (Minneapolis: Fortress Press, 2013), 211. "The historians and philosophers for most part talked past each other"; Sarah Hammerschlag, "Bad Jews, Authentic Jews, Figural Jews," in *Judaism, Liberalism, and Political Theology*, ed. Randi Rashkover and Martin Kavka (Bloomington: Indiana University Press, 2014), 231.

5. The responses from Dale Martin and Daniel Boyarin belong to these exceptions.

6. Fredriksen, "Historical Integrity, Interpretative Freedom," 61–62.

7. Notice that Fredriksen's focus is on the author and not the text.

8. Fredriksen, "Historical Integrity, Interpretative Freedom," 62.

9. Ibid.

10. An expression from Jacques Derrida, "Faith and Knowledge: The Two Sources of 'Religion' at the Limits of Reason Alone," in *Acts of Religion*, ed. Gil Anidjar (New York: Routledge, 2002), 43.

11. Blanton, *Displacing Christian Origins: Philosophy, Secularity, and the New Testament* (Chicago: University of Chicago Press, 2007), 9.

12. At the occasion of this conference at Syracuse in 2005 Sanders was interviewed about the academic event. Sophie Fuggle made the eloquent observation that "E. P. Sanders is engaging in a similar exercise of superiority when he implicitly compares Badiou's reading of Paul to the church sermons he has come to find so unbearable in light of his own context-enriched New

Testament scholarship"; Fuggle, "Negotiating Paul: Between Philosophy and Theology," *Paragraph* 31, no. 3 (2008): 368.

13. Blanton, *Displacing Christian Origins*, 17.

14. Alain Badiou, *Saint Paul: The Foundation of Universalism* (Stanford, Calif.: Stanford University Press, 2003), 66.

15. Slavoj Žižek, *The Puppet and the Dwarf: The Perverse Core of Christianity* (Cambridge, Mass.: MIT Press, 2003), 6.

16. Blanton, *Displacing Christian Origins*, 7. For one of the latest manifestations of this spiral, see Adam Y. Wells, *Phenomenologies of Scripture* (New York: Fordham University Press, 2017).

17. Blanton, *Displacing Christian Origins*, 17.

18. Ibid., 4.

19. Jacob Taubes, *The Political Theology of Paul* (Stanford, Calif.: Stanford University Press, 2004), 2.

20. Ibid., 4.

21. Ibid, 4.

22. Ibid., 5.

23. Taubes, *From Cult to Culture: Fragments Towards a Critique of Historical Reason* (Stanford, Calif.: Stanford University Press, 2010), 76–97. The essay derives from a presentation in the "Poetik und Hermeneutik" research group in 1966, but since the text that is discussed here was published two years after this meeting it will be referred to as "the 1968 essay."

24. Ibid., 77.

25. See "Method: The Art of True Disagreement," in Chapter 3.

26. Taubes's bibliography has the title from the 1913 edition, *Geschichte der Leben-Jesu-Forschung*; Taubes, *Occidental Eschatology* (Stanford, Calif.: Stanford University Press, 2009), 214.

27. Franz Rosenzweig, *The Star of Redemption* (Notre Dame, Ind.: Notre Dame Press, 1985), 102.

28. David N. Myers, *Resisting History: Historicism and Its Discontents in German-Jewish Thought* (Princeton, N.J.: Princeton University Press, 2003), 8.

29. Rosenzweig, *Star of Redemption*, 98–100.

30. Taubes, *Occidental Eschatology*, 13.

31. Taubes, *Political Theology of Paul*, 21.

32. "But at the moment of cultural civil war—this is something I also want to profess from the outset—I made—let this be clear—a clear choice. It was the student movement, no big deal, but it was something"; ibid., 98.

33. "Well, we're living in the evil Roman Empire. . . . Sure it's evil [*böse*], but—what are you going to do? I know this sort of mentality. It's not at all foreign to me. I have a passport. But what do I have to do with my country beyond my passport? My president's name is Reagan. Do I strike you as very American?"; ibid., 40–41. "I can imagine as an apocalyptic: let it go down. I have no spiritual investment in the world as it is"; ibid., 103. This disillusioned

Taubes is also observed by Agata Bielik-Robson, "Modernity: The Jewish Perspective," *New Blackfriars* 94, no. 1050 (2013): 206.

2. Jacob Taubes's Path to Paul: From the Eschatologist to the Paulinist

1. Jacob Taubes, *The Political Theology of Paul* (Stanford, Calif.: Stanford University Press, 2004), 3.
2. As the editors of the publication of Taubes's lecture also point out; ibid., 115.
3. Ibid., 2.
4. Taubes, *To Carl Schmitt: Letters and Reflections* (New York: Columbia University Press, 2013), 20.
5. Ibid., 22.
6. Taubes, *Occidental Eschatology* (Stanford, Calif.: Stanford University Press, 2009), 64.
7. Martin Treml, "Reinventing the Canonical: The Radical Reading of Jacob Taubes," in *"Escape to Life": German Intellectuals in New York; A Compendium on Exile after 1933*, ed. Eckart Goebel and Sigrid Weigel (Berlin and Boston: Gruyter, 2013), 461.
8. Taubes, *Political Theology of Paul*, 9.
9. Benjamin Lazier, *God Interrupted: Heresy and the European Imagination between the World Wars* (Princeton, N.J.: Princeton University Press, 2008), 7.
10. Susan Taubes, *Die Korrespondenz mit Jacob Taubes 1950–1951: Herausgegeben und Kommentiert von Christina Pareigis* (Paderborn: Wilhelm Fink, 2011), 275.
11. Taubes, *Occidental Eschatology*, xii.
12. Phillip Lopate, *Notes on Sontag* (Princeton, N.J.: Princeton University Press, 2009), 38.
13. Alan Unterman, *The Kabbalistic Tradition: An Anthology of Jewish Mysticism* (London: Penguin, 2008), xxxix.
14. Taubes, *From Cult to Culture: Fragments Towards a Critique of Historical Reason* (Stanford, Calif.: Stanford University Press, 2010), 9.
15. Susan Taubes, *Die Korrespondenz mit Jacob Taubes 1952: Herausgegeben und Kommentiert von Christina Pareigis* (Paderborn: Fink, 2013), 62.
16. Susan Taubes was working under the supervision of Paul Tillich. Her dissertation from 1956 bears the title "The Absent God: A Study of Simone Weil."
17. Susan Taubes, *Die Korrespondenz mit Jacob Taubes 1952*, 65.
18. Susan Taubes, *Die Korrespondenz mit Jacob Taubes 1950–1951*, 15.
19. Ibid., 16.
20. Taubes, *To Carl Schmitt*, 20.
21. Ibid., 22.
22. Carl Schmitt, *Political Theology: Four Chapters on the Concept of Sovereignty* (Chicago: University of Chicago Press, 2008), 36.
23. Karl Löwith, *From Hegel to Nietzsche: The Revolution in Nineteenth-Century Thought* (New York: Columbia University Press, 1991).

24. Taubes, *To Carl Schmitt*, 2.

25. Observed by Hans Blumenberg; Marc de Wilde, "Meeting Opposites: The Political Theologies of Walter Benjamin and Carl Schmitt," *Philosophy and Rhetoric* 44, no. 4 (2011): 368.

26. Ibid.

27. Schmitt, *Political Theology*, 36.

28. In 1970, after criticism from figures such as Erik Peterson and Hans Blumenberg, Schmitt will defend only the structural argument: "Everything I have said on the topic of political theology is statements of a jurist upon the obvious theoretical and practical legal structural resemblance between theological and juridical concepts"; Schmitt, *Political Theology II: The Myth of the Closure of Any Political Theology* (Cambridge: Polity Press, 2008), 148.

29. Schmitt, *Political Theology*, 36.

30. Löwith, "The Theological Background of the Philosophy of History," *Social Research* 13, no. 1 (1946): 58.

31. Löwith extended his line of eschatological meaning in philosophy, not limiting himself to modernity, but reaching back to the Middle Ages and Antiquity with his 1949 book. One could suspect a mutual influence between him and Taubes, given the footnotes to Taubes's dissertation; Löwith, *Meaning in History* (1949; Chicago; London: University of Chicago Press, 2006), 248, 55.

32. Perhaps one would be more cautious to state such allegations today when the intertextual nature of any academic work is more commonly recognized. In such an academic environment (for instance, marked by the influence of Derrida's deconstruction) one would rather appreciate Taubes as a representative of "the modern tradition of academic Jewish commentary"; Herbert Kopp-Oberstebrink, "Between Terror and Play: The Intellectual Encounter of Hans Blumenberg and Jacob Taubes," *Telos* 2012, no. 158 (2012): 125. Or as Jamie Martin points out, "Löwith's somewhat uncharitable characterization of Taubes's intellectual indebtedness obscures the fact that what Löwith called Taubes's 'penetrating study' itself shaped Löwith's thesis in *Meaning in History*. Löwith cited *Occidental Eschatology* as a source for his chapter on Augustine and for his argument about the secularization of Joachim's eschatology in Hegel"; Martin, "Liberalism and History after the Second World War: The Case of Jacob Taubes," *Modern Intellectual History* 12, no. 2 (2015): 9.

33. Taubes, *Occidental Eschatology*, xii.

34. Plagiarism may also be raised as an issue in this context. Christoph Schmidt states that *Occidental Eschatology* "owes far more than is fitting to the Jesuit Hans Urs von Balthasar's *Apocalypse of the German Soul*, a work that was completely unknown at the time"; Schmidt, "Review Essay on 'The Political Theology of Paul' by Jacob Taubes," *Hebrew Political Studies* 2, no. 2 (2007): 239.

35. Taubes, *Occidental Eschatology*, 15.

36. Ibid., 21.

37. Jacob Taubes, Carl Schmitt, and Mike Grimshaw, *To Carl Schmitt: Letters and Reflections* (New York: Columbia University Press, 2013), 2.
38. Ibid., 13.
39. Taubes, *Occidental Eschatology*, 87.
40. Ibid., 63.
41. Ibid., 35.
42. Ibid., 68.
43. Löwith, "Theological Background of the Philosophy of History," 58.
44. Taubes, *Occidental Eschatology*, 194.
45. John P. McCormick, "Transcending Weber's Categories of Modernity? The Early Lukács and Schmitt on the Rationalization Thesis," *New German Critique*, no. 75 (1998): 135.
46. Taubes, *To Carl Schmitt*, 4.
47. Ibid., 6.
48. On another level Taubes would two decades later attack Weber's use of the metaphor "the iron cage" because it described capitalism as a fate for humankind; Taubes, *From Cult to Culture*, 258–59.
49. Albert Salomon, "Eschatological Thinking in Western Civilization: Reflections on a Book," *Social Research* 16, no. 1 (1949): 97.
50. Lazier, *God Interrupted*, 6.
51. Anson Rabinbach, "Between Enlightenment and Apocalypse: Benjamin, Bloch and Modern German Jewish Messianism," *New German Critique*, no. 34 (1985): 78.
52. Lazier, *God Interrupted*, 6.
53. Rabinbach, "Between Enlightenment and Apocalypse," 88.
54. Lazier, *God Interrupted*, 31.
55. The pantheist is exemplified by Spinoza, a Jewish heretic who preoccupied Leo Strauss's writings; ibid., 18.
56. Though Jonas's appraisal of Heidegger would, naturally, be replaced by another tone after 1945.
57. Lazier, *God Interrupted*, 34.
58. Ibid., 13.
59. Friedrich Nietzsche, *Human, All Too Human: A Book for Free Spirits* (Cambridge and New York: Cambridge University Press, 1986), 182.
60. Taubes, *Occidental Eschatology*, 26.
61. Treml, "Reinventing the Canonical: The Radical Reading of Jacob Taubes," 463–64.
62. These were reports that Zwi Taubes shared with Karl Barth, the first one at his visit to Barth on June 25, 1944; Ward Blanton and Hent de Vries, *Paul and the Philosophers* (New York: Fordham University Press, 2013), 615.
63. Taubes, *Occidental Eschatology*, 27.
64. Karl Barth, *The Epistle to the Romans*, 6th ed. (London: Oxford University Press, 1968), 1.
65. Letter to Armin Mohler, February 14, 1952; Taubes, *To Carl Schmitt*, 23.

66. Christina Pareigis, "Letter from Susan Taubes to Jacob Taubes April 4, 1952," *Telos* 2010, no. 150 (2010): 112.

67. Gershom Scholem, A. D. Skinner, and A. David, *A Life in Letters, 1914–1982* (Cambridge, Mass.: Harvard University Press, 2002), 348.

68. Babette Babich, "Ad Jacob Taubes," *New Nietzsche Studies* 7, no. 3 (2007): 6.

69. For Taubes the real and more pressing issue between the two was the dead around them: five Jewish scholars with relations to the two of them, including Jacob's wife, whom Scholem, according to him, "traumatized to the end"; Scholem, Skinner, and David, *A Life in Letters, 1914–1982*, 468.

70. Treml, "Reinventing the Canonical," 464.

71. "He mysteriously succeeded in obtaining paid trips from all kinds of important foundations and corporations all over the world"; Albert I. Baumgarten, ed., *Self, Soul and Body in Religious Experience* (Leiden: E. J. Brill, 1998), 6–7.

72. Taubes, *To Carl Schmitt*, 10.

73. Taubes appears, however, in his writings from the '50s, to have shared Martin Buber's belief in Israel as a spiritual center.

74. Taubes, *From Cult to Culture*, 9.

75. Ibid., 58.

76. Taubes, *Political Theology of Paul*, 34. Lebovic observes this increasing interest in the same period of Taubes's career from his letters written in Jerusalem in the early '50s. Nitzan Lebovic, "The Jerusalem School: The Theopolitical Hour," *New German Critique*, no. 105 (2008).

77. Taubes, *Political Theology of Paul*, 64.

78. Franz Rosenzweig, *The Star of Redemption* (Notre Dame, Ind.: Notre Dame Press, 1985), 299.

79. Taubes, *Political Theology of Paul*, 143.

80. Sarah Hammerschlag, *The Figural Jew: Politics and Identity in Postwar French Thought* (Chicago: University of Chicago Press, 2010), 26.

81. Taubes, *Occidental Eschatology*, 3.

82. A crucial motivation was probably also his relation to Margareta von Brentano; Treml, "Reinventing the Canonical," 465.

83. Jerry Z. Muller's chapter in Monika Boll and Raphael Gross, *"Ich Staune, Dass Sie in Dieser Luft Atmen Können": Jüdische Intellektuelle in Deutschland Nach 1945* (Frankfurt am Main: S. Fischer Verlage, 2013).

84. Manfred Henningsen, *Eric Voegelin and the German Intellectual Left* (Munich: Eric-Voegelin-Archiv, 2008), 13.

85. Lebovic, "Jerusalem School," 108.

86. Baumgarten, *Self, Soul and Body in Religious Experience*, 5.

87. Treml, "Reinventing the Canonical," 465.

88. Taubes, *To Carl Schmitt*, 13.

89. His authority could often rely more on his skills as an orator than as a writer, as one example from the late '60s perhaps illustrates: "One student later

remembered that Taubes's speech at a sociology conference made Adorno's 'pale' in comparison"; Noah Benezra Strote, "Emigration and the Foundation of West Germany, 1933–1963" (Ph.D. diss., University of California, 2011), 178.

90. Taubes, *From Cult to Culture*, 45.
91. Ibid.
92. Ibid., 58.
93. Pareigis's translation of a letter written in German; Susan Taubes, *Die Korrespondenz mit Jacob Taubes 1952*, 80; Christina Pareigis, "Searching for the Absent God: Susan Taubes's Negative Theology," *Telos*, no. 150 (2010): 99.
94. Taubes, *To Carl Schmitt*, 23.
95. Taubes, *From Cult to Culture*, 54.
96. Taubes, *Political Theology of Paul*, 5.
97. Taubes, *From Cult to Culture*, 53.
98. Scholem, Skinner, and David, *A Life in Letters, 1914–1982*, 467.
99. Taubes, *From Cult to Culture*, 9.
100. Ibid.
101. Moshe Idel, *Messianic Mystics* (New Haven, Conn.: Yale University Press, 1998), 19.
102. Taubes, *Political Theology of Paul*, 5.
103. Once a communist, Mohler had moved to the right, even to the point of offering his services to the SS in Germany during the war in order to fight on the Eastern front.
104. Taubes, *To Carl Schmitt*, 20.
105. Susan Taubes, *Die Korrespondenz mit Jacob Taubes 1952*, 96.
106. Ibid., 103.
107. Ibid., 30. Letter to Susan Taubes, written January 7, 1952 in German; trans. in Pareigis, "Searching for the Absent God," 109.
108. Taubes, *To Carl Schmitt*, 21.
109. Ibid.
110. Ibid., 22.
111. Ibid., 22–23.
112. Ibid., 23.
113. Taubes, *Political Theology of Paul*, 61.
114. Ibid., 62.
115. Susan Taubes, *Die Korrespondenz mit Jacob Taubes 1952*, 50.
116. Taubes, *Political Theology of Paul*, 111.
117. Taubes, *To Carl Schmitt: Letters and Reflections*, 30.
118. Stephen R. Haynes, "'Between the Times': German Theology and the Weimar 'Zeitgeist,'" *Soundings: An Interdisciplinary Journal* 74, no. 1/2 (1991): 35.
119. Taubes, *Political Theology of Paul*, 60.
120. "The rejection of the Old Testament in the second century was a mistake which the great church rightly avoided; to maintain it in the sixteenth century was a fate from which Reformation was not yet able to escape; but to

still preserve it in Protestantism as a canonical document since the nineteenth century is the consequence of a religious and ecclesiastical crippling"; Adolf von Harnack, *Marcion: The Gospel of the Alien God*, trans. Lyle D. Bierma and John E. Steely (Eugene, Ore.: Wipf & Stock, 1990), 134. While Taubes considers Marcion a Gnostic, this is now a matter of debate that relates the question about the legitimacy of the concept and definition of "Gnosticism" as an ancient religion: "In Marcion's teaching, the salvation of the souls of humans is not a return to their original spiritual realm, for they did not originate there. There is no original affinity between humans and the Father. Such distinctions have some validity. Marcion definitely is different in some respects from some other sources. At the same time, the arguments that are often marshaled for distinguishing Marcion from 'gnosticism' also mask a more fundamental problem: the category of 'gnosticism' itself"; Michael A. Williams, *Rethinking "Gnosticism": An Argument for Dismantling a Dubious Category* (Princeton, N.J.: Princeton University Press, 1996), 27.

121. Taubes, *Political Theology of Paul*, 61.

122. This view is confirmed by historians such as Richard Weikart, "Book Review, The Holy Reich: Nazi Conceptions of Christianity, 1919–1945," *German Studies Review* 27, no. 1 (2004).

123. Taubes, *To Carl Schmitt*, 28. Taubes refers to Erik Peterson (1890–1960), who was a German theologian, scholar of early Christianity, and friend and colleague of Karl Barth and Carl Schmitt.

124. Taubes, *The Political Theology of Paul*, 3.

125. One notable exception is an essay from 1955 in which Jacob Taubes critiqued Schmitt for neglecting to reflect upon the Christian roots of democratic and nonhierarchical forms of political organization; see Taubes, "On the Symbolic Order of Modern Democracy," *Confluence: An International Forum* 4, no. 1 (1955): 57–71; Martin, "Liberalism and History after the Second World War: The Case of Jacob Taubes," 3.

126. Already in a letter from 1948 he indicated that he was identifying himself in a certain sense with Paul. "'New York is the Rome of the Imperial Era," he wrote to Martin Buber upon his arrival to that city from Europe in 1948, "newly opened up land—ripe for any seed. Paul would feel well here; certainly no one has sent an Epistle to the Romans to New York yet, but who knows"; Strote, "Emigration and the Foundation of West Germany, 1933–1963," 174.

127. With some notable exceptions, as will be indicated.

128. Scholem, Skinner, and David, *A Life in Letters, 1914–1982*, 348.

129. Taubes, *Political Theology of Paul*, 3.

130. Babich, "Arendt's Radical Good and the Banality of Evil: Echoes of Scholem and Jaspers in Margarethe von Trotta's Hannah Arendt," *Existenz* 9, no. 2 (2014): 19.

131. Paul Chodoff, "The Holocaust and Its Effects on Survivors: An Overview," *Political Psychology* 18, no. 1 (1997): 153–54.

132. Erika Bourguignon, "Bringing the Past into the Present: Family Narratives of Holocaust, Exile, and Diaspora; Memory in an Amnesic World: Holocaust, Exile, and the Return of the Suppressed," *Anthropological Quarterly* 78, no. 1 (2005): 69.

133. Aaron Hass, "Holocaust Survivor Testimony: The Psychological Implications," in *Remembering for the Future: The Holocaust in an Age of Genocide; Memory*, ed. Elisabeth Maxwell and John K. Roth (Basingstoke: Palgrave, 2001), 127–34.

"The initial Israeli reaction to the Shoah entailed survivors silencing themselves and being silenced by the Israeli society. During the 1948 War of Independence survivors were silenced not because they did not want to tell their stories, but because their story was not really acceptable, being very different from the heroic myths constructed around the European Jewry partisans and ghetto fighters on the one hand, and around the war fought by Eretz Israeli youth on the other"; Ronit Lentin, *Israel and the Daughters of the Shoah: Reoccupying the Territories of Silence* (New York: Berghahn, 2000), 119–20. See also the personal account from a Scandinavian context in Göran Rosenberg, *A Brief Stop on the Road from Auschwitz*, trans. Sarah Death (New York: Other Press, 2015).

134. Gabrielle M. Spiegel, *The Past as Text: The Theory and Practice of Medieval Historiography* (Baltimore: Johns Hopkins University Press, 1997), 36.

135. Ibid., 38.

136. Another striking similarity between the work of the two Jewish professors is the engagement of both with the thought of Carl Schmitt. This is evident in Jacques Derrida, *Rogues: Two Essays on Reason* (Stanford, Calif.: Stanford University Press, 2005); *Politics of Friendship* (London: Verso, 2006).

137. Babich, "Ad Jacob Taubes," 9.

3. Paul and Philosophy: Taubes's Contradictory Paul

1. The lecture given February 23, 1987, in Heidelberg; Jacob Taubes, *The Political Theology of Paul* (Stanford, Calif.: Stanford University Press, 2004), 103.

2. Ibid., 21.

3. Taubes, *From Cult to Culture: Fragments Towards a Critique of Historical Reason* (Stanford, Calif.: Stanford University Press, 2010), 77.

4. Taubes, *Occidental Eschatology* (Stanford, Calif.: Stanford University Press, 2009), 63.

5. Taubes, *The Political Theology of Paul*, 15.

6. Taubes, *From Cult to Culture*, xiii.

7. In these lectures he also confirms the view put forward by Charlotte Elisheva Fonrobert and Amir Engel that Taubes reads sources as "palimpsests." Taubes claims that the material conditions of writing before the destruction of the Temple in Jerusalem in the first century varied much more from after this

destruction than the written sources bear witness to. These sources, like any sources, are depicted as "ultimately distortions" that one has to read "against the grain"; Taubes, *Political Theology of Paul*, 20.

8. Ibid., 78.

9. From the Hebrew תכלית *takhlit*: "purpose, aim, object; end, limit."

10. The notion of texts as palimpsests is put into practice in one of Taubes's readings of Heidegger: "The way in which Heidegger, in his inaugural lecture, sets the scene for the question of Nothing is only really understandable when it is read as a palimpsestic (as there is no direct indication) a tract against Parmenides"; Taubes, *From Cult to Culture*, 127.

11. Taubes, *Political Theology of Paul*, 82.

12. Sergei Dolgopolski, *What Is Talmud? The Art of Disagreement* (New York: Fordham University Press, 2009), 238.

13. Ibid., 154.

14. "Since there is no longer any truth after Nietzsche, from Nietzsche to Weber, a new criterion arises, that of honesty"; Taubes, *Political Theology of Paul*, 41.

15. Friedrich Nietzsche, *Daybreak: Thoughts on the Prejudices of Morality*, ed. Maudemarie Clark and Brian Leiter, trans. R. J. Hollingdale (Cambridge: Cambridge University Press, 1997), 84.

16. Taubes, *Political Theology of Paul*, 116.

17. Jacques Derrida, *Of Grammatology* (1976; repr. Baltimore: Johns Hopkins University Press, 1997), 19.

18. Taubes, *Political Theology of Paul*, 77.

19. Ibid., 24.

20. Ibid., 85.

21. Ibid., 83.

22. Ibid., 79.

23. Franz Rosenzweig, *The Star of Redemption* (Notre Dame, Ind.: Notre Dame Press, 1985), 12.

24. Taubes, *Political Theology of Paul*, 77.

25. Rosenzweig, *Star of Redemption*, 12.

26. Taubes, *Political Theology of Paul*, 80.

27. Ibid.

28. "Oh well, he did pay the price for that. You can't get away with saying stuff like that for nothing. With a man like Nietzsche words like that have a price"; ibid.

29. Ibid., 84.

30. Ibid., 86.

31. Ibid., 82.

32. Taubes, *From Cult to Culture*, 76.

33. Taubes, *Political Theology of Paul*, 79.

34. Ibid., 87.

35. Nietzsche, *The Antichrist*, trans. H. L. Mencken (New York: Alfred A. Knopf, 1927), §51.

36. Taubes, *From Cult to Culture*, 79.

37. Although the label "Gnostic" as applicable to Marcion is debatable, Taubes's point about Marcion's distaste for Judaism is not up for discussion to the same degree. "Nothing is clearer about Marcion's teaching than his complete distaste for the God of Jewish Scripture"; Michael A. Williams, *Rethinking "Gnosticism": An Argument for Dismantling a Dubious Category* (Princeton, N.J.: Princeton University Press, 1996), 24.

38. Herbert Kopp-Oberstebrink, "Between Terror and Play: The Intellectual Encounter of Hans Blumenberg and Jacob Taubes," *Telos* 2012, no. 158 (2012): 119.

39. Taubes, *Political Theology of Paul*, 69.

40. Taubes, *From Cult to Culture*, 117–19.

41. Hans Jonas, *The Gnostic Religion: The Message of the Alien God & the Beginnings of Christianity* (Boston: Beacon Press, 2001), 326.

42. Ibid., xxiv–xxxv.

43. Hans Blumenberg, *The Legitimacy of the Modern Age* (Cambridge, Mass.: MIT Press, 1985), 126.

44. Taubes, *From Cult to Culture*, 138.

45. The "Gnosticism" overcome is mainly read by Blumenberg through Jonas, a construction of "Gnosticism" wholly based on the traces of this ancient heretical movement in the church fathers' polemic. This scholarly construction was made years before the discovery of the Nag Hammadi library and decades before the rise of the scholarly corpus on these discovered sources.

46. Benjamin Lazier quotes the Romanian scholar of religion, Ioan Culianu, who complains of this inflation and how Gnostics had "taken hold of the world" and categorized anything from the modern world as gnostic: "All things and their opposite are equally gnostic"; Lazier, *God Interrupted: Heresy and the European Imagination between the World Wars* (Princeton, N.J.: Princeton University Press, 2008), 21. Culianu's complaint is heard in new versions in recent scholarship, as Michael Allen Williams, who argues for the abandonment of the category "Gnosticism" altogether; Williams, *Rethinking "Gnosticism": An Argument for Dismantling a Dubious Category*; "Was There a Gnostic Religion? Strategies for a Clearer Analysis," in *Was There a Gnostic Religion?*, ed. Antti Marjanen (Helsinki; Finnish Exegetical Society; Göttingen: Vandenhoeck & Ruprecht, 2005).

47. Taubes, *Occidental Eschatology*, 37.

48. Taubes, *From Cult to Culture*, 123.

49. Kopp-Oberstebrink, "Between Terror and Play," 120.

50. Todd E. Klutz represents this minority position. It is discussed in Oh-Young Kwon, "A Critical Review of Recent Scholarship on the Pauline Opposition and the Nature of Its Wisdom (*Sophia*) in 1 Corinthians 1–4," *Currents in Biblical Research* 8, no. 3 (2010): 395–400.

51. Transcribed as "Notes on Surrealism," in Taubes, *From Cult to Culture*, 104–23.

52. Ibid., 122.

53. Angus Nicholls, *Myth and the Human Sciences: Hans Blumenberg's Theory of Myth* (Andover: Routledge, 2013), 215.

54. Blumenberg, quoted in ibid.

55. Taubes, *From Cult to Culture*, 62.

56. Kopp-Oberstebrink, "Between Terror and Play," 121.

57. Ibid., 130.

58. Adolf von Harnack, *Marcion: The Gospel of the Alien God*, trans. Lyle D. Bierma and John E. Steely. (Eugene, Ore.: Wipf & Stock, 1990), 1.

59. As revealed in a letter to Rudolf Bultmann, a correspondence that also confirms the image a common interest across the confessional borders of Judaism and Christianity; Lazier, *God Interrupted*, 42.

60. Jonas's Paul is interestingly countered by Jonas's philosophical biology with the flesh as the source of freedom, a covert anti-Paulinism in a nuclear age.

61. Taubes, *Occidental Eschatology*, 36.

62. Ibid., 31.

63. Taubes, *From Cult to Culture*, 137.

64. Ibid., 139–40.

65. Taubes, *Political Theology of Paul*, 61.

66. Ibid., 66.

67. Taubes, *From Cult to Culture*, 78–79.

68. As Walter Bauer, Wilhelm Bousset, Ernst Lohmeyer, Walter Schmithals, Johannes Weiss, and Ulrich Wilckens.

69. I will introduce other historical approaches to these texts and let them confront Taubes's approaches. The historical approaches are here primarily represented by Dale B. Martin's *The Corinthian Body* (New Haven, Conn.: Yale University Press, 1995), and Larry L. Welborn's *Paul, the Fool of Christ: A Study of 1 Corinthians 1–4 in the Comic-Philosophic Tradition* (London and New York: T. & T. Clark International, 2005). They can serve to demonstrate how Taubes relies on historical presuppositions about these texts and to situate his presuppositions with others, without assuming that these works are purely historical approaches, as these authors appear admirably aware of. Dale B. Martin's introduction refuses such a simple division of the historical and the philosophical-hermeneutical; Martin, *Corinthian Body*, xi.

70. Taubes, *Occidental Eschatology*, 52.

71. Ibid., 67.

72. Ibid., 68.

73. Ibid., 75.

74. Ibid., 82.

75. Taubes, *From Cult to Culture*, 77.

76. Taubes, *Occidental Eschatology*, 52.

77. Romans 13:1, as cited in ibid., 69.

78. Taubes, *From Cult to Culture*, 82.
79. Ibid., 79.
80. Ibid.
81. Ibid., 80.
82. Ibid.
83. Ibid., 81.
84. Ibid.
85. Ibid., 82.
86. Ibid., 82–83.
87. Hannah Arendt, "The Jew as Pariah: A Hidden Tradition," *Jewish Social Studies* 6, no. 2 (1944).
88. Taubes, *From Cult to Culture*, 84.
89. Ibid., 77.
90. For instance, in Hans Conzelmann, *1 Corinthians: A Commentary on the First Epistle to the Corinthians* (Philadelphia: Fortress, 1981).
91. Martin, *Corinthian Body*, 38.
92. Ibid., 40.
93. Ibid., 57.
94. Translation preferred by Martin, though not an exclusionary preference; ibid.
95. When writing about apocalypticism and eschatology at work in the Pauline texts I prefer to follow uses of this terminology in the works of New Testament scholars rather than in works of continental philosophers. It should be noted that in the works of, for instance, Jacques Derrida, the term "eschatology" takes on a very different meaning than in the works of a New Testament scholar like Dale B. Martin or Henrik Tronier. When Derrida detects logocentrism in the thought of Lévi-Strauss and the archeology of studying non-European peoples, Derrida affirms, "As always, this archeology is also a teleology and an eschatology; the dream of a full and immediate presence closing history, the transparence and indivision of a Parousia, the suppression of contradiction and difference"; Derrida, *Of Grammatology*, 115. In contrast, I treat eschatology here as a kind of theology that concerns the end of history or the last things. While the temporal dimension is dominant in eschatology, the apocalypse is a literary genre that may contain eschatological views but all the same has a more characteristic spatial element. Furthermore, the genre's accounts of heavenly or otherworldly events may occur in the future or end time. Nonetheless, they can also occur in the past or present. Apocalypticism is a social ideology and can have a timeless and vertical mode of perception. Social status reversal is another characteristic of apocalypticism, which might take spatial as well as temporal forms in their transcendent rupture with the common empirical experience; Martin, *Corinthian Body*, 57, 60; Henrik Tronier, "The Corinthian Correspondence between Philosophical Idealism and Apocalypticism," in *Paul Beyond the Judaism/Hellenism Divide*, ed. Troels Engberg-Pedersen (Louisville, Ky.: Westminster John Knox Press, 2001).

96. Taubes, *From Cult to Culture*, 79.

97. Welborn, *Paul, the Fool of Christ*, 252.

98. Taubes, *From Cult to Culture*, 85.

99. Welborn, "The Culture of Crucifixion," in *Paul and the Philosophers*, ed. Ward Blanton and Hent de Vries (New York: Fordham University Press, 2013), 135.

100. The prevailing silence had an exception in the well-known cases of high treason; ibid., 136.

101. Welborn, *Paul, the Fool of Christ*, 2–3.

102. "In my view, it was an historic moment when Paul, in the course of his correspondence with Corinth, began to articulate his gospel as a 'message of the cross' (1 Cor 1:18)"; Welborn, "Culture of Crucifixion," 137.

103. Nietzsche's *Antichrist*, quoted in Taubes, *From Cult to Culture*, 76.

104. Martin, *Corinthian Body*, 61.

105. Taubes, *From Cult to Culture*, 83.

106. Welborn, *Paul, the Fool of Christ*, 98.

107. Taubes, *From Cult to Culture*, 84.

108. Welborn, *Paul, the Fool of Christ*, 99.

109. A summary of this position and its adherents is found in Kwon, "A Critical Review of Recent Scholarship on the Pauline Opposition and the Nature of Its Wisdom (*Sophia*) in 1 Corinthians 1–4," 392–400.

110. Taubes, *Occidental Eschatology*, 72.

111. Albert Schweitzer, *The Mysticism of Paul the Apostle*, trans. William Montgomery (1931; repr. Baltimore: Johns Hopkins University Press, 1998), 71.

112. Taubes, *From Cult to Culture*, 80.

113. Ibid., 81.

114. Ibid.

115. Ibid.

116. For more on Taubes's Jewish Paul, see Chapter 4.

117. Taubes, *From Cult to Culture*, 86.

118. Ibid., 86–88.

119. Ibid., 95.

120. Ibid.

121. "Why is such a long latency necessary in order to carry through a subject once it has been raised, so that it finds its first 'pure' resonance in the post-Christian era, since Hamann and Hegel?"; ibid., 77.

122. Ibid., 80.

123. As is also the case in 2 Corinthians, according to L. L. Welborn: "Nor can Paul's Corinthian opponents be described as Gnostics, because Paul does not polemicize against *gnosis*, libertinism, or possession of the spirit"; Welborn, *An End to Enmity: Paul and the Wrongdoer of Second Corinthians* (Berlin: Gruyter, 2011), 126.

124. Martin, *Corinthian Body*, 62.

125. Taubes, *From Cult to Culture*, 86.

126. Ibid., 87.

127. Not only postcolonial theory. There is a wide range of theoretical approaches to texts that recognize the polysemy of meaning. The following anthology applies one of them, the postcolonial approach: Christopher D. Stanley, *The Colonized Apostle: Paul through Postcolonial Eyes* (Minneapolis: Fortress, 2011), 11.

128. Taubes, *Political Theology of Paul*, 57.

129. Charlotte Elisheva Fonrobert and Amir Engel, quoted earlier.

130. Taubes, *Political Theology of Paul*, 57.

131. Ibid.

132. Taubes, *From Cult to Culture*, 94. Paul's words in Galatians 3:1 about the crucified Christ as "publicly exhibited . . . before your eyes" sounds as if Paul could have held up a painted picture. This vivid image more likely exemplifies Paul's use of a rhetorical topos; Hans Dieter Betz, *Galatians: A Commentary on Paul's Letter to the Churches in Galatia* (Philadelphia: Fortress, 1979), 131.

133. Taubes, *From Cult to Culture*, 94.

134. Ibid., 89.

135. Taubes, *Political Theology of Paul*, 68.

136. Taubes, *Die Politische Theologie des Paulus* (Munich: Wilhelm Fink, 1993), 95.

137. Blumenberg, *Legitimacy of the Modern Age*, 134–35.

138. Welborn, "Jacob Taubes—Paulinist, Messianist," in *Paul in the Grip of the Philosophers*, ed. Peter Frick (Minneapolis: Fortress, 2013), 76.

139. Taubes, *Political Theology of Paul*, 69.

140. Ibid.

141. "How little Christianity cultivates the sense of honesty can be inferred from the character of the writings of its scholars. They set out their conjectures as audaciously as if they were dogmas and seldom find any difficulty in the interpretation of Scripture"; Nietzsche, *Daybreak*, §84.

142. Blumenberg, *Legitimacy of the Modern Age*, 6.

143. Ibid., 7.

144. Taubes argues that what lies behind some passages in Blumenberg's writings is "the interest in the state"; Taubes, *Political Theology of Paul*, 70. Taubes has not been alone in accusing Blumenberg of political conservatism. "Thus, despite his more or less open critique of Carl Schmitt . . . [Blumenberg] did not himself end up escaping allegations of political conservatism"; Nicholls, *Myth and the Human Sciences: Hans Blumenberg's Theory of Myth*, 217.

145. Taubes, *Political Theology of Paul*, 70.

146. Ibid., 72.

147. Ibid, 74.

148. Ibid.

149. Ibid.

150. Taubes, *From Cult to Culture*, 112–13.

151. These are words that also tend to be used as descriptions of messianic notions of time.

152. Taubes, *Political Theology of Paul*, 76.

153. Ibid., 75.

154. Taubes presents Adorno as a saint who is being revered through "hagiographies written under the direction of Mr. Horkheimer"; ibid., 98.

155. Ibid., 75.

156. Ibid., 76.

157. Kopp-Oberstebrink, "Between Terror and Play," 132.

158. Taubes, *Political Theology of Paul*, 98.

159. Astrid Deuber-Mankowsky, "Walter Benjamin's Theological-Political Fragment as a Response to Ernst Bloch's Spirit of Utopia," *Leo Baeck Institute Yearbook* 47, no. 1 (2002): 6.

160. Taubes, *Political Theology of Paul*, 80.

161. Welborn, "Jacob Taubes—Paulinist, Messianist," 76.

162. Ibid., 78.

163. Such a revision or originary influence seems to be implied by Welborn's emphasis on Benjamin's influence on Scholem and upon Scholem's chapter on Sabbatianism as Taubes's "clue to 'the inner logic of the messianic' at work in Paul's notion of faith": ibid., 76–77.

4. Paul as Predecessor to Psychoanalysis: Taubes's Introspective Paul

1. Jacob Taubes, *The Political Theology of Paul* (Stanford, Calif.: Stanford University Press, 2004), 4.

2. Taubes's 1968 essay on 1 Corinthians will not be discussed in this chapter, as the focus will be on other interpretations of Paul in Taubes.

3. Although this study is dedicated to Taubes's construction of Paul, his contributions also affect conceptions of Judaism. Here Paul is also used as an instrument to "build a case for the categorization of antinomianism as a legitimately *Jewish* enterprise"; Daniel R. Langton, *The Apostle Paul in the Jewish Imagination: A Study in Modern Jewish-Christian Relations* (New York: Cambridge University Press, 2010), 255.

4. Taubes, *Political Theology of Paul*, 88.

5. "This disagreement is not an intermediary point to consensus, but rather becomes an end in itself"; Sergei Dolgopolski, *What Is Talmud? The Art of Disagreement* (New York: Fordham University Press, 2009), 187.

6. Taubes was mainly intervening in intellectual debates in Germany, though "The Price of Messianism" is a fine example of an intervention in another context: the Jewish World Congress in Jerusalem in 1981.

7. Taubes, *Political Theology of Paul*, 28.

8. Augustine retrospectively changes his view of Romans 7 concerning a sinner under the law who freely can choose not to sin to Paul's autobiography and a stage in the process of conversion; Paula Fredriksen, "Paul and Augustine:

Conversion Narratives, Orthodox Traditions, and the Retrospective Self," *Journal of Theological Studies* 37, no. 1 (1986): 20–27.

9. Krister Stendahl, "The Apostle Paul and the Introspective Conscience of the West," *Harvard Theological Review* 56, no. 3 (1963): 205.

10. Stendahl asks, "Does he ever intimate that he is aware of any sins of his own that would trouble his conscience? It is actually easier to find statements to the contrary. The tone in Acts 23:1, 'Brethren, I have lived before God in all good conscience up to this day' (cf. 24:16), prevails also throughout his letters."

11. Stendahl, "The Apostle Paul and the Introspective Conscience of the West."

12. Taubes, *From Cult to Culture: Fragments Towards a Critique of Historical Reason* (Stanford, Calif.: Stanford University Press, 2010), 337.

13. Ibid., 4.

14. The exact expression for the title of Stendahl's essay, clearly an allusion to Stendahl, though his essay is not explicitly referred to in Taubes's talk at the World Congress of Jewish Studies.

15. Taubes, *From Cult to Culture*, 5.

16. In contrast to the early Taubes in *Occidental Eschatology* (Stanford, Calif.: Stanford University Press, 2009), who develops a narrative of the Fall, where the messianic revolution that Jesus proclaimed ends with Paul's turn inward (which reflects "the spirit" of his age) and is even more effectively suppressed by Augustine.

17. This Talmudic expression was frequently used in Zionist discourse. This appears directed against Scholem and his Zionist convictions, as part of Taubes's overall attack.

18. Taubes, *From Cult to Culture*, 9.

19. Ibid., 6.

20. Taubes, *Political Theology of Paul*, 21.

21. Ibid., 11.

22. Ibid., 14.

23. J. Louis Martyn, *Galatians: A New Translation with Introduction and Commentary*, 1st ed. (New York: Doubleday, 1998), 156.

24. Robert Jewett, *Romans: A Commentary* (Minneapolis: Fortress, 2007), 102.

25. Stendahl, "The Apostle Paul and the Introspective Conscience of the West," 204–5. This point has been a crucial one for the views of the scholars of the New Perspective and the Radical Perspective of Paul.

26. Dieter Georgi argues against the notion that "those believing in Jesus as a divine agent were part of a new religion"; Dieter Georgi, "The Early Church: Internal Jewish Migration or New Religion?," *Harvard Theological Review* 88, no. 1 (1995): 37. Georgi contributed to a conference Taubes arranged that resulted in "Gott auf den Kopf Stellen: Überlegungen zu Tendenz und Kontext des Theokratiegedankens in Paulinischer Praxis und Theologie," in *Religionstheorie und Politische Theologie*, Band 3, *Theokratie*, ed. Jacob Taubes (Munich:

Wilhelm Fink Verlag, 1987). Georgi's influence on Taubes's views on Paul is acknowledged by Taubes in his *Political Theology of Paul*, 17.

27. Taubes, *From Cult to Culture*, 5.

28. Taubes, *Political Theology of Paul*, 66.

29. Within New Testament studies a reaction against Bultmann's individualism can be detected in Halvor Moxnes, *Theology in Conflict: Studies in Paul's Understanding of God in Romans* (Leiden: E. J. Brill, 1980). "In the introduction we suggested that Bultmann's thesis was inadequate, when he said that 'if a man will speak of God, he must evidently speak of himself.' From the texts that we have discussed it is more to the point to say that, for Paul, to speak about God is to speak about his people!"; ibid., 99.

30. Taubes, *Political Theology of Paul*, 36.

31. Ibid., 37.

32. Ibid., 38.

33. Pamela Michelle Eisenbaum, *Paul Was Not a Christian: The Real Message of a Misunderstood Apostle* (New York: HarperOne, 2009), 236.

34. "Commentaries have generally opened the way to a depoliticizing of Paul's view by the manifold ways that being justified or justification is interpreted, interpretations that result in severing the connection between justification and justice. Thus, so-called forensic justification has God declaring people to be just who manifestly are not just, thereby vitiating the claim for justice itself"; Theodore W. Jennings, *Outlaw Justice: The Messianic Politics of Paul* (Stanford, Calif.: Stanford University Press, 2013), 62. See also José Porfirio Miranda, *Marx y la Biblia: Crítica a la Filosofía de la Opresión* (Salamanca: Ediciones Sígueme, 1972), 206; Elsa Tamez, *Contra Toda Condena: La Justificación por la Fe Desde los Excluidos*, 2nd ed. (San José: Depto Ecuménico de Investigaciones [DEI], 1991), 125.

35. Jewett, *Romans: A Commentary*, 150.

36. "Instead of an individual-universal perspective of the human essence, Paul's perspective is collective and historical"; Stanley K. Stowers, *A Rereading of Romans: Justice, Jews, and Gentiles* (New Haven, Conn.: Yale University Press, 1994), 108.

37. Ibid., 144.

38. Contra Luther, who summarizes Romans 2 in this manner: "The apostle refutes the faults of the Jews, saying that as far as their guilt is concerned they are the same as the Gentiles and in a certain respect even worse"; Martin Luther and Jaroslav Pelikan, "Lectures on Romans," in *The Works of Martin Luther*, ed. Jaroslav Pelikan and Helmut T. Lehmann (Charlottesville: InteLex, 2013), 15. Contra Ernst Käsemann's claim that Rom 2:1–3:20 constitutes a "judgement on the Jews"; Käsemann, *Commentary on Romans*, trans. G. W. Bromiley (Grand Rapids, Mich.: Eerdmans, 1980). Contra Heikki Räisänen's affirmation that Paul "goes on to demonstrate the sinfulness of the Jews (2.1–29)"; Räisänen, *Paul and the Law* (Tübingen: Mohr, 1983), 97–98. In agreement with Mark D. Nanos that the description of the Judaic example begins in

Romans 2:17 and not 2:1; Nanos, *The Mystery of Romans: The Jewish Context of Paul's Letter* (Minneapolis: Fortress, 1996), 10. "It is a question of using Judean norms to test Judaism after using pagan norms to test paganism"; Jennings, *Outlaw Justice: The Messianic Politics of Paul*, 51.

39. In contrast to the traditional view of the interlocutor as referring to a universal human condition; Stowers, *Rereading of Romans: Justice, Jews, and Gentiles*, 104.

40. Contra Eisenbaum: "Romans 1 is not a description of the corruption of humanity; it's a description of the corruption of the Gentiles, as made clear by the fact that Paul begins his description with the ungodly behavior of idolatry (1:18–19)"; Eisenbaum, *Paul Was Not a Christian*, 236. "For Paul, God's wrath, that had long and justly been stored up against the gentiles, was an obvious and acute problem. Paul thought that God was at present also angry with Israel but for different reasons (chapters 9–11). Both peoples need salvation from God's wrath"; Stowers, *Rereading of Romans*, 108.

41. Taubes, *Political Theology of Paul*, 37.

42. Taubes, *From Cult to Culture: Fragments Towards a Critique of Historical Reason*, 84.

43. Ibid., 4.

44. Ibid.

45. Taubes, *Political Theology of Paul*, 23–24.

46. Ibid.

47. Ibid., 23.

48. Taubes, *From Cult to Culture*, 5.

49. Ibid.

50. Thus it is implied by Taubes's reading that what is often translated as the *end* of the law in Romans 10:4 must refer to the end of the use or validity of the law. The Greek *telos*, however, could also point in the opposite direction to the fulfillment or fullness of the law as its end.

51. Jewett, *Romans*, 227.

52. Partly, therefore, the reader of Romans could be open to Mark D. Nanos's "working hypothesis" that Paul may have been "a practicing Jew" and not in dispute with "righteous Torah-observant behavior" of his day; Nanos, *Mystery of Romans*, 9.

53. "Thus Jews frequently wrote that circumcision was a matter of the heart without ever supposing an elimination of physical circumcision"; Stowers, *Rereading of Romans*, 155.

54. Jewett, *Romans*, 233.

55. Jennings, *Outlaw Justice*, 53.

56. "In this regard, Paul was hardly radical or innovative, although his admonitory diatribal language is sharp and forceful. The theme 'circumcision of the heart' comes directly from the Jewish scriptures, and many varieties of ancient Judaism emphasized it"; Stowers, *Rereading of Romans*, 155.

57. Stanley Stowers calls this a "redeeming merciful justice"; ibid., 196.

58. This is the preferred term over the more forensic "righteousness."

59. Nanos, *Mystery of Romans*, 10.

60. "Only from the perspective of the Jew as the representative of the religious person can universal godlessness be proclaimed"; Käsemann, *Commentary on Romans*, 85.

61. Nanos, "Paul's Non-Jews Do Not Become 'Jews,' but Do They Become 'Jewish'?: Reading Romans 2:25–29 within Judaism, Alongside Josephus," *Journal of the Jesus Movement in Its Jewish Setting* 1, no. 1 (2014): 42.

62. Jennings, *Outlaw Justice*, 52.

63. Alan F. Segal, *Paul the Convert: The Apostolate and Apostasy of Saul the Pharisee* (New Haven, Conn.: Yale University Press, 1990). Segal distinguishes his version of Paul's conversion from the version in Acts; Segal, *The Other Judaisms of Late Antiquity*, Brown Judaic Studies (Atlanta: Scholars, 1987), 145.

64. Jewett, *Romans*, 232.

65. An expression possibly employed in an argument against the social boundaries justified in Qumran writings; James D. G. Dunn, *The New Perspective on Paul: Collected Essays* (Tübingen: Mohr Siebeck, 2005), 117.

66. Taubes, *From Cult to Culture*, 4.

67. Taubes, *The Political Theology of Paul*, 23.

68. Neil Elliott compares Taubes to Stanley K. Stowers on this point. Referring to Taubes, Elliott writes, "Stanley K. Stowers has made a comparable suggestion regarding a pervasive Hellenistic ethos that valued self-mastery (*enkrateia*)—an ethos cultivated among the Roman (and Romanizing) elite in the provinces, and adapted by some Jews in terms of the cultural excellence of Jewish law"; Elliott, "The Question of Politics," in *Paul within Judaism: Restoring the First-Century Context to the Apostle*, ed. Mark D. Nanos and Magnus Zetterholm (Minneapolis: Fortress, 2015), 231.

69. This is a reading of Galatians inspired by Taubes's lectures on Romans; Brigitte Kahl, *Galatians Re-Imagined: Reading with the Eyes of the Vanquished* (Minneapolis: Fortress, 2010), 9.

70. J. Louis Martyn, "Christ, the Elements of the Cosmos, and the Law in Galatians," in *The Social World of the First Christians: Essays in Honor of Wayne A. Meeks*, ed. L. Michael White and O. Larry Yarbrough (Minneapolis: Fortress, 1995).

71. Taubes, *Political Theology of Paul*, 26.

72. Taubes, *From Cult to Culture*, 337.

73. Taubes, *Political Theology of Paul*, 89.

74. Ibid., 90.

75. Ibid., 89.

76. In Taubes's 1957 essay; *From Cult to Culture*, 340.

77. Taubes, *Political Theology of Paul*, 90.

78. Ibid., 89.

79. Ibid., 87.

80. Nietzsche, quoted in ibid.

81. In this regard we follow Stendahl's call for distinguishing more clearly figures like Augustine and Luther from Paul.

82. Taubes, *From Cult to Culture*, 337.

83. Sigmund Freud, *Moses and Monotheism*, trans. Katherine Jones (Letchworth: Hogarth, 1939), 139. Taubes quotes the same excerpt in the Heidelberg lectures, only adding one comment to it: "Pay attention: every word is important to me here. 'Correctly'—this is historical truth"; Taubes, *Political Theology of Paul*, 91.

84. Taubes, *From Cult to Culture*, 338.

85. Ibid., 335.

86. Jewett, *Romans*, 249.

87. Ibid., 280.

88. Nietzsche, quoted in Taubes, *Political Theology of Paul*, 87.

89. Ibid.

90. Stendahl, "The Apostle Paul and the Introspective Conscience of the West," 199.

91. Ibid., 211.

92. Ibid., 205–6.

93. Stowers, *Rereading of Romans*, 273.

94. See, for instance, the explicitly Jewish perspective on Romans 7 encountered in Eisenbaum, *Paul Was Not a Christian*, 226–39.

95. "Luther's experience enforced the impression that Judaism, not least the Judaism of Paul's time, was a *degenerate religion*"; Dunn, *New Perspective on Paul*, 192.

96. Freud, *Moses and Monotheism*, 143.

97. Ibid., 139.

98. Taubes, *Political Theology of Paul*, 94.

99. Ward Blanton, *A Materialism for the Masses: Saint Paul and the Philosophy of Undying Life* (New York: Columbia University Press, 2014), 184.

100. See "Romans 13 as Covert Freudianism," in this chapter.

101. Taubes, *Political Theology of Paul*, 3.

102. Ibid., 51.

103. *To Carl Schmitt: Letters and Reflections* (New York: Columbia University Press, 2013), 13.

104. Taubes, *Political Theology of Paul*, 51.

105. Ibid., 38.

106. Ibid., 50.

107. Ibid., 51.

108. Ibid., 25.

109. Ibid., 48.

110. Ibid., 47.

111. Especially pages 46–51, in ibid.

112. Ibid., 41.

113. Ibid., 28.

114. Ibid.
115. Ibid., 27.
116. Jewett, *Romans*, 543.
117. Taubes, *Political Theology of Paul*, 49.
118. Nietzsche, *Daybreak: Thoughts on the Prejudices of Morality*, ed. Maudemarie Clark and Brian Leiter, trans. R. J. Hollingdale (Cambridge: Cambridge University Press, 1997), §84.
119. Taubes, *Political Theology of Paul*, 45.
120. Except for a brief remark that does not seem to relate to Romans 9–11; ibid., 46.
121. Nietzsche, *Daybreak*, §84.
122. Although Taubes is careful not to bypass the typological aspects of Paul's hermeneutics: "Paul is a very particular mixture of allegoresis and typology"; Taubes, *Political Theology of Paul*, 46.
123. "It was on the basis of Romans 9:14 that Augustine became convinced that grace comes as a result of divine predestination"; Daniel Patte and Eugene TeSelle, *Engaging Augustine on Romans: Self, Context, and Theology in Interpretation* (Harrisburg: Trinity, 2002), 26.
124. Taubes, *Political Theology of Paul*, 148, n. 27.
125. Ibid., 47.
126. Ibid., 49.
127. Noah Benezra Strote, "Emigration and the Foundation of West Germany, 1933–1963" (Ph.D. diss., University of California, 2011), 160.
128. Taubes, *Political Theology of Paul*, 47.
129. Ibid., 52–53.
130. Kenneth Reinhard, "Paul and the Political Love of the Neighbour," in *Paul and the Philosophers*, ed. Ward Blanton and Hent de Vries (New York: Fordham University Press, 2013), 452.
131. Freud, *Moses and Monotheism*, 141.
132. Taubes, *Political Theology of Paul*, 92.
133. Ibid., 89.
134. Taubes, *From Cult to Culture*, 340.
135. Taubes, *Political Theology of Paul*, 95.
136. Reinhard, "Paul and the Political Love of the Neighbour," 461.
137. Jacques Derrida, *Archive Fever: A Freudian Impression*, trans. Eric Prenowitz (Chicago: University of Chicago Press, 1996), 42.
138. Yosef Hayim Yerushalmi, *Freud's Moses: Judaism Terminable and Interminable* (New Haven, Conn.: Yale University Press, 1991).

5. Paul against Empire: Taubes's Political Paul

1. Richard A. Horsley, "General Introduction," in *Paul and Empire: Religion and Power in Roman Imperial Society*, ed. Richard A. Horsley (Harrisburg: Trinity, 1997), 3.

2. Ibid., 5. In writing of "The New Perspective," Horsley refers to E. P. Sanders, *Paul and Palestinian Judaism: A Comparison of Patterns of Religion* (Philadelphia: Fortress, 1977).

3. Horsley, "General Introduction," 1.

4. Neil Elliott, *Liberating Paul: The Justice of God and the Politics of the Apostle* (1994; repr. Minneapolis: Fortress, 2006), 215.

5. Elliott, *The Arrogance of Nations: Reading Romans in the Shadow of Empire* (Minneapolis: Fortress, 2008), 15.

6. N. T. Wright, *Pauline Perspectives: Essays on Paul, 1978–2013* (Minneapolis: Fortress, 2013), 403.

7. Wright, "Paul's Gospel and Caesar's Empire," in *Paul and Politics: Ekklesia, Israel, Imperium, Interpretation: Essays in Honor of Krister Stendahl*, ed. Richard A. Horsley (Harrisburg: Trinity, 2000), 164.

8. During the 2008 annual meeting (November 22–25) at the Society of Biblical Literature (SBL), John M. G. Barclay polemically stated that Wright was "hallucinating" (!) with such claims.

9. John M. G. Barclay, *Pauline Churches and Diaspora Jews* (Tübingen: Mohr Siebeck, 2011), 376.

10. Georgi, "Gott auf den Kopf Stellen: Überlegungen zu Tendenz und Kontext des Theokratiegedankens in Paulinischer Praxis und Theologie," in *Religionstheorie und Politische Theologie*, Band 3, *Theokratie*, ed. Jacob Taubes (Munich: Wilhelm Fink Verlag, 1987).

11. Georgi, *The Opponents of Paul in Second Corinthians: A Study of Religious Propaganda in Late Antiquity* (Philadelphia: Fortress, 1986).

12. Georgi, *Theocracy in Paul's Praxis and Theology* (Minneapolis: Fortress, 1991).

13. Georgi, "God Turned Upside Down," in *Paul and Empire: Religion and Power in Roman Imperial Society*, ed. Richard A. Horsley (Harrisburg: Trinity, 1997).

14. Jacob Taubes, *The Political Theology of Paul* (Stanford, Calif.: Stanford University Press, 2004), 16.

15. Elliott, *Arrogance of Nations*, 62.

16. James R. Harrison, *Paul and the Imperial Authorities at Thessalonica and Rome: A Study in the Conflict of Ideology* (Tübingen: Mohr Siebeck, 2011), 11.

17. Ibid., 8.

18. Giorgio Agamben, *The Time That Remains: A Commentary on the Letter to the Romans* (Stanford, Calif.: Stanford University Press, 2005), 33.

19. Peter Oakes, "Re-Mapping the Universe: Paul and the Emperor in 1 Thessalonians and Philippians," *Journal for the Study of the New Testament* 27, no. 3 (2005): 301–2.

20. Taubes, *Occidental Eschatology* (Stanford, Calif.: Stanford University Press, 2009), 48.

21. Early Christianity is inescapably political in this view, since "all attempts to separate the political messianic movement from the transcendent apocalypse in the eschatology of Jesus have failed"; ibid., 45.

22. Ibid.

23. Taubes, *From Cult to Culture: Fragments Towards a Critique of Historical Reason* (Stanford, Calif.: Stanford University Press, 2010), 79.

24. Friedrich Nietzsche, *The Antichrist*, trans. H. L. Mencken (New York: Alfred A. Knopf, 1927), §58.

25. The editors of the Heidelberg lectures also draw attention to this aphorism, which follows the aphorism "The First Christian," that Taubes quotes in the lectures; Taubes, *Political Theology of Paul*, 121.

26. Nietzsche, *Daybreak: Thoughts on the Prejudices of Morality*, ed. Maudemarie Clark and Brian Leiter, trans. R. J. Hollingdale (Cambridge: Cambridge University Press, 1997), §71.

27. Not dissimilar to Taubes, Auerbach was an émigré from the German-speaking Jewry, exiled on the American East Coast after the Second World War. Auerbach left Turkey for the United States in 1946.

28. Erich Auerbach, *Literary Language and Its Public in Late Latin Antiquity and in the Middle Ages* (Princeton, N.J.: Princeton University Press, 1993), 37.

29. Ibid., 66.

30. Nietzsche, *Antichrist*, § 51.

31. Taubes, *From Cult to Culture: Fragments Towards a Critique of Historical Reason*, 82–83.

32. Taubes, *Political Theology of Paul*, 14.

33. Ibid., 15–16.

34. Ibid., 23.

35. Ibid., 24–25.

36. ". . . those holy anarchists made it a matter of 'piety' to destroy 'the world,' *that is to say*, the *imperium Romanum*, so that in the end not a stone stood upon another"; Nietzsche, *Antichrist*, §58.

37. Taubes, *Political Theology of Paul*, 16.

38. "Christianity is the formula for exceeding *and* summing up the subterranean cults of all varieties, that of Osiris, that of the Great Mother, that of Mithras, for instance: in his discernment of this fact the genius of Paul showed itself"; Nietzsche, *Antichrist*, § 58.

39. Taubes, *Political Theology of Paul*, 16.

40. Ibid., 24.

41. Nietzsche, *Antichrist*, §43. Another inspiration for this notion may be Karl Barth: ". . . the real revolution comes from God and not from human revolt"; Barth, *The Epistle to the Romans*, 6th ed. (London: Oxford University Press, 1968), 485.

42. Georgi, *Theocracy in Paul's Praxis and Theology*, 83.

43. The similarities with the historical reconstruction undertaken by Georgi and the one presented by Taubes indicate that the latter derived his

views mainly from the German biblical scholar; ibid., 81–82, 86. Taubes's reliance on Georgi is further indicated by the exact same presentation of the historical events following Claudius's death in Taubes as in Georgi; see Taubes, *Political Theology of Paul*, 16.

44. Taubes, *Political Theology of Paul*, 24–25; Georgi, *Theocracy in Paul's Praxis and Theology*, 86.

45. Taubes, *Political Theology of Paul*, 16.

46. Ibid., 52.

47. Horsley, "General Introduction," 184.

48. Taubes, *Political Theology of Paul*, 74. Such readings are complicit in distorting Paul's message and in monstrous abuses of power, according to Taubes.

49. Ibid., 52.

50. The commentator Joseph A. Fitzmyer also relates Romans 13 to 1 Corinthians 7. Upon 1 Corinthians 7:29 he comments, "Cf. Rom 13:1. He wants to express freedom to engage in life in this world as if one were not in it, and so he takes an apocalyptic view of the world"; Fitzmyer, *First Corinthians: A New Translation with Introduction and Commentary* (New Haven, Conn.: Yale University Press, 2008), 317.

51. Taubes, *Political Theology of Paul*, 53.

52. Ibid.

53. Nitzan Lebovic and Roy Ben-Shai, *The Politics of Nihilism: From the Nineteenth Century to Contemporary Israel* (New York: Bloomsbury, 2014), 2.

54. Taubes, *Political Theology of Paul*, 40.

55. Mattias Martinson, "Atheism as Culture and Condition: Nietzschean Reflections on the Contemporary Invisibility of Profound Godlessness," *Approaching Religion* 2, no. 1 (2012): 83.

56. Taubes, *Political Theology of Paul*, 40.

57. Ibid., 52.

58. Barth, *Epistle to the Romans*.

59. Ibid., 483.

60. Ibid., 477.

61. Ibid., 478.

62. Ibid., 479–80.

63. Ibid., 481.

64. Ibid., 481–82.

65. Taubes, *Political Theology of Paul*, 54.

66. Considering that Benjamin's thought has been regarded as inherently Jewish. This image has been particularly shaped by Gershom Scholem's depictions of the young Benjamin; see Scholem, *Walter Benjamin* (1965; repr. New York: New York Review of Books, 2012). Taubes's invocation of Benjamin here should not be seen as isolated from the personal and intellectual rift between Taubes and Scholem and both thinkers' claim to Benjamin's legacy.

67. Taubes, *Political Theology of Paul*, 74.

68. See Chapter 3, under "To Immerse Oneself Talmudically."

69. Taubes, *From Cult to Culture: Fragments Towards a Critique of Historical Reason* (Stanford, Calif.: Stanford University Press, 2010), 112–13.

70. Walter Benjamin, *Reflections: Essays, Aphorisms, Autobiographical Writings* (New York: Schocken, 2007), 313.

71. Taubes, *Political Theology of Paul*, 72.

72. In the following, I will rely on other and more extensive readings of Walter Benjamin: Uwe Steiner, "The True Politician: Walter Benjamin's Concept of the Political," *New German Critique*, no. 83 (2001); Sami R. Khatib, "A Non-Nullified Nothingness: Walter Benjami and Messianic," *Stasis*, no. 1 (2013): 82–139; Eric Jacobsen, "Understanding Walter Benjamin's Theologico-Political Fragment," *Jewish Studies Quarterly* 8 (2001).

73. Benjamin, *Reflections*, 313.

74. Steiner, "True Politician," 77.

75. Nietzsche's reading of ancient tragedies was particularly influential upon philosophers that were of utmost importance for the development of Benjamin's thought: "Rosenzweig, Bloch, Lukács, and Benjamin were all concerned with the relationship between tragedy and the messianic structure of the solitary individual"; Jacobsen, "Understanding Walter Benjamin's Theologico-Political Fragment," 230.

76. Benjamin, *Reflections*, 313.

77. Khatib, "A Non-Nullified Nothingness."

78. Jacobsen, "Understanding Walter Benjamin's Theologico-Political Fragment," 205.

79. Taubes, *Occidental Eschatology*, 19.

80. Ibid.

81. Benjamin, *Reflections*, 312.

82. Taubes, *Political Theology of Paul*, 71.

83. Ibid., 14.

84. Ibid., 16.

85. Jewett, *Romans: A Commentary* (Minneapolis: Fortress, 2007), 783.

86. See Chapter 3.

87. Taubes, *Political Theology of Paul*, 44.

88. Jewett, *Romans*, 2.

89. Barclay, *Pauline Churches and Diaspora Jews*, 386.

90. Ibid., 375.

91. Harrison, *Paul and the Imperial Authorities at Thessalonica and Rome: A Study in the Conflict of Ideology*, 309; D. G. Horrell, "The Peaceable, Tolerant Community and the Legitimate Role of the State: Ethics and Ethical Dilemmas in Romans 12:1–15:13," *Review & Expositor* 100, no. 1 (2003): 88.

92. Taubes, *Political Theology of Paul*, 53.

93. This section can be further delineated into two main parts, based on Paul's call to be united in love (Rom 12:13: "Contribute to the needs of the saints; extend hospitality to strangers"). While the assembly's social relation to

the saints is the theme of 14:1–15:13, the relation to the strangers is the concern of 12:14–13:14.

94. Jewett, *Romans*.

95. This is especially the case from verse 14 onward; ibid., 765.

96. Ibid., 779.

97. There might well be remnants or residues from the Jesus tradition in the admonition to love your enemies.

98. Mark D. Nanos, *The Mystery of Romans: The Jewish Context of Paul's Letter* (Minneapolis: Fortress, 1996), 289–336.

99. This political dimension of legitimation appears absent in Nanos's argument for reading the authorities in Romans 13:1 as synagogue authorities, in ibid.

100. The role of this motif in Paul's thought is an object of major disagreement within New Testament studies. It concerns the fundamental question about the reason for Paul's mission among the Gentiles in the first place. Matthew V. Novenson has suggested that there are three solutions circulating within scholarly discussions of this problem: The first is the vision of an eschatological pilgrimage of Gentiles, who in the end-time come to Zion to join in worshipping together with Jews. The first articulation of this position can be seen in Halvor Moxnes, *Theology in Conflict: Studies in Paul's Understanding of God in Romans* (Leiden: E. J. Brill, 1980), 95. It was confirmed by E. P. Sanders, *Paul, the Law, and the Jewish People* (Philadelphia: Fortress, 1983), 171–206. Thereafter it was further elaborated in Paula Fredriksen, "Judaism, the Circumcision of Gentiles, and Apocalyptic Hope: Another Look at Galatians 1 and 2," *Journal of Theological Studies* 42, no. 2 (1991). It has been rejected by Terence Donaldson, "Proselytes or 'Righteous Gentiles'? The Status of Gentiles in Eschatological Pilgrimage Patterns of Thought," *Journal for the Study of the Pseudepigrapha* 4, no. 7 (1990): 3–27. Because of what Donaldson held to be a lack of evidence in Paul's letters, the scholar proposed proselytization as the most plausible solution. Novenson, however, opts for Moxnes's solution, but with a complementary perspective: the messianic belief in "a political and military rule of the scion of the house of David over the pagan nations." Novenson acknowledges that Donaldson's objection to the eschatological pilgrimage thesis is substantial, since "Paul cites few if any eschatological-pilgrimage texts." This is also the case for the messianic tradition, which Paul according to Novenson also seldom cites. Romans 15 is an exception in this regard, as are the Davidic references in Rom 1:3–4; Novenson, "The Jewish Messiahs, the Pauline Christ, and the Gentile Question," *Journal of Biblical Literature* 128, no. 2 (2009): 366. Novenson's hypothesis for a solution to Paul and the Gentile question is an argument for the legitimacy of Taubes's political-messianic reading of Paul.

101. Harrison, *Paul and the Imperial Authorities at Thessalonica and Rome*, 300–2; Theodore W. Jennings, *Outlaw Justice: The Messianic Politics of Paul* (Stanford, Calif.: Stanford University Press, 2013), 192; Horrell, "The Peaceable, Tolerant Community and the Legitimate Role of the State," 88.

102. Taubes, *Political Theology of Paul*, 54.

103. Ibid., 16.

104. Tacitus, quoted in Harrison, *Paul and the Imperial Authorities at Thessalonica and Rome*, 320.

105. "The term *hypotage* [for "subjection"] is frequent in military discussions and indicates the assumption and acceptance of a submissive rank in an established hierarchy"; Lewis R. Donelson, *Colossians, Ephesians, First and Second Timothy, and Titus* (Louisville, Ky.: Westminster John Knox Press, 1996), 129.

106. Jewett, *Romans*, 790.

107. Ibid.

108. In agreement with one aspect of James R. Harrison's reading. This scholar claims that Paul's exhortation "alerts his readers to the dangers posed by the imperial authorities, and spells out the ruler's limitations of power so that Roman believers might learn how to placate the authorities by astute civic behavior"; Harrison, *Paul and the Imperial Authorities at Thessalonica and Rome*, 308. Also, in accordance with Neil Elliott, "Romans 13:1–7 in the Context of Imperial Propaganda," in *Paul and Empire: Religion and Power in Roman Imperial Society*, ed. Richard A. Horsley (Harrisburg: Trinity, 1997).

109. According to Tacitus (*exitiabilis superstitio*), quoted in Harrison, *Paul and the Imperial Authorities at Thessalonica and Rome*, 320.

110. The anti-imperial meaning in Paul, detected by James R. Harrison, does also rely on this notion of intentional meaning. He is not content himself with plausibilities of how the apostle's message might have been heard and interpreted by his contemporaries: "It is Paul who, through the rich presentation of his eschatology, *intentionally* drove home the ideological collision"; ibid., 40. The same basis of the anti-imperial meaning of Paul's letters is presupposed by N. T. Wright: Paul's message "could not but be construed as deeply counter-imperial, as subversive to the whole edifice of the Roman Empire; and there is in fact plenty of evidence that Paul intended it to be so construed"; Wright, "Paul's Gospel and Caesar's Empire," 162.

111. Samuel Sandmel, "Parallelomania," *Journal of Biblical Literature* 81, no. 1 (1962): 1–13; Seyoon Kim, *Christ and Caesar: The Gospel and the Roman Empire in the Writings of Paul and Luke* (Grand Rapids, Mich.: William B. Eerdmans, 2008), 28–33. The problem is encapsulated in John M. G. Barclay's statement: "Overlaps in terminology (between the divine and human spheres of power or between human possessors of the same title) do not of themselves indicate a competitive relationship"; Barclay, *Pauline Churches and Diaspora Jews*, 378.

112. "To read a book is to consider its author as already dead and the book as posthumous"; Paul Ricoeur, *Hermeneutics and the Human Sciences: Essays on Language, Action, and Interpretation*, trans. John B. Thompson (Cambridge: Cambridge University Press, 1981), 147. "And yet Rousseau, caught, like the logic of identity, *within* the graphic of supplementarity, says what he does not

wish to say, describes what he does not wish to conclude. . . . There is not, strictly speaking, a text whose author or subject is Jean-Jacques Rousseau"; Jacques Derrida, *Of Grammatology* (1976; repr. Baltimore: Johns Hopkins University Press, 1997), 246.

113. Barclay describes literary echoes as Wright's "chief theoretical tool." Moreover, he states that "Wright is working from nothing explicit in the text," while the source of Wright's theoretical tool, Hays, had proceeded "from numerous and explicit citations of Scripture to echoes that surround and supplement that solid sound of citation"; Barclay, *Pauline Churches and Diaspora Jews*, 380.

114. The classicist Karl Galinsky has warned New Testament scholars, in particular, against bold notions of "*the* imperial cult" (it was neither a single nor a centrally planned phenomenon), "imperial theology" or "the gospel of Caesar." Although Galinsky is not arguing against explorations of linguistic parallels between Roman and Pauline discourse, he calls for more nuanced approaches; Galinsky, "The Cult of the Roman Emperor: Uniter or Divider?," in *Rome and Religion: A Cross-Disciplinary Dialogue on the Imperial Cult*, ed. Jeffrey Brodd and Jonathan L. Reed (Atlanta: Society of Biblical Literature, 2011).

115. John M. G. Barclay has argued that there was no need for "coding" a subversive message in the Roman Empire, since it was entirely possible to level criticism against the Roman Empire in public. Barclay writes, "There is no indication, for instance, that early Christian letters were likely to be intercepted by Roman secret agents"; Barclay, *Pauline Churches and Diaspora Jews*, 380.

116. A line of scholars from Dieter Georgi to James R. Harrison draws on this contrast, but the role of Roman "propaganda" or ideology in Paul's writings is an object of heated debate among scholars. See, for instance, J. Albert Harrill's claim: "The highly integrated connotations of the modern term *imperialism*, therefore, are inappropriate for a Roman context. . . . Likewise problematic when applied to the Roman Empire is *propaganda*. . . . There was no central office in Augustan rule to coordinate a single propagandistic message, nor the technology of mass media"; Harrill, "Paul and Empire: Studying Roman Identity after the Cultural Turn," *Early Christ Early Christianity* 2, no. 3 (2011): 289–90.

117. Taubes, *Political Theology of Paul*, 72.
118. Ibid., 103.
119. Benjamin, *Reflections*, 312.
120. Oakes, "Re-Mapping the Universe."
121. "My thesis thus implies that Christianity has its origin not properly in Jesus but in Paul"; Taubes, *Political Theology of Paul*, 40.
122. Barclay, *Pauline Churches and Diaspora Jews*, 362.

Conclusion

1. Ward Blanton, *Displacing Christian Origins: Philosophy, Secularity, and the New Testament* (Chicago: University of Chicago Press, 2007), 7.

2. Ibid., 169.

3. Alain Badiou, *Saint Paul: The Foundation of Universalism* (Stanford, Calif.: Stanford University Press, 2003), 66.

4. Jacob Taubes, *The Political Theology of Paul* (Stanford, Calif.: Stanford University Press, 2004), 66.

5. One of the main sources for Badiou's book on Paul, Günther Bornkamm, was a student of Bultmann. This Bultmannianism lives on in Žižek's Paulinism; Ole Jakob Løland, *Reception of Paul the Apostle in the Works of Slavoj Žižek* (London: Palgrave Macmillan, 2018).

6. Taubes, *Political Theology of Paul*, 89.

7. Daniel Boyarin, *Border Lines: The Partition of Judaeo-Christianity* (Philadelphia: University of Pennsylvania Press, 2004), 1.

8. Kenneth Reinhard, "Paul and the Political Love of the Neighbour," in *Paul and the Philosophers*, ed. Ward Blanton and Hent de Vries (New York: Fordham University Press, 2013), 461.

9. Jacques Derrida, "Faith and Knowledge: The Two Sources of 'Religion' at the Limits of Reason Alone," in *Acts of Religion*, ed. Gil Anidjar (New York: Routledge, 2002), 45.

10. Antonio Negri is an exception to this; Negri, *The Labor of Job: The Biblical Text as a Parable of Human Labor*, trans. Michael Hardt (Durham, N.C.: Duke University Press, 2009).

11. Mika Ojakangas, "Apostle Paul and the Profanation of the Law," *Distinktion: Scandinavian Journal of Social Theory* 10, no. 1 (2009): 48.

12. Slavoj Žižek, *The Fragile Absolute, or, Why Is the Christian Legacy Worth Fighting For?* (2000; repr. London and New York: Verso, 2008), 57–58.

13. Blanton, *A Materialism for the Masses: Saint Paul and the Philosophy of Undying Life* (New York: Columbia University Press, 2014), 16–17.

14. Ibid., 36.

Bibliography

Agamben, Giorgio. *The Time That Remains: A Commentary on the Letter to the Romans*. Stanford, Calif.: Stanford University Press, 2005.
Arendt, Hannah. "The Jew as Pariah: A Hidden Tradition." *Jewish Social Studies* 6, no. 2 (1944): 99–122.
Auerbach, Erich. *Literary Language & Its Public in Late Latin Antiquity and in the Middle Ages*. Princeton, N.J.: Princeton University Press, 1993.
Babich, Babette. "Ad Jacob Taubes." *New Nietzsche Studies* 7, no. 3 (2007): 5–10.
———. "Arendt's Radical Good and the Banality of Evil: Echoes of Scholem and Jaspers in Margarethe von Trotta's Hannah Arendt." *Existenz* 9, no. 2 (2014): 13–26.
Badiou, Alain. *Saint Paul: The Foundation of Universalism*. Stanford, Calif.: Stanford University Press, 2003.
Barclay, John M. G. "Paul and the Philosophers: Alain Badiou and the Event." *New Blackfriars* 91, no. 1032 (2010): 171–84.
———. *Pauline Churches and Diaspora Jews*. Tübingen: Mohr Siebeck, 2011.
Barth, Karl. *The Epistle to the Romans*. 6th ed. London: Oxford University Press, 1968.
Baumgarten, Albert I., ed. *Self, Soul and Body in Religious Experience*. Leiden: E. J. Brill, 1998.
Beal, Timothy. "Reception History and Beyond: Toward the Cultural History of Scriptures." *Biblical Interpretation* 19, no. 4 (2011): 357–72.
Benjamin, Walter. *Reflections: Essays, Aphorisms, Autobiographical Writings*. New York: Schocken, 2007.

Betz, Hans Dieter. *Galatians: A Commentary on Paul's Letter to the Churches in Galatia*. Philadelphia: Fortress, 1979.

Bielik-Robson, Agata. "Modernity: The Jewish Perspective." *New Blackfriars* 94, no. 1050 (2013): 188–207.

Blanton, Ward. *Displacing Christian Origins: Philosophy, Secularity, and the New Testament*. Chicago: University of Chicago Press, 2007.

———. "Mad with the Love of Undead Life." In *Paul in the Grip of the Philosophers: The Apostle and Contemporary Continental Philosophy*. Minneapolis: Fortress, 2013.

———. *A Materialism for the Masses: Saint Paul and the Philosophy of Undying Life*. New York: Columbia University Press, 2014.

Blanton, Ward, and Hent de Vries, eds. *Paul and the Philosophers*. New York: Fordham University Press, 2013.

Blumenberg, Hans. *The Legitimacy of the Modern Age*. Cambridge, Mass.: MIT Press, 1985.

Boll, Monika, and Raphael Gross. *"Ich Staune, Dass Sie in Dieser Luft Atmen Können": Jüdische Intellektuelle in Deutschland Nach 1945*. Frankfurt am Main: S. Fischer Verlage, 2013.

Bourguignon, Erika. "Bringing the Past into the Present: Family Narratives of Holocaust, Exile, and Diaspora; Memory in an Amnesic World: Holocaust, Exile, and the Return of the Suppressed." *Anthropological Quarterly* 78, no. 1 (2005): 63–88.

Boyarin, Daniel. *Border Lines: The Partition of Judaeo-Christianity*. Philadelphia: University of Pennsylvania Press, 2004.

Breed, Brennan W. *Nomadic Text: A Theory of Biblical Reception History*. Bloomington: Indiana University Press, 2014.

Chodoff, Paul. "The Holocaust and Its Effects on Survivors: An Overview." *Political Psychology* 18, no. 1 (1997): 147–57.

Conzelmann, Hans. *1 Corinthians: A Commentary on the First Epistle to the Corinthians*. Philadelphia: Fortress, 1981.

Derrida, Jacques. *Archive Fever: A Freudian Impression*. Translated by Eric Prenowitz. Chicago: University of Chicago Press, 1996.

———. "Faith and Knowledge: The Two Sources of 'Religion' at the Limits of Reason Alone." In *Acts of Religion*, edited by Gil Anidjar, 40–101. New York: Routledge, 2002.

———. *Of Grammatology*. Baltimore: Johns Hopkins University Press, 1997. Originally published in 1976.

———. *Politics of Friendship*. London: Verso, 2006.

———. *Rogues: Two Essays on Reason*. Stanford, Calif.: Stanford University Press, 2005.

———. "Three Questions to Hans-Georg Gadamer." In *Dialogue and Deconstruction: The Gadamer-Derrida Encounter*, edited by Diane P. Michelfelder and Richard E. Palmer, 52–54. Albany: State University of New York Press, 1989.

Deuber-Mankowsky, Astrid. "Walter Benjamin's Theological-Political Fragment as a Response to Ernst Bloch's Spirit of Utopia." *Leo Baeck Institute Yearbook* 47, no. 1 (2002): 3–19.

De Vries, Hent. *Philosophy and the Turn to Religion.* Baltimore: Johns Hopkins University Press, 1999.

De Wilde, Marc. "Meeting Opposites: The Political Theologies of Walter Benjamin and Carl Schmitt." *Philosophy and Rhetoric* 44, no. 4 (2011): 363–81.

Dolgopolski, Sergei. *What Is Talmud? The Art of Disagreement.* New York: Fordham University Press, 2009.

Donaldson, Terence. "Proselytes or 'Righteous Gentiles'? The Status of Gentiles in Eschatological Pilgrimage Patterns of Thought." *Journal for the Study of the Pseudepigrapha* 4, no. 7 (1990): 3–27.

Donelson, Lewis R. *Colossians, Ephesians, First and Second Timothy, and Titus.* Louisville, Ky.: Westminster John Knox Press, 1996.

Dunn, James D. G. *The New Perspective on Paul: Collected Essays.* Tübingen: Mohr Siebeck, 2005.

Eisenbaum, Pamela Michelle. *Paul Was Not a Christian: The Real Message of a Misunderstood Apostle.* New York: HarperOne, 2009.

Elliott, Neil. *The Arrogance of Nations: Reading Romans in the Shadow of Empire.* Minneapolis: Fortress, 2008.

———. *Liberating Paul: The Justice of God and the Politics of the Apostle.* Minneapolis: Fortress, 2006. Originally published in 1994.

———. "The Question of Politics." In *Paul within Judaism: Restoring the First-Century Context to the Apostle*, edited by Mark D. Nanos and Magnus Zetterholm, 203–43. Minneapolis: Fortress, 2015.

———. "Romans 13:1–7 in the Context of Imperial Propaganda." In *Paul and Empire: Religion and Power in Roman Imperial Society*, edited by Richard A. Horsley. Harrisburg: Trinity, 1997.

Fitzmyer, Joseph A. *First Corinthians: A New Translation with Introduction and Commentary.* New Haven, Conn.: Yale University Press, 2008.

Foucault, Michel. *The Essential Works of Michel Foucault, 1954–1984.* Vol. 2. London: Penguin, 2000.

———. "The Order of Discourse." In *Untying the Text: A Post-Structuralist Reader*, edited by Robert Young, 51–78. Boston: Routledge & Kegan Paul, 1981.

Fredriksen, Paula. "Historical Integrity, Interpretative Freedom: The Philosopher's Paul and the Problem of Anachronism." In *St. Paul among the Philosophers*, edited by John D. Caputo and Linda Martín Alcoff. Bloomington: Indiana University Press, 2009.

———. "Judaism, the Circumcision of Gentiles, and Apocalyptic Hope: Another Look at Galatians 1 and 2." *Journal of Theological Studies* 42, no. 2 (1991): 532–64.

———. "Paul and Augustine: Conversion Narratives, Orthodox Traditions, and the Retrospective Self." *Journal of Theological Studies* 37, no. 1 (1986): 3–34.

Freud, Sigmund. *Moses and Monotheism*. Translated by Katherine Jones. Letchworth: Hogarth, 1939.

Fuggle, Sophie. "Negotiating Paul: Between Philosophy and Theology." *Paragraph* 31, no. 3 (2008): 365–74.

Galinsky, Karl. "The Cult of the Roman Emperor: Uniter or Divider?" In *Rome and Religion: A Cross-Disciplinary Dialogue on the Imperial Cult*, edited by Jeffrey Brodd and Jonathan L. Reed, 1–22. Atlanta: Society of Biblical Literature, 2011.

Georgi, Dieter. "The Early Church: Internal Jewish Migration or New Religion?" *Harvard Theological Review* 88, no. 1 (1995): 35–68.

———. "God Turned Upside Down." In *Paul and Empire: Religion and Power in Roman Imperial Society*, edited by Richard A. Horsley, 148–57. Harrisburg: Trinity, 1997.

———. "Gott auf den Kopf Stellen: Überlegungen zu Tendenz und Kontext des Theokratiegedankens in Paulinischer Praxis und Theologie." In *Religionstheorie und Politische Theologie*. Band 3, *Theokratie*, edited by Jacob Taubes. Munich: Wilhelm Fink Verlag, 1987.

———. *The Opponents of Paul in Second Corinthians: A Study of Religious Propaganda in Late Antiquity*. Philadelphia: Fortress, 1986.

———. *Theocracy in Paul's Praxis and Theology*. Minneapolis: Fortress, 1991.

Hammerschlag, Sarah. "Bad Jews, Authentic Jews, Figural Jews." In *Judaism, Liberalism, and Political Theology*, edited by Randi Rashkover and Martin Kavka. Bloomington: Indiana University Press, 2014.

———. *The Figural Jew: Politics and Identity in Postwar French Thought*. Chicago: University of Chicago Press, 2010.

Harrill, J. Albert. "Paul and Empire: Studying Roman Identity after the Cultural Turn." *Early Christ Early Christianity* 2, no. 3 (2011): 281–311.

Harrison, James R. *Paul and the Imperial Authorities at Thessalonica and Rome: A Study in the Conflict of Ideology*. Tübingen: Mohr Siebeck, 2011.

Hass, Aaron. "Holocaust Survivor Testimony: The Psychological Implications." In *Remembering for the Future: The Holocaust in an Age of Genocide; Memory*, edited by Elisabeth Maxwell and John K. Roth, 127–34. Basingstoke: Palgrave, 2001.

Haynes, Stephen R. "'Between the Times': German Theology and the Weimar 'Zeitgeist.'" *Soundings: An Interdisciplinary Journal* 74, no. 1/2 (1991): 9–44.

Henningsen, Manfred. *Eric Voegelin and the German Intellectual Left*. Munich: Eric-Voegelin-Archiv, 2008.

Horrell, D. G. "The Peaceable, Tolerant Community and the Legitimate Role of the State: Ethics and Ethical Dilemmas in Romans 12:1–15:13." *Review & Expositor* 100, no. 1 (2003): 81–99.

Horsley, Richard A., ed. *Paul and Empire: Religion and Power in Roman Imperial Society*. Harrisburg: Trinity, 1997.
Idel, Moshe. *Messianic Mystics*. New Haven, Conn.: Yale University Press, 1998.
Jacobsen, Eric. "Understanding Walter Benjamin's Theologico-Political Fragment." *Jewish Studies Quarterly* 8 (2001): 205–47.
Jennings, Theodore W. *Outlaw Justice: The Messianic Politics of Paul*. Stanford, Calif.: Stanford University Press, 2013.
Jewett, Robert. *Romans: A Commentary*. Minneapolis: Fortress, 2007.
Jonas, Hans. *The Gnostic Religion: The Message of the Alien God & the Beginnings of Christianity*. Boston: Beacon Press, 2001.
Kahl, Brigitte. *Galatians Re-Imagined: Reading with the Eyes of the Vanquished*. Minneapolis: Fortress, 2010.
Käsemann, Ernst. *Commentary on Romans*. Translated by G. W. Bromiley. Grand Rapids, Mich.: Eerdmans, 1980.
Khatib, Sami R. "A Non-Nullified Nothingness: Walter Benjamin and Messianic." *Stasis*, no. 1 (2013): 82–139.
Kim, Seyoon. *Christ and Caesar: The Gospel and the Roman Empire in the Writings of Paul and Luke*. Grand Rapids, Mich.: William B. Eerdmans, 2008.
Knight, Mark. "Wirkungsgeschichte, Reception History, Reception Theory." *Journal for the Study of the New Testament* 33, no. 2 (2010): 137–46.
Kopp-Oberstebrink, Herbert. "Between Terror and Play: The Intellectual Encounter of Hans Blumenberg and Jacob Taubes." *Telos* 2012, no. 158 (2012): 119–34.
Kwon, Oh-Young. "A Critical Review of Recent Scholarship on the Pauline Opposition and the Nature of Its Wisdom (*Sophia*) in 1 Corinthians 1–4." *Currents in Biblical Research* 8, no. 3 (2010): 386–427.
Langton, Daniel R. *The Apostle Paul in the Jewish Imagination: A Study in Modern Jewish-Christian Relations*. New York: Cambridge University Press, 2010.
Lazier, Benjamin. *God Interrupted: Heresy and the European Imagination between the World Wars*. Princeton, N.J.: Princeton University Press, 2008.
Lebovic, Nitzan. "The Jerusalem School: The Theopolitical Hour." *New German Critique*, no. 105 (2008): 97–120.
Lebovic, Nitzan, and Roy Ben-Shai. *The Politics of Nihilism: From the Nineteenth Century to Contemporary Israel*. New York: Bloomsbury, 2014.
Lentin, Ronit. *Israel and the Daughters of the Shoah: Reoccupying the Territories of Silence*. New York: Berghahn, 2000.
Løland, Ole Jakob. *Reception of Paul the Apostle in the Works of Slavoj Žižek*. London: Palgrave Macmillan, 2018.
Lopate, Phillip. *Notes on Sontag*. Princeton, N.J.: Princeton University Press, 2009.

Löwith, Karl. *From Hegel to Nietzsche: The Revolution in Nineteenth-Century Thought*. New York: Columbia University Press, 1991.

———. *Meaning in History*. Chicago and London: University of Chicago Press, 2006. Originally published in 1949.

———. "The Theological Background of the Philosophy of History." *Social Research* 13, no. 1 (1946): 51–80.

Luther, Martin, and Jaroslav Pelikan. "Lectures on Romans." In *The Works of Martin Luther*, edited by Jaroslav Pelikan and Helmut T. Lehmann. Charlottesville: InteLex, 2013.

Martin, Dale B. *The Corinthian Body*. New Haven, Conn.: Yale University Press, 1995.

Martin, Jamie. "Liberalism and History after the Second World War: The Case of Jacob Taubes." *Modern Intellectual History* 12, no. 2 (2015): 1–22.

Martinson, Mattias. "Atheism as Culture and Condition: Nietzschean Reflections on the Contemporary Invisibility of Profound Godlessness." *Approaching Religion* 2, no. 1 (2012).

Martyn, J. Louis. "Christ, the Elements of the Cosmos, and the Law in Galatians." In *The Social World of the First Christians: Essays in Honor of Wayne A. Meeks*, edited by L. Michael White and O. Larry Yarbrough. Minneapolis: Fortress, 1995.

———. *Galatians: A New Translation with Introduction and Commentary*. 1st ed. New York: Doubleday, 1998.

McCormick, John P. "Transcending Weber's Categories of Modernity? The Early Lukács and Schmitt on the Rationalization Thesis." *New German Critique*, no. 75 (1998): 133–77.

Miranda, José Porfirio. *Marx y la Biblia: Crítica a la Filosofía de la Opresión*. Salamanca: Ediciones Sígueme, 1972.

Moxnes, Halvor. *Theology in Conflict: Studies in Paul's Understanding of God in Romans*. Leiden: E. J. Brill, 1980.

Myers, David N. *Resisting History: Historicism and Its Discontents in German-Jewish Thought*. Princeton, N.J.: Princeton University Press, 2003.

Nanos, Mark D. *The Mystery of Romans: The Jewish Context of Paul's Letter*. Minneapolis: Fortress, 1996.

———. "Paul's Non-Jews Do Not Become 'Jews,' but Do They Become 'Jewish'?: Reading Romans 2:25–29 within Judaism, Alongside Josephus." *Journal of the Jesus Movement in Its Jewish Setting* 1, no. 1 (2014): 26–53.

Negri, Antonio. *The Labor of Job: The Biblical Text as a Parable of Human Labor*. Translated by Michael Hardt. Durham, N.C.: Duke University Press, 2009.

Nicholls, Angus. *Myth and the Human Sciences: Hans Blumenberg's Theory of Myth*. Andover: Routledge, 2013.

Nietzsche, Friedrich. *The Antichrist*. Translated by H. L. Mencken. New York: Alfred A. Knopf, 1927.

———. *Daybreak: Thoughts on the Prejudices of Morality*. Edited by Maudemarie Clark and Brian Leiter. Translated by R. J. Hollingdale. Cambridge: Cambridge University Press, 1997.

———. *Human, All Too Human: A Book for Free Spirits*. Cambridge and New York: Cambridge University Press, 1986.

Novenson, Matthew V. "The Jewish Messiahs, the Pauline Christ, and the Gentile Question." *Journal of Biblical Literature* 128, no. 2 (2009): 357–73.

Oakes, Peter. "Re-Mapping the Universe: Paul and the Emperor in 1 Thessalonians and Philippians." *Journal for the Study of the New Testament* 27, no. 3 (2005): 301–22.

Ojakangas, Mika. "Apostle Paul and the Profanation of the Law." *Distinktion: Scandinavian Journal of Social Theory* 10, no. 1 (2009): 47–68.

Økland, Jorunn. "Setting the Scene: The End of the Bible, the End of the World." In *The Way the World Ends: The Apocalypse of John in Culture and Ideology*, edited by William John Lyons and Jorunn Økland, 1–30. Sheffield: Sheffield Phoenix Press, 2009.

Pareigis, Christina. "Letter from Susan Taubes to Jacob Taubes April 4, 1952." *Telos* 2010, no. 150 (2010): 111–14.

———. "Searching for the Absent God: Susan Taubes's Negative Theology." *Telos* 2010, no. 150 (2010): 97–110.

Patte, Daniel, and Eugene TeSelle. *Engaging Augustine on Romans: Self, Context, and Theology in Interpretation*. Harrisburg: Trinity, 2002.

Rabinbach, Anson. "Between Enlightenment and Apocalypse: Benjamin, Bloch and Modern German Jewish Messianism." *New German Critique*, no. 34 (1985): 78–124.

Räisänen, Heikki. "The 'Effective History' of the Bible." In *Challenges to Biblical Interpretation: Collected Essays, 1991–2000*, edited by Heikki Räisänen. Leiden: E. J. Brill, 2001.

———. *Paul and the Law*. Tübingen: Mohr, 1983.

Reinhard, Kenneth. "Paul and the Political Love of the Neighbour." In *Paul and the Philosophers*, edited by Ward Blanton and Hent de Vries. New York: Fordham University Press, 2013.

Ricoeur, Paul. *Hermeneutics and the Human Sciences: Essays on Language, Action, and Interpretation*. Translated by John B. Thompson. Cambridge: Cambridge University Press, 1981.

Rosenberg, Göran. *A Brief Stop on the Road from Auschwitz*. Translated by Sarah Death. New York: Other Press, 2015.

Rosenzweig, Franz. *The Star of Redemption*. Notre Dame, Ind.: Notre Dame Press, 1985.

Salomon, Albert. "Eschatological Thinking in Western Civilization: Reflections on a Book." *Social Research* 16, no. 1 (1949): 90–98.

Sanders, E. P. *Paul and Palestinian Judaism: A Comparison of Patterns of Religion*. Philadelphia: Fortress, 1977.

———. *Paul, the Law, and the Jewish People*. Philadelphia: Fortress, 1983.

Sandmel, Samuel. "Parallelomania." *Journal of Biblical Literature* 81, no. 1 (1962): 1–13.
Schmitt, Carl. *Political Theology: Four Chapters on the Concept of Sovereignty.* Chicago: University of Chicago Press, 2008.
———. *Political Theology II: The Myth of the Closure of Any Political Theology.* Cambridge: Polity Press, 2008.
Scholem, Gershom. *Walter Benjamin.* New York: New York Review of Books, 2012. Originally published in 1965.
Scholem, Gershom, A. D. Skinner, and A. David. *A Life in Letters, 1914–1982.* Cambridge, Mass.: Harvard University Press, 2002.
Schweitzer, Albert. *The Mysticism of Paul the Apostle.* Translated by William Montgomery. Baltimore: Johns Hopkins University Press, 1998. Originally published in 1931.
Segal, Alan F. *The Other Judaisms of Late Antiquity.* Brown Judaic Studies. Atlanta: Scholars, 1987.
———. *Paul the Convert: The Apostolate and Apostasy of Saul the Pharisee.* New Haven, Conn.: Yale University Press, 1990.
Spiegel, Gabrielle M. *The Past as Text: The Theory and Practice of Medieval Historiography.* Baltimore: Johns Hopkins University Press, 1997.
Stanley, Christopher D. *The Colonized Apostle: Paul through Postcolonial Eyes.* Minneapolis: Fortress, 2011.
Steiner, Uwe. "The True Politician: Walter Benjamin's Concept of the Political." *New German Critique*, no. 83 (2001): 43–88.
Stendahl, Krister. "The Apostle Paul and the Introspective Conscience of the West." *Harvard Theological Review* 56, no. 3 (1963): 199–215.
Stowers, Stanley K. *A Rereading of Romans: Justice, Jews, and Gentiles.* New Haven, Conn.: Yale University Press, 1994.
Strote, Noah Benezra. "Emigration and the Foundation of West Germany, 1933–1963." Ph.D. diss., University of California, 2011.
Tamez, Elsa. *Contra Toda Condena: La Justificación por la Fe Desde los Excluidos.* 2nd ed. San José: Depto Ecuménico de Investigaciones (DEI), 1991.
Taubes, Jacob. *Die Politische Theologie des Paulus.* Munich: Wilhelm Fink, 1993.
———. *From Cult to Culture: Fragments Towards a Critique of Historical Reason.* Stanford, Calif.: Stanford University Press, 2010.
———. *Occidental Eschatology.* Stanford, Calif.: Stanford University Press, 2009.
———. "On the Symbolic Order of Modern Democracy." *Confluence: An International Forum* 4, no. 1 (1955), 57–71.
———. *The Political Theology of Paul.* Stanford, Calif.: Stanford University Press, 2004.
———. *To Carl Schmitt: Letters and Reflections.* New York: Columbia University Press, 2013.
Taubes, Jacob, Carl Schmitt, and Mike Grimshaw. *To Carl Schmitt: Letters and Reflections.* New York: Columbia University Press, 2013.

Taubes, Susan. *Die Korrespondenz mit Jacob Taubes 1950–1951: Herausgegeben und Kommentiert von Christina Pareigis*. Paderborn: Wilhelm Fink, 2011.

———. *Die Korrespondenz mit Jacob Taubes 1952: Herausgegeben und Kommentiert von Christina Pareigis*. Paderborn: Fink, 2013.

Treml, Martin. "Reinventing the Canonical: The Radical Reading of Jacob Taubes." In *"Escape to Life": German Intellectuals in New York; A Compendium on Exile after 1933*, edited by Eckart Goebel and Sigrid Weigel, 457–78. Berlin and Boston: Gruyter, 2013.

Tronier, Henrik. "The Corinthian Correspondence between Philosophical Idealism and Apocalypticism." In *Paul Beyond the Judaism/Hellenism Divide*, edited by Troels Engberg-Pedersen, 165–96. Louisville, Ky.: Westminster John Knox Press, 2001.

Unterman, Alan. *The Kabbalistic Tradition: An Anthology of Jewish Mysticism*. London: Penguin, 2008.

von Harnack, Adolf. *Marcion: The Gospel of the Alien God*. Translated by Lyle D. Bierma and John E. Steely. Eugene, Ore.: Wipf & Stock, 1990.

Weikart, Richard. "Book Review: The Holy Reich: Nazi Conceptions of Christianity, 1919–1945." *German Studies Review* 27, no. 1 (2004): 174–76.

Welborn, Larry L. "The Culture of Crucifixion." In *Paul and the Philosophers*, edited by Ward Blanton and Hent de Vries, 127–40. New York: Fordham University Press, 2013.

———. *An End to Enmity: Paul and the Wrongdoer of Second Corinthians*. Berlin: Gruyter, 2011.

———. "Jacob Taubes—Paulinist, Messianist." In *Paul in the Grip of the Philosophers*, edited by Peter Frick. Minneapolis: Fortress, 2013.

———. *Paul, the Fool of Christ: A Study of 1 Corinthians 1–4 in the Comic-Philosophic Tradition*. London and New York: T. & T. Clark International, 2005.

Wells, Adam Y. *Phenomenologies of Scripture*. New York: Fordham University Press, 2017.

Williams, Michael A. *Rethinking "Gnosticism": An Argument for Dismantling a Dubious Category*. Princeton, N.J.: Princeton University Press, 1996.

———. "Was There a Gnostic Religion? Strategies for a Clearer Analysis." In *Was There a Gnostic Religion?*, edited by Antti Marjanen, 55–79. Helsinki: Finnish Exegetical Society; Göttingen: Vandenhoeck & Ruprecht, 2005.

Wright, N. T. *Pauline Perspectives: Essays on Paul, 1978–2013*. Minneapolis: Fortress, 2013.

———. "Paul's Gospel and Caesar's Empire." In *Paul and Politics: Ekklesia, Israel, Imperium, Interpretation: Essays in Honor of Krister Stendahl*, edited by Richard A. Horsley, 160–83. Harrisburg: Trinity, 2000.

Yerushalmi, Yosef Hayim. *Freud's Moses: Judaism Terminable and Interminable*. New Haven, Conn.: Yale University Press, 1991.

Žižek, Slavoj. *The Fragile Absolute, or, Why Is the Christian Legacy Worth Fighting For?* London and New York: Verso, 2008. Originally published in 2000.

———. *The Puppet and the Dwarf: The Perverse Core of Christianity.* Cambridge, Mass.: MIT Press, 2003.

———. *Revolution at the Gates: A Selection of Writings from February to October 1917.* London: Verso, 2004. Originally published in 2002.

Index of Biblical References

Exodus: *32–34*, 107
Numbers: *14–15*, 107
Deuteronomy: *10:16*, 114
Ezra: *44:9*, 114
Book of Psalm: *2*, 147
Jeremiah: *1:5*, 106; *4:4*, 114; *9:26*, 114; *31:33*, 114
Matthew: *6*, 128; *6:1–6*, 115
Romans: 17, 22, 88, 95, 101, 102, 104; *1:1*, 106; *1:3*, 147; *1:3–4*, 150, 151; *1:4*, 147, 149; *1:5*, 148; *1:16*, 109, 110, 131; *1:1–7*, 143, 147; *1:16–17*, 168; *1:17*, 109; *1:18*, 107, 108, 110, 119, 122, 124, 129; *1:18–2:16*, 109; *1:23–32*, 109; *1:32*, 108; *2:1–5*, 109; *2:5*, 109; *2:7–8*, 129; *2:9*, 110; *2:12*, 123; *2:14*, 114; *2:15*, 114; *2:17–24*, 109, 113, 117; *2:17–3:20*, 109; *2:25*, 113; *2:25–29*, 117; *2:28*, 112, 113; *2:29*, 114; *3:1–2*, 117; *3:3*, 131; *3:7*, 123; *3:19–21*, 117; *3:21*, 115; *3:23–25*, 123; *3:25*, 124; *3:27*, 117; *3:28*, 117; *3:31*, 116; *4:15*, 110; 109; *5*, 119, 122, 123; *5:12–14*, 123; *5:12–21*, 124; *7*, 102, 103, 119, 121, 122, 124, 125, 126, 131, 139; *7:7*, 131; *7:7–25*, 125, 131; *8*, 91, 96, 107, 130, 131, 159; *8:35*, 130; *8:35–38*, 168; *8:37–39*, 130; *8:38*, 131; *9–11*, 21, 48, 103, 108, 125, 127, 128, 129, 131, 133, 134, 135, 136; *9*, 103; *9:1–3*, 103; *9:1–5*, 131, 133; *9:6*, 134; *9:14*, 131; *10:4*, 112, 113; *10:19*, 129; *10:20–21*, 128; *11:7*, 128; *11:11*, 128, 129; *11:14*, 129; *11:15*, 128; *11:25*, 129, 135; *11:28*, 127, 129, 133, 134; *12:1–2*, 168; *12:1–15:13*, 168; *12:2*, 169; *12:3–7*, 169; *12:19*, 169; *12:19–21*, 167, 168; *12:20*, 169; *12:21*, 155, 166, 169, 174; *12:21–3:7*, 156; *13*, 47, 48, 71, 96, 135, 143, 144, 152, 155, 157, 158, 159, 160, 166, 169, 176; *13:1*, 152, 153, 155, 166, 169, 172, 173; *13:1–7*, 166, 167, 168, 169; *13:1–10*, 172; *13:2*, 172; *13:4*, 169; *13:8*, 135, 136, 137, 166; *13:11*, 152, 153; *13:11–14*, 169, 172; *15:6*, 106
1 Corinthians: 18, 58, 59, 60, 69, 77, 78, 86, 88, 89, 93, 146, 167; *1–2*, 52, 53, 54, 97, 99; *1:4–9*, 76; *1:5*, 84; *1:17–2:5*, 58, 72–73, 75, 79, 84; *1:18*, 77, 79; *1:20*, 3, 58, 97, 99, 144, 177; *1:22*, 77; *1:23*, 59, 73; *1:25*, 79; *1:26*, 79; *1:26–31*, 73, 74, 78, 79; *1:27–28*,

1 Corinthians (cont.)
 71; *2:1*, 73; *2:1–5*, 74, 75, 79, 80; *2:2*,
 80, 82; *2:3*, 74, 80; *2:5*, 85; *2:6*, 85,
 98, 166, 177; *2:6–10*, 80, 82, 83, 84,
 85; *2:7*, 84; *2:8*, 166, 168; *2:9*, 85; *4:8*,
 84; *7:29*, 91, 143, 153, 158; *15*, 85

2 Corinthians: 73, 74
Galatians: 113; *1:15*, 106; *3:10*, 117; *4:10*,
 118; *4:8*, 118; *4:10*, 118; *6:2*, 117; *6:15*,
 119
Ephesians: *5:21*, 172
Philippians: *2:5–11*, 77; *2:8*, 77; *3:5*, 106

General Index

Adorno, Theodor, 39, 88, 91–94, 96, 98, 159, 160, 178
aesthetics, 59, 63, 65, 87, 92–93, 97, 99
Agamben, Giorgio, 1, 2, 11, 143, 159, 181–84
Alcoff, Linda Martín, 13
anarchism, 145, 153
antinomianism, 43, 46, 112–13, 115, 117, 119, 148
anti-semitism, 32, 50, 127, 129, 134, 136, 139, 179
apocalypticism, 20–21, 23, 28–30, 33–35, 38–39, 66–67, 70, 76–80, 83–87, 96, 101, 105, 109, 111, 141, 144–45, 151–55, 158, 160, 162, 164, 166–69, 172–75, 181
Aquinas, Thomas, 7
Arendt, Hannah, 74
Aristotle, 57
asceticism, Jewish, 25
assimilation, Jewish, 32, 38
Assmann, Aleida, 51
atheism, 33, 120, 180
atonement, 124
Auerbach, Erich, 71, 146

Augustine, 7, 30, 46, 71, 82, 89, 103–4, 121–26, 138, 146, 181
authorial intention, 173

Baader-Meinhof group, 39
Babich, Babette, 49, 50, 51
Badiou, Alain, 1, 8–9, 13–16, 181–82
Baeck, Leo, 28, 43
Balthasar, Hans Urs von, 28, 30, 135
Barclay, John M. G., 1, 2, 141, 168, 174, 176
Barth, Karl, 10, 20, 28, 31, 33–35, 47, 65–66, 88, 90, 93–94, 96, 98, 152, 155–59, 162, 168, 174–75
Basilides, 82
Bauer, Bruno, 149
Benjamin, Walter, 10, 33, 47, 65, 88, 90–99, 152–53, 159–64, 174–75, 179
Bergman, Hugo, 26
biblical criticism, 3, 6–7, 14, 18, 52, 54, 63, 140, 153, 167, 173
biblical exegesis, 13, 92, 152
biblical reception, 3–8, 52, 69–70, 99, 102, 135, 139, 177–80, 183–84

231

Blanton, Ward, 6, 8, 15–17, 126, 179–80, 183–84
Bloch, Ernst, 33, 65, 91
Blumenberg, Hans, 3, 40, 53, 61–67, 88, 90–92, 96, 98, 178
Bornkamm, Günther, 18
Boyarin, Daniel, 182
Breed, Brennan W., 6–7, 13
Brentano, Margareta von, 36
Buber, Martin, 24–26, 28, 32, 37, 41, 43
Bultmann, Rudolf, 34, 134, 181

Calvin, Jean, 7
Caputo, John, 13
Catholicism, 24
Christianity, relationship with Judaism, 21, 40–41, 45, 61, 66–67, 100, 104, 106, 108, 133, 135, 178, 182
Cicero, 77
circumcision, 113–17
class, 87
Cohen, Geulah, 39
Cohen, Hermann, 43, 46
commentary; genre of, 4, 102
communism, 30
conservatism, 156
Constantine, 83, 87
conversion, 8, 107, 115–16
Conzelmann, Hans, 63
cosmology, 95, 109, 111, 118, 119
covenant, 100, 115, 130
Critchley, Simon, 182
cross, Paul's doctrine of the, 3, 71–78, 82–83, 88, 98, 111–12, 144–45, 148, 174, 177, 184

deconstruction, 4, 51, 56, 99, 100–1
Deismann, Adolf, 141
demytologization, 64, 181
Derrida, Jacques, 5, 15, 16, 50–51, 138, 180, 182
Dibelius, Martin, 18
disenchantment, 30, 33
doctrine of the two kingdoms, Lutheran, 152, 166
Dolgopolski, Sergei, 55, 180
Dutschke, Rudi, 37

ecumenism, 40, 135
election, of Israel, 100–1, 129–31, 134, 139, 178–79
Elliott, Neil, 140, 142, 152, 158
Engel, Amir, 54
enlightenment, European, and Judaism, 23–25
Erikson, Erik H., 103
eschatology, 20, 23, 31, 67, 70, 84, 112, 132, 163
exile, 34, 38, 51, 67
existentialism, 61, 108

Feuerbach, Ludvig, 136
Fonrobert, Charlotte Elisheva, 54
Foucault, Michel, 4–6
Frankfurt school, 96
Fredriksen, Paula, 13–16
Free University, of Berlin, 39, 40
Freud, Jakob, 138
Freud, Sigmund, 1, 10, 38, 54, 101, 104, 119–24, 126, 135–39, 178, 181–84

genealogy, 4–5, 28, 60, 69–70
Georgi, Dieter, 142, 144, 147, 150, 175
Gnosticism, 29, 33–35, 52–53, 60–64, 66–68, 80–86, 92
grace, 16, 78, 100
guilt, 103–4, 119–21, 123–24

Habermas, Jürgen, 40
Habsburg Empire, 34
Hapoel Hatzair, 24
Harnack, Adolf von, 34, 48, 65, 68
Harrison, James R., 142–43, 158
Hasidism, 24–25, 32, 37
Hebrew University, of Jerusalem, 26, 36–37
Hegel, G. W. F., 18, 27, 29, 45–46, 54, 62, 120, 180
Heidegger, Martin, 23, 30, 34, 45, 53, 67–68, 75, 180
Heidelberg, University of, 17–18
Hellenism, 76–77, 149
hermeneutics, 111; of authorial intention, 173; of suspicion, 55
historicism, 16–21, 52–54, 56, 60, 63, 92, 98, 161–62

historiography, of New Testament studies, 15–16
Hitler, Adolf, 46
hope, 20, 58
Horsley, Richard A., 140–42
humanism, 44, 45

Idel, Moshe, 42
imperial cult, 141, 147, 149, 152, 154
incarnation, 146
introspection, Pauline, 101, 103–7, 117, 121, 125, 127, 163
Iser, Wolfgang, 3, 61

Jauss, Hans Robert, 3, 61
Jewish Theological Seminary, 25
Jewish World Congress, 42, 104, 105
Joachim of Fiore, 70
Jonas, Hans, 19, 34, 61–62, 66–67
Judaism: Liberal, 43, 47; Modern, 26; Rabbinic, 21, 25; Second Temple, 21, 77, 170
justice, 108–9, 113–17, 123, 168, 171
justification, theological, 107, 132

Kant, Immanuel, 15
Kelsen, Hans, 45
Kierkegaard, Søren, 27, 29, 54
Kopp-Oberstebrink, Herbert, 63, 65, 94
Koselleck, Reinhard, 3, 61

Latte, Kurt, 100
law, 100, 102–3, 110–19, 121, 123, 125, 136–37, 139, 148, 157
Levinas, Emmanuel, 26
liberalism, 32–33, 43–45, 47, 111, 148
logocentrism, 56
Löwith, Karl, 27–30, 62
Lukács, Georg,
Luther, Martin, 7, 103, 107, 121, 124, 133, 138
Lyons, John, 7

Maimonides, 46
Maison des Sciences de l'Homme, 51
Marburg, University of, 28
Marcion, 61, 65–67, 88–89
Marcuse, Herbert, 39

Martin, Dale B., 75, 78, 83
Marx, Karl, 1, 27, 62
Mendelssohn, Moses, 32
messianism, 36–37, 42, 60, 70–71, 91–92, 96, 104–5, 110, 159–67
millenarian puritanism, 42
mimicry, 86–87
miracle, 28, 58, 120
modernity, 28, 30–32, 46, 57, 61–64, 66–67, 95, 178, 182–83
Mohler, Armin, 23, 26, 39, 41, 43–46, 49, 51
myth, 71

Nanos, Mark D., 169–70
Nathan of Gaza, 112
Nazism, 22–23, 30, 34–35, 41, 43–48, 53, 61, 68, 99, 135, 178
Nietzsche, Friedrich, 1, 3, 10, 18, 19, 27, 34, 40, 53–60, 69, 71–72, 75, 78, 82–83, 90–91, 95, 97–99, 101, 120–22, 124–27, 132–33, 138–39, 142, 144–46, 149–50, 152–53, 156, 159–63, 174–81, 183–84
nihilism, 61, 91, 153–55, 178

Oakes, Peter, 143, 147, 176
Ojakangas, Mika 183
Økland, Jorunn, 7
original sin, 89, 122–24

paradigm shift, 140
Pareigis, Christina, 35
Peterson, Erik, 48
philology, 56, 73, 82, 90, 132, 155, 167–68, 173, 180
plagiarism, 28
Plato, 57
platonism, 80, 82, 184
polemics, 56, 60, 69, 72, 78, 82, 98, 101
political theology, 27, 31, 45–47, 62, 70, 142–43, 179
postcolonial theory, 86
predestination, 89, 134–35
prohibition, of images, 87
Protestantism, Liberal, 28, 31, 46–48, 66–67, 90
psychoanalysis, 103–4, 119–21, 126, 137–39, 180, 183

Räisänen, Heikki, 8, 10
rebellion, 145, 150–51, 154, 172
redemption, 20, 42, 46, 73, 91 104–5, 108, 120, 123–24
Reinhard, Kenneth, 137
revelation, 20
rhetorical criticism, 167
Roman Empire, 70, 97, 112, 118, 140–44, 149–50, 153–55, 165–66, 168, 174–76, 179
Rosenzweig, Franz, 19–20, 28, 37–38, 41, 57, 65, 108

sabbatianism, 24–25, 41–42
Salomon, Albert, 31
Sanders, E. P., 16
Santner, Eric, 182
Schmithals, Walter, 63
Schmitt, Carl, 9, 22, 23, 27, 28, 29, 31, 37, 39, 45, 46, 47, 48, 49, 53, 62, 65, 89, 90, 93, 94, 96, 97, 98, 101, 127, 128, 134, 135, 139, 178
Scholem, Gerschom, 25–26, 33, 36–37, 41–42, 49–50, 65, 91, 94–95, 104–5, 111
Schweitzer, Albert, 19, 29, 31, 81
secularism, 45
secularity; and religion, 1, 174
secularization, 23, 27, 62, 65, 88, 90, 180–81
Septuagint, 150
Shoah, 31, 46, 49, 50, 51, 178
Spiegel, Gabrielle, 50–51
spirituality, 26
Staiger, Emil, 100
Stendahl, Krister, 9, 102–3, 107, 121, 125, 132, 137, 139
Strauss, David Friedrich, 180
Strauss, Leo, 65
supersessionism, 128, 132, 184

surrealism, 64, 92
survival guilt, 49–50
Syracuse, University of, 13
Szondi, Peter, 39

Tacitus, 171
Talmud, 24, 28, 55, 99, 107
Taubes, Chaim Zwi Hirsch, 24
Taubes, Fanny, 24
Taubes, Susan, 7, 25–26, 35, 41, 44, 47
Theissen, Gerd, 18
theocracy, 142, 162–65, 174, 179
theodicy, 135, 171
theology, 17–18, 23–33, 45–48, 56, 58, 60, 80–81, 90, 108, 113, 125, 140
Tillich, Paul, 20, 28
tradition, 6

universalism, 78, 129

Valentinus, 82
Viennese Hebrew Pädagogium, 24
Voegelin, Eric, 62
Vries, Hent de, 2

wandering Jew, the legend of, 38
Weber, Max, 30–31, 33, 74
Weimar Republic, 32, 34, 53, 61
Weiss, Joseph, 36
Welborn, Larry L., 75, 78, 95–96
Wilckens, Ulrich, 63
Wirkungsgeschichte, 5
Wright, Nicholas Thomas, 141, 168, 174, 176

Yerushalmi, Yosef Hayim, 138

Zevi, Sabbatai, 41, 43, 112
Zionism, 36–37
Žižek, Slavoj, 1–2, 8, 13, 16, 180

Ole Jakob Løland holds a postdoc position at the Faculty of Theology, University of Oslo. He has written extensively on the role and reception of biblical texts within modern contexts. He is the author of *The Reception of Paul the Apostle in the Works of Slavoj Žižek* (2018).

Perspectives in Continental Philosophy
John D. Caputo, series editor

Recent titles:

Ole Jakob Løland, *Pauline Ugliness: Jacob Taubes and the Turn to Paul.*
Marika Rose, *A Theology of Failure: Žižek against Christian Innocence.*
Marc Crépon, *Murderous Consent: On the Accommodation of Violent Death.* Translated by Michael Loriaux and Jacob Levi, Foreword by James Martel
Emmanuel Falque, *The Guide to Gethsemane: Anxiety, Suffering, and Death.* Translated by George Hughes.
Emmanuel Alloa, *Resistance of the Sensible World: An Introduction to Merleau-Ponty.* Translated by Jane Marie Todd. Foreword by Renaud Barbaras.
Françoise Dastur, *Questions of Phenomenology: Language, Alterity, Temporality, Finitude.* Translated by Robert Vallier.
Jean-Luc Marion, *Believing in Order to See: On the Rationality of Revelation and the Irrationality of Some Believers.* Translated by Christina M. Gschwandtner.
Adam Y. Wells, ed., *Phenomenologies of Scripture.*
An Yountae, *The Decolonial Abyss: Mysticism and Cosmopolitics from the Ruins.*
Jean Wahl, *Transcendence and the Concrete: Selected Writings.* Edited and with an Introduction by Alan D. Schrift and Ian Alexander Moore.
Colby Dickinson, *Words Fail: Theology, Poetry, and the Challenge of Representation.*
Emmanuel Falque, *The Wedding Feast of the Lamb: Eros, the Body, and the Eucharist.* Translated by George Hughes.
Emmanuel Falque, *Crossing the Rubicon: The Borderlands of Philosophy and Theology.* Translated by Reuben Shank. Introduction by Matthew Farley.

Colby Dickinson and Stéphane Symons (eds.), *Walter Benjamin and Theology.*
Don Ihde, *Husserl's Missing Technologies.*
William S. Allen, *Aesthetics of Negativity: Blanchot, Adorno, and Autonomy.*
Jeremy Biles and Kent L. Brintnall, eds., *Georges Bataille and the Study of Religion.*
Tarek R. Dika and W. Chris Hackett, *Quiet Powers of the Possible: Interviews in Contemporary French Phenomenology.* Foreword by Richard Kearney.
Richard Kearney and Brian Treanor, eds., *Carnal Hermeneutics.*

A complete list of titles is available at http://fordhampress.com.

www.ingramcontent.com/pod-product-compliance
Lightning Source LLC
Chambersburg PA
CBHW030439300426
44112CB00009B/1071